The Ultimate
Plant-Based
Cookbook for Beginners

1800+ Days of Easy and Flavorful Recipes for Embracing a Plant-Based Lifestyle. Incl. 30 Days Meal Plan for a Vibrant and Energized You

Luther Tuma

Warning-Disclaimer

The purpose of this book is to educate and entertain. The author or publisher does not guarantee that anyone following the techniques, suggestions, tips, ideas, or strategies will become successful. The author and publisher shall have neither liability or responsibility to anyone with respect to any loss or damage caused, or alleged to be caused, directly or indirectly by the information contained in this book.

Table of Contents

Introduction

Welcome to the world of plant-based eating! This cookbook is your guide to a healthier and more sustainable way of living. Whether you are a seasoned vegan or just starting out, this book will provide you with delicious and nutritious recipes that are easy to make and will leave you feeling satisfied and energized.

By choosing to eat a plant-based diet, you are not only improving your own health, but also contributing to the health of our planet. Plant-based foods require fewer resources to produce and generate less greenhouse gas emissions than animal-based foods. Plus, they are packed with vitamins, minerals, and fiber that are essential for optimal health.

This cookbook features a wide range of recipes that showcase the versatility and deliciousness of plant-based ingredients. From hearty soups and stews to fresh salads and flavorful curries, there is something for everyone in these pages. So grab your apron and get ready to explore the wonderful world of plant-based cooking!

It all started with a health scare. I was in my mid-thirties, working long hours at a stressful job and not taking care of myself the way I should have been. One day, I collapsed at work and was rushed to the hospital. The doctors told me that I had high blood pressure and high cholesterol, and that if I didn't make some serious lifestyle changes, I was at risk for heart disease.

That was a wake-up call for me. I knew I needed to do something to get my health back on track, but I wasn't sure where to start. That's when I stumbled upon the idea of a plant-based diet. I had always thought of myself as a meat-and-potatoes kind of guy, but as I started to research the benefits of a plant-based diet, I realized that it might be just what I needed.

At first, it was tough. I missed the taste of meat and dairy, and I wasn't sure how to cook without them. But as I started to experiment with different plant-based ingredients and recipes, I discovered a whole new world of flavors and textures that I had never experienced before.

Not only did I start to feel better physically, but I also felt more connected to the world around me. Eating a plant-based diet made me more aware of the impact that my food choices were having on the environment, and I felt like I was doing my part to make a difference.

As I continued on my plant-based journey, I started to share my recipes and experiences with friends and family. They were amazed at how delicious and satisfying plant-based food could be, and many of them started to incorporate more plant-based meals into their own diets.

That's when I realized that I wanted to write this cookbook. I wanted to share my story and my recipes with as many people as possible, to show them that eating a plant-based diet doesn't have to be difficult or boring. With this cookbook, I hope to inspire others to take control of their health and make a positive impact on the world around them.

History of Plant-Based Diet

The idea of a plant-based diet has been around for centuries, with various cultures and religions promoting the consumption of fruits, vegetables, grains, and legumes. In ancient Greece, philosopher Pythagoras was known to follow a vegetarian diet, and in India, the practice of ahimsa (non-violence) has long been associated with a plant-based diet.

In the 1800s, Sylvester Graham, a Presbyterian minister and health reformer, advocated for a vegetarian diet as a way to improve physical and moral health. His ideas were later popularized by John Harvey Kellogg, who founded the Battle Creek Sanitarium in Michigan, where patients were prescribed a plant-based diet as part of their treatment.

In the early 20th century, the term "vegan" was coined by Donald Watson, who founded the Vegan Society in England in 1944. The society promoted a plant-based diet that excluded all animal products, including dairy and eggs.

In the 1970s, the concept of a plant-based diet gained popularity with the publication of Frances Moore Lappé's book, "Diet for a Small Planet," which argued that a vegetarian diet was not only healthier, but also more sustainable for the planet.

More recently, scientific studies have shown that a plant-based diet can help prevent and even reverse chronic diseases such as heart disease, diabetes, and certain types of cancer. As a result, more people are turning to plant-based diets as a way to improve their health and reduce their environmental impact.

Today, there are many variations of a plant-based diet, including vegetarian, vegan, and flexitarian (which includes some animal products in moderation). Regardless of the specific approach, the benefits of a plant-based diet are clear, and the movement shows no signs of slowing down.

Why Plant-Based Diet

A plant-based diet, which focuses on whole foods such as fruits, vegetables, whole grains, legumes, nuts, and seeds, has been shown to have numerous health benefits. Here are some of the most significant benefits of a plant-based diet:

1. Reduced risk of chronic diseases: Plant-based diets have been associated with a lower risk of chronic diseases such as heart disease, type 2 diabetes, and certain types of cancer. This is because plant-based diets tend to be lower in saturated fat, cholesterol, and processed foods, and higher in fiber, antioxidants, and other nutrients that promote good health.

2. Improved weight management: Plant-based diets are often lower in calories than diets that include meat and dairy products, which can help with weight management. Additionally, plant-based diets tend to be more filling due to their high fiber content, which can reduce hunger and prevent overeating.

3. Lowered blood pressure: Plant-based diets have been shown to lower blood pressure, which is a major risk factor for heart disease and stroke. This is likely due to the high potassium content of many plant-based foods, which can help counteract the effects of sodium.

4. Better digestion: Plant-based diets are rich in fiber, which promotes good digestion and regular bowel movements. This can reduce the risk of constipation, hemorrhoids, and other digestive issues.

5. Improved mood: Some studies have suggested that plant-based diets may improve mood and reduce symptoms of depression. This may be due to the high levels of antioxidants and other nutrients found in plant-based foods, which can support brain health and function.

6. Environmental sustainability: Plant-based diets are more environmentally sustainable than diets that include meat and dairy products. Animal agriculture is a major contributor to greenhouse gas emissions, deforestation, and water pollution, so reducing or eliminating animal products

from your diet can have a positive impact on the planet.

Overall, a plant-based diet can provide numerous health benefits and is a sustainable choice for both your own health and the health of the planet.

Key Aspects to Maintain a Healthy Plant-Based Diet

Maintaining a healthy plant-based diet requires attention to several key aspects. Here are some of the most important things to keep in mind:

1. Eat a variety of whole foods: A healthy plant-based diet should include a variety of whole foods such as fruits, vegetables, whole grains, legumes, nuts, and seeds. Eating a variety of these foods ensures that you get all the nutrients your body needs.

2. Get enough protein: Protein is an essential nutrient that is needed for building and repairing tissues in the body. While animal products are a common source of protein, plant-based sources such as beans, lentils, tofu, and tempeh can provide all the protein your body needs.

3. Pay attention to iron and calcium intake: Iron and calcium are two important nutrients that can be more challenging to get on a plant-based diet. Good sources of iron include dark leafy greens, beans, and fortified cereals. Calcium can be found in leafy greens, almonds, and fortified plant milks.

4. Watch your fat intake: While plant-based diets tend to be lower in saturated fat than animal-based diets, it's still important to watch your overall fat intake. Focus on healthy fats such as those found in nuts, seeds, avocados, and olive oil.

5. Avoid processed foods: Processed plant-based foods such as vegan burgers, sausages, and cheese substitutes can be high in salt, sugar, and unhealthy fats. While they can be convenient and tasty, it's best to limit them and focus on whole, unprocessed foods.

6. Supplement when necessary: Some nutrients, such as vitamin B12 and vitamin D, may be more difficult to get on a plant-based diet. It's important to talk to your healthcare provider about whether you need to supplement with these nutrients.

By paying attention to these key aspects, you can maintain a healthy and balanced plant-based diet that supports your overall health and wellbeing.

Chapter 1

Tips for Success

Stocking a Plant-Based Pantry

Stocking a plant-based pantry is essential for maintaining a healthy and nutritious diet. Here are some tips on how to stock your pantry with plant-based essentials:

1. Grains: Whole grains such as brown rice, quinoa, and whole wheat pasta are great staples to have in your pantry. They are versatile and can be used in a variety of dishes.

2. Legumes: Beans, lentils, and chickpeas are excellent sources of protein and fiber. Canned versions are convenient, but dried beans are more economical and can be cooked in bulk and frozen for later use.

3. Nuts and seeds: Nuts and seeds are a great source of healthy fats and protein. Almonds, walnuts, cashews, and sunflower seeds are all good options to have on hand.

4. Nut butters: Peanut butter, almond butter, and other nut butters are great for adding flavor and nutrition to smoothies, oatmeal, and other dishes.

5. Plant-based milks: Soy milk, almond milk, and oat milk are all good alternatives to dairy milk. They can be used in cooking and baking, as well as in smoothies and other drinks.

6. Spices and herbs: A well-stocked spice cabinet can add flavor and depth to any dish. Some key spices to have on hand include cumin, coriander, paprika, and chili powder. Fresh herbs like basil, parsley, and cilantro can also add flavor and nutrition to meals.

7. Condiments: Stock up on condiments like mustard, ketchup, hot sauce, and soy sauce. These can be used to add flavor to sandwiches, salads, and other dishes.

8. Baking supplies: For baking, you'll want to have flour, baking powder, baking soda, and sweeteners like sugar or maple syrup. You may also want to have plant-based substitutes for eggs and butter, such as applesauce and coconut oil.

By stocking your pantry with these essentials, you'll have the ingredients on hand to create a variety of delicious and nutritious plant-based meals. Be sure to check expiration dates regularly and rotate items to ensure that everything stays fresh.

Meal Planning and Prepping

Meal planning and prepping can be helpful strategies for maintaining a healthy plant-based diet. Here are some tips to get started:

1. Plan your meals in advance: Take some time at the beginning of each week to plan out your meals for the coming days. This will help you stay on track and avoid last-minute decisions that may lead to less healthy choices.

2. Choose recipes that use similar ingredients: To save time and money, choose recipes that use similar ingredients. For example, if you're making a stir-fry one night, you could use the leftover vegetables in a salad the next day.

3. Prep ingredients in advance: Spend some time chopping vegetables, cooking grains, and preparing other ingredients in advance. This will make meal prep much faster and easier throughout the week.

4. Cook in bulk: Cooking in bulk is a great way to save time and ensure that you have healthy meals ready to go. Make a big batch of soup, chili, or stew and freeze portions for later use.

5. Use a slow cooker or pressure cooker: Slow cookers and pressure cookers are great tools for meal prep. You can set them up in the morning and come home to a hot meal in the evening.

6. Keep healthy snacks on hand: Stock your pantry and fridge with healthy snacks like cut-up veggies, fruit, hummus, and nuts. This will help you resist the temptation to reach for less healthy options when hunger strikes.

7. Don't be afraid to experiment: Trying new recipes and ingredients can keep things interesting and prevent boredom with your plant-based diet. Don't be afraid to experiment with new flavors and cuisines.

By following these tips, you can make meal planning and prepping a regular part of your routine and enjoy the benefits of a healthy and nutritious plant-based diet.

Smart Substitutions for Common Ingredients

Substituting common ingredients with plant-based alternatives is a great way to make your favorite recipes healthier and more sustainable. Here are some smart substitutions for common ingredients in a plant-based diet:

1. Meat: Substitute meat with plant-based proteins such as tofu, tempeh, seitan, lentils, beans, and chickpeas. These options are high in protein and can be used in a variety of dishes.

2. Dairy milk: Substitute dairy milk with plant-based milks such as soy, almond, oat, or coconut milk. These options are lower in calories and saturated fat and can be used in cooking and baking.

3. Butter: Substitute butter with plant-based alternatives such as coconut oil, olive oil, or vegan margarine. These options are lower in saturated fat and can be used in cooking and baking.

4. Eggs: Substitute eggs with mashed bananas, applesauce, flaxseed meal, or chia seeds. These options work well in baked goods and can help bind ingredients together.

5. Cheese: Substitute cheese with plant-based alternatives such as nutritional yeast, tofu, or vegan cheese. These options provide a similar texture and flavor to cheese but without the animal products.

6. Cream: Substitute cream with plant-based alternatives such as coconut cream or cashew cream. These options can be used in soups, sauces, and desserts.

7. Honey: Substitute honey with plant-based sweeteners such as maple syrup, agave nectar, or date syrup. These options are lower in calories and can be used in baking and cooking.

By making these smart substitutions, you can enjoy all of your favorite foods while maintaining a healthy and sustainable plant-based diet.

Eating out and traveling on a plant-based diet

Eating out and traveling can be challenging when following a plant-based diet, but with a little planning, it's possible to find delicious and nutritious options. Here are some tips for eating out and traveling on a plant-based diet:

1. Research restaurants in advance: Before heading out to eat, research restaurants in the area that offer plant-based options. Many restaurants now have vegan or vegetarian menus or can accommodate special requests.

2. Ask for modifications: Don't be afraid to ask for modifications to menu items to make them plant-based. For example, you could ask for a salad without cheese or a veggie burger without mayo.

3. Look for ethnic cuisine: Ethnic cuisines such as Indian, Thai, and Middle Eastern often have many plant-based options. Look for dishes that feature vegetables, legumes, and grains.

4. Pack snacks: When traveling, pack healthy snacks such as cut-up veggies, fruit, nuts, and seeds. This will help you resist the temptation to reach for less healthy options when hunger strikes.

5. Bring your own food: If you're traveling by car or plane, consider bringing your own food. Pack sandwiches, wraps, or salads that can be eaten on the go.

6. Use food delivery services: Many cities now have food delivery services that offer plant-based options. This is a great way to enjoy healthy meals from the comfort of your hotel room.

7. Be prepared to explain your dietary needs: When dining out, be prepared to explain your dietary needs to the server or chef. They may not be familiar with a plant-based diet, so be clear about what you can and cannot eat.

By following these tips, you can enjoy delicious and nutritious plant-based meals while eating out or traveling. Remember to plan ahead and be flexible, and you'll be able to stick to your plant-based diet no matter where you are.

Overcoming Challenges and Staying Motivated

Following a plant-based diet can be challenging at times, but there are many ways to overcome these challenges and stay motivated. Here are some tips:

1. Educate yourself: Learn as much as you can about the health and environmental benefits of a plant-based diet. This knowledge will help keep you motivated and committed to your dietary choices.

2. Connect with others: Join online communities or local groups of people who follow a plant-based diet. This will provide you with support, motivation, and inspiration.

3. Be prepared: Plan ahead for meals and snacks by stocking your pantry and fridge with healthy plant-based options. This will make it easier to resist temptation and stick to your dietary goals.

4. Experiment with new recipes: Keep things interesting by trying new plant-based recipes and experimenting with different ingredients and flavors.

5. Focus on whole foods: Avoid processed plant-based foods that are high in salt, sugar, and unhealthy fats. Instead, focus on whole foods such as fruits, vegetables, whole grains, legumes, nuts, and seeds.

6. Don't be too hard on yourself: Remember that nobody is perfect, and slip-ups happen. If you do indulge in something non-plant-based, don't beat yourself up about it. Just get back on track with your next meal.

7. Celebrate your successes: Take time to celebrate your successes and milestones along the way. Whether it's losing weight, feeling more energized, or simply sticking to your dietary goals for a certain period of time, acknowledge and celebrate your achievements.

By following these tips, you can overcome challenges and stay motivated when following a plant-based diet. Remember that every small step counts, and with time and commitment, you'll be able to achieve your dietary goals and enjoy the many benefits of a plant-based lifestyle.

Recommended Exercises

When following a plant-based diet, it's important to engage in regular exercise to support overall health and wellbeing. Here are some recommended exercises:

1. Cardiovascular exercise: Cardiovascular exercise, such as running, cycling, or swimming, is great for improving heart health, burning calories, and reducing stress. Aim for at least 30 minutes of moderate-intensity cardio exercise most days of the week.

2. Strength training: Strength training, such as weightlifting or bodyweight exercises, can help build muscle mass, increase metabolism, and improve bone density. Aim for at least two strength-training sessions per week, targeting all major muscle groups.

3. Yoga: Yoga is a great way to improve flexibility, balance, and mental wellbeing. It can also help reduce stress and anxiety. Try to incorporate yoga into your routine at least once or twice a week.

4. Pilates: Pilates is another low-impact exercise that focuses on strengthening the core muscles and improving posture. It can also help reduce back pain and improve flexibility.

5. Outdoor activities: Hiking, biking, or kayaking are great ways to get outside and enjoy nature while getting exercise. These activities can also help improve cardiovascular health and reduce stress.

Remember to consult with a healthcare provider before starting any new exercise program, especially if you have any underlying health conditions. By incorporating these exercises into your routine, you can support your overall health and wellbeing while following a plant-based diet.

30-Day Meal Plan

DAYS	BREAKFAST	LUNCH	DINNER	SNACK/DESSERT
1	Fruity Granola P 10	Whole-Grain Corn Muffins P 21	Classic French Vinaigrette P 70	Pepita and Almond Squares P 31
2	Baked Deep-Dish Apple Pancake P 10	BLAT (Bacon, Lettuce, Avocado and Tomato) Pitas P 21	Tabbouleh Salad P 69	Great Smoky Almonds P 31
3	Ful Medames (Egyptian Breakfast Beans) P 10	Slow Cooker Black Bean and Lentil Super Burritos P 22	Orange, Fennel and White Bean Salad P 65	Spiced Glazed Carrots P 31
4	Avocado Toast P 11	Smoky Cajun Bowl P 23	Warm Lentil Salad P 68	Seeded Bars P 32
5	Hemp and Vanilla Bircher Breakfast P 11	Cabbage and Millet Pilaf P 21	Lemon Garlic Chickpeas Salad P 67	Choco Almond Bars P 32
6	Stuffed Breakfast Sweet Potatoes P 11	Koshari (Lentils with Rice and Macaroni) P 22	Chickpea Apple Salad P 67	Carrot Cake Two-Bite Balls P 33
7	Peanut Butter and Strawberry Jam Oatmeal P 12	Cuban-Style Black Beans with Cilantro Rice P 23	Orange, Beet and Bean Salad P 70	Over-the-Top Bars to Go P 33
8	Chocolate Quinoa Breakfast Bowl P 12	Smoked Tofu and Beans Bowl P 23	Sweet Potato, Kale, and Red Cabbage Salad P 67	Greens and Beans Dip P 32
9	Liver Flush Juice P 12	Marinated Tempeh P 24	Lentil Cranberry Salad P 66	Tamari Toasted Almonds P 39
10	Granola P 13	Marinated Beans P 24	Detox Salad P 70	Guacamole P 32
11	Fruited Barley P 13	Quinoa Tabouli P 64	Vegan "Toona" Salad P 64	Garlic Hummus P 34
12	Vanilla Buckwheat Porridge P 13	Smoky Potato Salad over Greens P 65	Tangy Cabbage, Apples, and Potatoes P 46	Maple-Glazed Mixed Nuts P 13
13	Sweet Potato and Black Bean Hash P 12	Rice Salad with Fennel, Orange and Chickpeas P 13	Roasted Carrots with Ginger Maple Cream P 47	Seeded Whole-Grain Crackers P 34
14	Grain-Free Porridge P 13	Zingy Melon and Mango Salad P 66	Delicata Squash Boats P 48	Raw Date Chocolate Balls P 33
15	Breakfast Potatoes P 66	Creamy Chickpea and Avocado Salad P 64	Grilled Vegetable Kabobs P 44	Basic Oil-Free Hummus P 66
16	Almond and Protein Shake P 15	Bean and Corn Salad P 80	Ratatouille P 49	Superfood Caramels P 82
17	Walnut Crunch Banana Bread P 11	Winter Sunshine Salad P 70	Teriyaki Mushrooms P 66	Stone Fruit Chia Pudding P 82

DAYS	BREAKFAST	LUNCH	DINNER	SNACK/DESSERT
18	A.M. Breakfast Scramble P 66	Bulgur Lettuce Cups P 68	Provençal Potato Gratin P 43	Caramel-Coconut Frosted Brownies P 66
19	Easy Gluten-Free Waffles P 15	Beet, Cabbage, and Black Bean Salad P 66	Fluffy Mashed Potatoes with Gravy P 47	Zesty Orange-Cranberry Energy Bites P 83
20	Paradise Island Overnight Oatmeal P 66	Thai-ish Cabbage Salad P 68	Roasted Carrots with Ginger Maple Cream P 66	Nutty Raspberry Thumbprint Cookies P 82
21	Cherry Pecan Granola Bars P 66	Radish Turmeric Pickle P 45	Soy Mince Noodle Bowl P 25	Chocolate Lava Mug Cake P 66
22	Savory Oatmeal P 14	Loaded Frijoles P 44	Fancy Rice P 24	Nice Cream P 83
23	Lazy Steel-Cut Oatmeal P 16	Savory Sweet Potato Casserole P 44	Red Curry "Fried" Rice P 25	Chocolate Lava Mug Cake P 84
24	Plant-Powered Pancakes P 11	Fennel and Green Cabbage Kraut P 45	Barley and Sweet Potato Pilaf P 45	Molasses-Ginger Oat Cookie Balls P 84
25	Stovetop Blueberry Oatmeal P 13	Garlicky Winter Vegetable and White Bean Mash P 43	Oil-Free Rice-and-Vegetable Stir-Fry P 26	Vanilla Corn Cake with Roasted Strawberries P 84
26	Vanilla Protein Pancakes P 17	Oven-Roasted Dijon Veggies P 47	Mexican Quinoa Bowl P 27	Triple Chocolate Icebox Cake P 85
27	Zucchini Bread Oatmeal P 19	Vegan Goulash P 46	Fava Bean Ratatouille P 27	Blueberry-Lime Sorbet P 82
28	Banana-Date Shake with Oats P 19	Baked Sweet Potato Fries P 47	Mango Satay Tempeh Bowl P 27	Golden Banana Bread P 85
29	Slow Cooker Apples and Oats P 19	Cauliflower and Pine Nut "Ricotta" Toasts P 45	Green Chile Rice with Black Beans P 28	Chocolate-Covered Strawberries P 86
30	Tofu Rancheros P 17	Garlic Toast P 46	Nut-Crusted Tofu P 27	Baked Apples P 83

Chapter

2

Breakfasts

Fruity Granola

Prep time: 15 minutes | Cook time: 45 minutes | Makes 5 cups

2 cups rolled oats
¾ cup whole-grain flour
1 tablespoon ground cinnamon
1 teaspoon ground ginger (optional)
½ cup sunflower seeds or walnuts, chopped
½ cup almonds, chopped
½ cup pumpkin seeds
½ cup unsweetened shredded coconut
1¼ cups pure fruit juice (cranberry, apple, or something similar)
½ cup raisins or dried cranberries
½ cup goji berries (optional)

1. Preheat the oven to 350ºF (180ºC). 2. In a large bowl, combine oats, flour, cinnamon, ginger, sunflower seeds, almonds, pumpkin seeds, and coconut. 3. Sprinkle juice over the mixture and stir until it is just moistened. Adjust the liquid amount based on the absorption of oats and flour. 4. Spread the granola evenly on a large baking sheet. After approximately 15 minutes, use a spatula to turn the granola to ensure even drying. Bake for an additional 30 minutes or until desired crunchiness is achieved. 5. Remove the granola from the oven and mix in raisins and goji berries (if using). 6. Store any leftovers in an airtight container for up to 2 weeks.

Per Serving: (½ cup)

calories: 222 | fat: 10g | protein: 9g | carbs: 32g | fiber: 6g

Baked Deep-Dish Apple Pancake

Prep time: 10 minutes | Cook time: 35 minutes | Serves 8

4 tart apples, peeled, cored, and thinly sliced
¼ cup chopped walnuts or pecans (optional)
1 teaspoon ground cinnamon
1½ cups whole wheat flour
2 teaspoons baking powder
¼ teaspoon plus ⅛ teaspoon salt (optional)
1 cup light or full-fat coconut milk
2 tablespoons maple syrup (optional)
1 tablespoon plus 1 teaspoon fresh lemon juice
1 teaspoon vanilla extract
¼ cup coconut sugar (optional)

1. Begin by preheating the oven to 375ºF (190ºC) and placing a deep cast-iron skillet over medium heat. Once the skillet is warm, add the apples, ½ teaspoon of cinnamon, and optionally, walnuts in a single layer. Allow the apples to cook while you prepare the batter. 2. In a medium bowl, combine the flour, baking powder, and ¼ teaspoon of salt (if desired). In a separate bowl, mix the coconut milk, maple syrup (if desired), 1 tablespoon of lemon juice, and vanilla together. Pour the wet mixture into the dry ingredients and whisk until just combined. 3. Sprinkle the sugar, remaining 1 teaspoon of lemon juice, and remaining ⅛ teaspoon of salt (if desired) over the apples. 4. Now, pour the batter on top of the apples and place the skillet in the oven. Bake for 30 to 35 minutes, or until the pancake is thoroughly cooked and has a golden brown color. 5. Once done, slice the pancake into wedges, scoop onto plates, and serve. Enjoy your delicious cast-iron skillet apple pancake!

Per Serving:

calories: 233 | fat: 10g | protein: 4g | carbs: 37g | fiber: 6g

Ful Medames (Egyptian Breakfast Beans)

Prep time: 15 minutes | Cook time: 2 hours | Serves 4

1½ pounds (680 g) dried fava beans, soaked for 8 to 10 hours
1 medium yellow onion, peeled and diced small
4 cloves garlic, peeled and minced
1 teaspoon ground cumin
Zest and juice of 1 lemon
Salt, to taste (optional)
1 lemon, quartered

1. Start by draining and rinsing the beans, then place them in a large pot. Add enough water to cover the beans by 4 inches and bring it to a boil over high heat. Once boiling, reduce the heat to medium, cover the pot, and let the beans cook until they become tender, which usually takes about 1½ to 2 hours. 2. While the beans are cooking, take a medium skillet or saucepan and sauté the onion over medium heat for about 8 to 10 minutes, or until the onion becomes tender and begins to brown. Add the garlic, cumin, lemon zest, and juice to the skillet and continue cooking for an additional 5 minutes. Set this mixture aside until the beans are fully cooked. 3. Once the beans are tender, drain all but ½ cup of the cooking liquid from the pot. Now, add the sautéed onion mixture to the beans and mix everything well. If desired, season with salt to taste. Finally, serve the dish garnished with lemon quarters for an extra zesty touch.

Per Serving:

calories: 170 | fat: 1g | protein: 14g | carbs: 35g | fiber: 13g

To the Power of Four Overnight Oats

Prep time: 10 minutes | Cook time: 0 minutes | Serves 2

3½ cups unsweetened almond milk
2 cups old-fashioned oats
¼ cup maple syrup (optional)
2 tablespoons chia seeds
2 tablespoons unsweetened
shredded coconut
¼ cup sunflower seed kernels
4 tablespoons peanut butter, divided
Sunflower seed kernels, for garnish (optional)

1. Add all the ingredients except for 2 tablespoons of the peanut butter and the sunflower seeds to a large bowl. Mix well. It will seem very wet but the chia seeds and oats will absorb some of the milk. Cover and place in the refrigerator to set overnight. 2. To serve in the morning, dot the remaining 2 tablespoons peanut butter around the inside of two bowls and fill each with the overnight oats. Garnish with sunflower seeds, if desired.

Per Serving:

calories: 559 | fat: 21g | protein: 24g | carbs: 46g | fiber: 10g

Avocado Toast

Prep time: 10 minutes | Cook time: 0 minutes | Makes 2 slices

1 ripe avocado, halved, pitted, and sliced	2 large slices toast
	Salt (optional)

1. In a small bowl, mash the avocado and spread it evenly onto the toast. If you prefer, sprinkle some salt on top to taste.

Per Serving: (1 slice)

calories: 243 | fat: 16g | protein: 5g | carbs: 24g | fiber: 9g

Hemp and Vanilla Bircher Breakfast

Prep time: 15 minutes | Cook time: 0 minutes | Serves 1

⅓ cup certified gluten-free rolled oats	(optional)
1 tablespoon hulled hemp seeds	1 cup unsweetened almond milk
1 tablespoon chia seeds	1 teaspoon pure maple syrup, or to taste (optional)
¼ teaspoon vanilla powder or pure vanilla extract	Serve:
⅛ teaspoon fine sea salt	Chopped fresh fruit
	Nut or seed butter

1. In a small sealable jar or any other container, mix together the oats, hemp seeds, chia seeds, vanilla powder, and, if preferred, a pinch of sea salt. Pour in the almond milk and stir everything until well combined. Put the lid on the container and refrigerate it for at least 4 hours, preferably overnight. 2. Once the bircher breakfast has chilled, take it out of the refrigerator and remove the lid. Add the maple syrup to the jar and give it a good stir to blend the flavors. Serve the bircher with fresh fruit and, if desired, a spoonful of nut or seed butter for added richness. Enjoy your delicious and nutritious breakfast!

Per Serving:

calories: 302 | fat: 12g | protein: 10g | carbs: 33g | fiber: 9g

Stuffed Breakfast Sweet Potatoes

Prep time: 5 minutes | Cook time: 10 minutes | Serves 2

2 medium sweet potatoes	2 tablespoons maple syrup
2 tablespoons almond butter	(optional)
2 tablespoons plain plant-based yogurt	½ cup store-bought granola

1. Begin by thoroughly scrubbing the sweet potatoes to clean them. Then, take a fork and poke holes all over each potato. 2. Next, place the prepared sweet potatoes on a microwave-safe plate. Microwave them on high for 2-minute intervals, making sure to turn them over after each interval. Keep microwaving until the sweet potatoes are easily pierced with a fork. Alternatively, you can bake them in the oven on a sheet pan at 400ºF (205ºC) for approximately 40 minutes or until they can be easily pierced with a fork. 3. Once the sweet potatoes are cooked, allow them to cool for a few minutes until they are easy to handle. Cut each potato lengthwise down the middle to expose the insides. Use a fork to lightly mash the insides and open the potato wider. 4. Drizzle each sweet potato half with almond butter, yogurt, and maple syrup (if using), and then sprinkle some granola on top for added texture and flavor. 5. Serve the sweet potatoes while still hot and enjoy this delicious and nutritious treat!

Per Serving:

calories: 410 | fat: 16g | protein: 9g | carbs: 62g | fiber: 8g

Plant-Powered Pancakes

Prep time: 5 minutes | Cook time: 15 minutes | Makes 8 pancakes

1 cup whole-wheat flour	½ cup unsweetened applesauce
1 teaspoon baking powder	¼ cup maple syrup (optional)
½ teaspoon ground cinnamon	1 teaspoon vanilla extract
1 cup plant-based milk	

1. In a large bowl, combine the flour, baking powder, and cinnamon. 2. Stir in the milk, applesauce, maple syrup (if desired), and vanilla until no dry flour is left and the batter is smooth. 3. Heat a large, nonstick skillet or griddle over medium heat. For each pancake, pour ¼ cup of batter onto the hot skillet. Once bubbles form over the top of the pancake and the sides begin to brown, flip and cook for 1 to 2 minutes more. 4. Repeat until all of the batter is used, and serve.

Per Serving: (2 pancakes)

calories: 210 | fat: 2g | protein: 5g | carbs: 44g | fiber: 5g

Walnut Crunch Banana Bread

Prep time: 5 minutes | Cook time: 1 hour | Makes 1 loaf

4 ripe bananas	1½ cups whole-wheat flour
¼ cup maple syrup (optional)	½ teaspoon ground cinnamon
1 tablespoon apple cider vinegar	½ teaspoon baking soda
1 teaspoon vanilla extract	¼ cup walnut pieces (optional)

1. To start, preheat your oven to 350ºF (180ºC). 2. In a large bowl, take a fork or a mixing spoon to mash the bananas until they turn into a smooth purée. Then, stir in the maple syrup (if desired), apple cider vinegar, and vanilla to enhance the flavor. 3. Add the flour, cinnamon, and baking soda to the bowl and mix everything together until well combined. If you choose to include walnut pieces, gently fold them into the batter. 4. Carefully pour the batter into a loaf pan, making sure not to fill it more than three-quarters of the way full. Bake the loaf for approximately 1 hour or until a knife inserted into the middle comes out clean. 5. Once done, remove the loaf from the oven and let it cool on the countertop for at least 30 minutes before serving.

Per Serving: (⅛ loaf)

calories: 178 | fat: 1g | protein: 4g | carbs: 40g | fiber: 5g

Peanut Butter and Strawberry Jam Oatmeal

Prep time: 5 minutes | Cook time: 20 minutes | Serves 4

2 cups rolled oats
4 cups water
½ cup unsweetened plant-based milk
1 tablespoon maple syrup (optional)
Pinch of salt (optional)
4 tablespoons natural peanut butter, divided
4 tablespoons no-sugar-added strawberry jam, divided

1. Start by combining the oats and water in a medium saucepan. Bring it to a boil over medium-high heat. Once boiling, reduce the heat to medium-low and let it simmer, stirring often, until the oats become soft and creamy, which usually takes about 15 minutes. Once done, remove the saucepan from the heat. Now, add the plant-based milk, maple syrup, and salt (if desired), and stir everything together until well combined. 2. Divide the oatmeal equally among four bowls. On top of each serving, add 1 tablespoon of peanut butter and 1 tablespoon of jam. Serve immediately for a warm and delightful breakfast. 3. If you have leftovers, you can store the oatmeal in an airtight container in the refrigerator for up to 4 days. To serve again, simply reheat the oatmeal in a medium saucepan over low heat, adding 2 tablespoons of water to loosen it up, as chilled oatmeal tends to become solid. Just before serving, add the peanut butter and jam to enjoy the delicious flavors.

Per Serving:
calories: 284 | fat: 12g | protein: 11g | carbs: 35g| fiber: 6g

Sweet Potato and Black Bean Hash

Prep time: 10 minutes | Cook time: 2 to 3 hours | Serves 4 to 6

1 shallot, diced
2 cups peeled, chopped sweet potatoes (about 1 large or 2 small)
1 medium bell pepper (any color), diced
2 garlic cloves, minced
1 (14½-ounce / 411-g) can black beans, drained and
rinsed
1 teaspoon paprika
½ teaspoon onion powder
½ teaspoon garlic powder
¼ cup store-bought low-sodium vegetable broth
4 to 6 tablespoons unsweetened plant-based milk

1. In the slow cooker, combine the shallot, sweet potatoes, bell pepper, garlic, beans, paprika, onion powder, garlic powder, and broth. Stir everything together to ensure they are well mixed. Cover the slow cooker and cook on Low for 2 to 3 hours, or until the sweet potatoes become tender. 2. Once the cooking time is up, remove the lid and add the milk, starting with 4 tablespoons. Stir everything together to develop a creamy sauce. If needed, you can add more milk to achieve the desired consistency. Allow the mixture to heat through for a few minutes before serving.

Per Serving:

calories: 251 | fat: 1g | protein: 9g | carbs: 53g | fiber: 14g

Chocolate Quinoa Breakfast Bowl

Prep time: 5 minutes | Cook time: 25 to 30 minutes | Serves 2

1 cup quinoa
1 teaspoon ground cinnamon
1 cup nondairy milk
1 cup water
1 large banana
2 to 3 tablespoons unsweetened cocoa powder
1 to 2 tablespoons almond butter, or other nut or seed butter
1 tablespoon ground flaxseed, or chia or hemp seeds
2 tablespoons walnuts
¼ cup raspberries

1. In a medium pot, combine the quinoa, cinnamon, milk, and water. Bring the mixture to a boil over high heat, and then reduce the heat to low, covering the pot. Let it simmer for 25 to 30 minutes until the quinoa is fully cooked. 2. While the quinoa is simmering, take a medium bowl and either purée or mash the banana. Stir in the cocoa powder, almond butter, and flaxseed until well combined. 3. To serve, spoon 1 cup of the cooked quinoa into a bowl. Top it with half of the prepared pudding mixture and half of the walnuts and raspberries.

Per Serving:
calories: 564 | fat: 17g | protein: 21g | carbs: 86g | fiber: 13g

Liver Flush Juice

Prep time: 15 minutes | Cook time: 0 minutes | Serves 1

1 beet, scrubbed and trimmed
1 (1-inch) piece fresh turmeric, or 1 teaspoon ground turmeric
5 carrots, scrubbed and trimmed
1 grapefruit, peeled
1 lemon, peeled
¼ cup purified water, if using a blender

Using a Juicer:
1. Simply feed all the ingredients through your juicer. Give the juice a quick stir and serve immediately for a refreshing drink.
Without a Juicer:
1. Begin by cutting the vegetables into bite-sized pieces. 2. In a blender, combine all the ingredients and blend until you achieve a smooth consistency. To help with blending, you can add about ¼ cup of purified water. 3. Place a fine-mesh strainer over a large bowl and carefully pour the blended juice through it. Then, using a wooden spoon or spatula, press the pulp down to extract all the juice and ensure none goes to waste. 4. Allow the juice to sit for 2 to 3 minutes, giving it time to drain and separate further. Afterward, discard the pulp from the strainer. 5. Finally, pour the freshly extracted juice into a serving glass and drink it immediately to enjoy its wholesome goodness.

Per Serving:
calories: 261 | fat: 1g | protein: 6g | carbs: 60g | fiber: 14g

Granola

Prep time: 15 minutes | Cook time: 35 minutes | Makes 15 cups

4 cups rolled oats	seeds
2 cups raw buckwheat groats	¼ cup chia seeds
4 cups unsweetened flaked	1 teaspoon fine sea salt
dried coconut	(optional)
1 cup whole raw almonds	1 teaspoon ground cinnamon
1 cup raw nuts, roughly	¾ cup brown rice syrup or
chopped	yacon syrup (optional)
1 cup raw pumpkin seeds	½ cup melted extra-virgin
½ cup raw sunflower seeds	coconut oil (optional)
½ cup raw unhulled sesame	1 tablespoon vanilla extract

1. To start, preheat your oven to 300ºF (150ºC). Line two rimmed baking sheets with parchment paper and set them aside. 2. In a large bowl, combine the oats, buckwheat, coconut, almonds, raw nuts, pumpkin seeds, sunflower seeds, sesame seeds, chia seeds, and, if desired, a pinch of salt and cinnamon. Mix everything together thoroughly and set it aside. If you choose to use brown rice syrup, gently warm it with the coconut oil in a small saucepan over low heat, stirring until smooth. Then, add the vanilla and stir again. Alternatively, if you opt for yacon syrup, simply stir the syrup and oil together in a small bowl, and then mix in the vanilla. Pour this syrup mixture over the oat-nut mixture and mix everything well to combine. 3. Now, divide the combined mixture between the prepared baking sheets and spread it out evenly. Bake in the preheated oven for 15 minutes. Then, take the trays out, give the granola a stir, rotate the trays, and return them to the oven for another 15 minutes or until the granola turns golden and emits a delightful fragrance. Be cautious during this step as it can easily burn. Remember that the granola will continue to crisp up as it cools. 4. Once you've achieved the desired color and crispness, remove the granola from the oven and let it cool completely. After cooling, transfer it to airtight jars for storage. Properly stored, this delicious homemade granola can stay fresh for up to 6 weeks.

Per Serving: (1 cup)

calories: 343 | fat: 22g | protein: 12g | carbs: 37g | fiber: 8g

Fruited Barley

Prep time: 10 minutes | Cook time: 55 minutes | Serves 2

1 to 1½ cups orange juice	1 small cinnamon stick
1 cup pearled barley	⅛ teaspoon ground cloves
2 tablespoons dried currants	Pinch salt, or to taste
3 to 4 dried unsulfured	(optional)
apricots, chopped	

1. In a medium saucepan over medium heat, bring 1 cup of water and 1 cup of orange juice to a boil. Add the barley, currants, apricots, cinnamon stick, cloves, and, if desired, a pinch of salt. Bring the mixture to a boil again, then cover the saucepan, reduce the heat to medium-low, and let it cook for 45 minutes.

If after 45 minutes the barley is not tender, you can add up to an additional ½ cup of orange juice and continue cooking for another 10 minutes to ensure it reaches the desired texture. 2. Before serving the dish, remember to remove the cinnamon stick to prevent it from being served accidentally.

Per Serving:

calories: 420 | fat: 1g | protein: 10g | carbs: 93g | fiber: 16g

Vanilla Buckwheat Porridge

Prep time: 5 minutes | Cook time: 25 minutes | Serves 4

3 cups water	1 tablespoon hemp seeds
1 cup raw buckwheat groats	1 tablespoon sesame seeds,
1 teaspoon ground cinnamon	toasted
1 banana, sliced	½ cup unsweetened nondairy
¼ cup golden raisins	milk
¼ cup dried currants	1 tablespoon pure maple syrup
¼ cup sunflower seeds	(optional)
2 tablespoons chia seeds	1 teaspoon vanilla extract

1. Place an 8-quart pot over high heat and bring the water to a boil. Stir in the buckwheat, cinnamon, and banana. Continue stirring as the mixture comes to a boil, then reduce the heat to medium-low. Cover the pot and let the mixture cook for about 15 minutes or until the buckwheat becomes tender. Once done, remove the pot from the heat. 2. Now, add the raisins, currants, sunflower seeds, chia seeds, hemp seeds, sesame seeds, milk, and, if you prefer, maple syrup for sweetness. Also, stir in the vanilla to enhance the flavor. Cover the pot again and let everything sit for about 10 minutes before serving. 3. You can serve this delightful buckwheat dish as is or top it with your favorite toppings as desired.

Per Serving:

calories: 353 | fat: 11g | protein: 10g | carbs: 61g | fiber: 10g

Stovetop Blueberry Oatmeal

Prep time: 10 minutes | Cook time: 8 minutes | Serves 2

1½ cups plant-based milk	1 teaspoon cinnamon or
1 cup old-fashioned rolled oats	pumpkin pie spices
½ cup fresh or frozen	2 tablespoons chopped nuts
blueberries	2 to 3 tablespoons granola
Optional Toppings:	1 tablespoon coconut shreds
1 tablespoon maple syrup	2 tablespoons raw sunflower
(optional)	seeds

1. In a medium saucepan over medium-high heat, bring the milk to a boil. 2. Stir in the oats and frozen blueberries and reduce the heat to low. 3. Simmer for 5 minutes, stirring occasionally. 4. Remove from the heat and serve with optional toppings.

Per Serving:

calories: 227 | fat: 7g | protein: 15g | carbs: 44g | fiber: 8g

Grain-Free Porridge

Prep time: 10 minutes | Cook time: 20 minutes | Makes 3½ cups

½ cup whole raw almonds, soaked overnight in 2 cups filtered water
3 cups filtered water
¼ cup coconut flour
Pinch of fine sea salt (optional)

½ cup raw sunflower seeds, soaked overnight in 2 cups filtered water
½ cup unsweetened flaked dried coconut
3 tablespoons whole flaxseeds
2 tablespoons chia seeds

1. Start by draining and rinsing the almonds. Transfer them to an upright blender and add 3 cups of water, coconut flour, and, if desired, a pinch of salt. Blend the mixture until it becomes smooth and creamy. Next, drain and rinse the sunflower seeds and add them to the blender along with the coconut. Pulse the blender until the seeds and coconut are coarsely ground. 2. Pour the blended mixture into a medium pot and bring it to a boil over high heat, whisking frequently to ensure even cooking. Once it reaches a boil, remove the pot from the heat and whisk in the flax and chia seeds until they are thoroughly combined. Cover the pot and set it aside for about 5 minutes, allowing the porridge to thicken. 3. After the brief resting period, give the porridge another whisk to achieve the desired consistency and texture. Serve the creamy and nutritious porridge as a delicious breakfast option. 4. For any leftover porridge, transfer it into a wide-mouthed glass jar or any other container. Allow it to cool before covering it tightly and storing it in the refrigerator for up to 4 days.

Per Serving: (½ cup)
calories: 181 | fat: 15g | protein: 6g | carbs: 9g | fiber: 5g

Breakfast Potatoes

Prep time: 10 minutes | Cook time: 20 minutes | Serves 4 to 6

1½ pounds (680 g) Yukon Gold potatoes, cut into bite-size pieces
½ cup vegetable broth
1 teaspoon dried parsley
¼ teaspoon freshly ground

black pepper
½ teaspoon garlic powder
½ teaspoon onion powder
½ teaspoon paprika
¼ teaspoon dried sage
¼ teaspoon dried thyme

1. Take a nonstick sauté pan or skillet and combine the potatoes, broth, parsley, and pepper in it. Place the pan over medium heat and bring the mixture to a simmer. Cover the pan and let it cook for approximately 15 to 20 minutes, or until the potatoes become tender enough for a knife to easily slide into them. Once done, remove the pan from the heat. 2. While the potatoes are cooking, in a small bowl, mix together the garlic powder, onion powder, paprika, sage, and thyme to create a flavorful spice blend. 3. After removing the pan from the heat, sprinkle the prepared spice mixture over the potatoes and stir thoroughly to ensure they are evenly coated.

Per Serving:
calories: 95 | fat: 0g | protein: 3g | carbs: 21g | fiber: 2g

A.M. Breakfast Scramble

Prep time: 5 minutes | Cook time: 15 minutes | Serves 2

1 (14-ounce / 397-g) package firm or extra-firm tofu
4 ounces (113 g) sliced mushrooms
½ diced bell pepper
2 tablespoons nutritional yeast
1 tablespoon vegetable broth

or water
½ teaspoon garlic powder
½ teaspoon onion powder
⅛ teaspoon freshly ground black pepper
1 cup fresh spinach

1. Begin by heating a large skillet over medium-low heat. 2. Drain the tofu and place it in the skillet. Using a fork or a mixing spoon, mash the tofu down to achieve a crumbled texture. Stir in the mushrooms, bell pepper, nutritional yeast, broth, garlic powder, onion powder, and pepper. Cover the skillet and let the mixture cook for 10 minutes, stirring once around the 5-minute mark. 3. After 10 minutes, uncover the skillet and stir in the spinach. Cook for an additional 5 minutes to allow the flavors to meld and the spinach to wilt.

Per Serving:
calories: 230 | fat: 10g | protein: 27g | carbs: 16g | fiber: 7g

Savory Oatmeal

Prep time: 10 minutes | Cook time: 10 minutes | Makes 2 bowls

1 cup gluten-free old-fashioned rolled oats
1 carrot, peeled and shredded
1½ cups water
1 cup stemmed and chopped kale
¼ cup salsa or marinara sauce
2 tablespoons nutritional yeast

½ chopped avocado
2 tablespoons roasted pumpkin seeds
Smoked paprika or crushed red pepper (optional)
Salt and black pepper (optional)

1. In a small saucepan over medium heat, combine the oats and carrot. Add water, adjusting the amount to achieve your desired oatmeal consistency (approximately 1½ cups of water for a fairly thick oatmeal). 2. Heat the mixture until it starts simmering, then continue to cook, stirring often, until both the oats and carrot become tender, which usually takes about 5 minutes. 3. Once everything is tender, stir in the kale, salsa, and nutritional yeast to add a burst of flavors. 4. Pour the oatmeal into a bowl and generously top it with avocado and pumpkin seeds. For an extra kick, you can sprinkle some smoked paprika and crushed red pepper if desired. Add salt (if desired) and pepper to taste, and your savory oatmeal is ready to be served.

Per Serving: (½ bowl)
calories: 153 | fat: 7g | protein: 9g | carbs: 24g | fiber: 7g

Easy Gluten-Free Waffles

Prep time: 15 minutes | Cook time: 20 minutes | Makes 6 waffles

1 cup almond flour
1¼ cups certified gluten-free oat flour
½ cup finely shredded unsweetened coconut
2 teaspoons aluminum-free baking powder
1½ teaspoons arrowroot powder
1 teaspoon ground cinnamon
½ teaspoon fine sea salt (optional)
2 tablespoons ground flaxseed
½ cup mashed ripe banana
1¼ cups unsweetened almond milk
2 tablespoons liquid virgin coconut oil (optional)
1 tablespoon pure maple syrup (optional)
1 teaspoon pure vanilla extract
Serve:
Nut or seed butter
Sliced fresh fruit or whole berries
Pure maple syrup (optional)
Others toppings of your choice

1. Start by preheating your oven to 275ºF (135ºC) and place a baking sheet inside to warm up. 2. In a large bowl, whisk together the almond flour, oat flour, shredded coconut, baking powder, arrowroot powder, cinnamon, and, if desired, a pinch of sea salt. 3. In a blender or food processor, combine the ground flaxseed, mashed banana, almond milk, coconut oil, maple syrup (if using), and vanilla. Blend on high for about a minute until well mixed. 4. Add the flax and banana mixture to the dry ingredients and gently stir until just combined. Allow the batter to sit for 12 to 15 minutes to thicken. 5. Heat your waffle iron to a setting in the higher range; a slightly hotter setting works best for these waffles. Once the waffle iron is ready, lightly grease the irons with some coconut oil using either a pastry brush or a paper towel. Drop ½ cup of the batter into the center of the bottom iron and close the lid. Remove the waffle when the timer goes off or when it appears golden brown all across the top. 6. Keep the cooked waffles warm on the baking sheet in the oven while you repeat the cooking process with the remaining batter. 7. Serve the delicious waffles with your choice of nut or seed butter, fresh fruit, maple syrup, or any other accompaniments you enjoy.

Per Serving:

½ cup: calories: 302 | fat: 11g | protein: 7g | carbs: 35g | fiber: 5g

Almond and Protein Shake

Prep time: 5 minutes | Cook time: 0 minutes | Serves 2

1½ cups soy milk
3 tablespoons almonds
1 teaspoon maple syrup (optional)
1 tablespoon coconut oil (optional)
2 scoops of chocolate or vanilla flavor vegan protein powder
2 to 4 ice cubes
1 teaspoon cocoa powder (optional)

1. Place all the necessary ingredients in a blender, and if you'd like, add the optional cocoa powder. Blend the mixture for 2 minutes until smooth and well combined. Transfer the shake to a large cup or shaker. Serve and savor the delightful flavors!

Per Serving:

calories: 340 | fat: 17g | protein: 32g | carbs: 15g | fiber: 2g

Cherry Pecan Granola Bars

Prep time: 10 minutes | Cook time: 45 minutes | Makes 12 bars

2 cups rolled oats
½ cup dates, pitted and coarsely chopped
½ cup orange juice
¼ cup chopped pecans
1 cup fruit-sweetened dried
cherries
½ teaspoon ground cinnamon
¼ teaspoon ground allspice
Pinch salt, or to taste (optional)

1. Begin by preheating your oven to 325ºF (165ºC). 2. Spread the oats evenly on a 13 × 18-inch baking sheet and bake them for about 10 minutes or until they start to turn slightly brown. Once done, remove the oats from the oven and transfer them to a large mixing bowl. 3. In a small saucepan, combine the dates and orange juice. Cook the mixture over medium-low heat for approximately 15 minutes until the dates soften. Pour the cooked date mixture into a blender and process it until it becomes smooth and creamy. 4. Add the date mixture to the bowl with the oats. Also, add the pecans, dried cherries, cinnamon, allspice, and, if desired, a pinch of salt. Mix everything together well. 5. Press the oat mixture into a nonstick 8 × 8-inch baking pan, ensuring it is evenly distributed. Bake the mixture for around 20 minutes or until the top turns lightly golden. 6. Allow the baked bars to cool before slicing them into individual bars.

Per Serving:

calories: 92 | fat: 2g | protein: 3g | carbs: 20g | fiber: 3g

Overnight Pumpkin Spice Chia Pudding

Prep time: 10 minutes | Cook time: 0 minutes | Serves 4

¾ cup chia seeds
2 cups unsweetened plant-based milk
1 (15-ounce / 425-g) can unsweetened pumpkin purée
¼ cup maple syrup (optional)
1 tablespoon pumpkin pie spice blend
1 cup water
½ cup pecans, for serving

1. In a large bowl, combine the chia seeds, plant-based milk, pumpkin purée, and, if desired, maple syrup. Sprinkle in the pumpkin pie spice and add water to the mixture. Whisk everything together until well blended. 2. Divide the chia seed mixture evenly among 4 mason jars or containers with lids. Let the mixture sit for about 10 minutes to allow the chia seeds to absorb the liquid. Afterward, stir each container to break up any clumps of chia seeds. Cover the jars or containers with lids and refrigerate them overnight to allow the mixture to firm up. To serve, garnish each jar with some of the pecans for added texture and flavor.

Per Serving:

calories: 421 | fat: 23g | protein: 12g | carbs: 47g | fiber: 20g

Sunshine Muffins

Prep time: 15 minutes | Cook time: 30 minutes | Makes 6 muffins

1 teaspoon coconut oil, for greasing muffin tins (optional)
2 tablespoons almond butter or sunflower seed butter
¼ cup nondairy milk
1 orange, peeled
1 carrot, coarsely chopped
2 tablespoons chopped dried apricots or other dried fruit
3 tablespoons molasses
2 tablespoons ground flaxseed
1 teaspoon apple cider vinegar
1 teaspoon pure vanilla extract
½ teaspoon ground cinnamon
½ teaspoon ground ginger (optional)
¼ teaspoon ground nutmeg (optional)
¼ teaspoon allspice (optional)
¾ cup rolled oats or whole-grain flour
1 teaspoon baking powder
½ teaspoon baking soda
Mix-Ins (optional):
½ cup rolled oats
2 tablespoons raisins or other chopped dried fruit
2 tablespoons sunflower seeds

1. Preheat the oven to 350°F (180°C). Prepare a 6-cup muffin tin by rubbing the insides of the cups with coconut oil (if using) or using silicone or paper muffin cups. 2. Purée the nut butter, milk, orange, carrot, apricots, molasses, flaxseed, vinegar, vanilla, cinnamon, ginger, nutmeg, and allspice in a food processor or blender until somewhat smooth. 3. Grind the oats in a clean coffee grinder until they're the consistency of flour (or use whole-grain flour). In a large bowl, mix the oats with the baking powder and baking soda. 4. Mix the wet ingredients into the dry ingredients until just combined. Fold in the mix-ins (if using). 5. Spoon about ¼ cup batter into each muffin cup and bake for 30 minutes, or until a toothpick inserted into the center comes out clean. The orange creates a very moist base, so the muffins may take longer than 30 minutes, depending on how heavy your muffin tin is.

Per Serving: (1 muffin)
calories: 226 | fat: 8g | protein: 7g | carbs: 34g | fiber: 6g

Lazy Steel-Cut Oatmeal

Prep time: 15 minutes | Cook time: 30 minutes | Serves 1

1 teaspoon virgin coconut oil (optional)
½ teaspoon ground cinnamon
¼ cup certified gluten-free steel-cut oats
2 tablespoons dried sour cherries or other dried fruit
⅛ teaspoon fine sea salt
(optional)
1 cup unsweetened almond milk, plus extra for reheating if necessary
1 tablespoon pure maple syrup, or to taste (optional)
Chopped fresh fruit, for serving (optional)

1. Begin by heating the coconut oil in a small saucepan over medium heat. Stir in the cinnamon, and let it become fragrant for about 30 seconds. Add the oats to the pan, stirring them to coat them in the delightful cinnamon flavor. Then, add the dried cherries, and if desired, a pinch of sea salt. Pour in the almond milk and give everything a good stir. 2. Bring the mixture to a gentle boil. Once it starts boiling, turn off the heat, remove the saucepan from the burner, and cover it with a lid. Leave the oats on the cold stove overnight to soak. 3. The next morning, place the saucepan back on the burner over medium heat. If you prefer a creamier consistency, feel free to add more almond milk. Allow the porridge to come to a boil again, and once it reaches the desired consistency, remove it from the heat. 4. Now, scrape the warm and creamy porridge into your serving bowl. For added sweetness and flavor, top the porridge with maple syrup and your favorite chopped fruits if you like.

Per Serving:
calories: 283 | fat: 9g | protein: 6g | carbs: 35g | fiber: 6g

Apple-Cinnamon French Toast Bake

Prep time: 10 minutes | Cook time: 20 minutes | Serves 4

⅓ cup unsweetened applesauce
⅓ cup unsweetened soy milk
2 tablespoons pure maple syrup, plus more for serving
8 whole-grain bread slices, each cut into 9 squares
½ teaspoon ground cinnamon
¼ cup unsweetened raisins
2 tablespoons rolled oats

1. Start by preheating your oven to 350°F (180°C). 2. In a small bowl, combine the applesauce, soy milk, and maple syrup, mixing them well. 3. Place the bread in a large bowl and sprinkle it with cinnamon. 4. Add the raisins to the large bowl with the bread. 5. Gently fold in the applesauce mixture, making sure the bread absorbs the liquid evenly. 6. Transfer the bread mixture into an 8-by-8-inch glass baking dish, spreading it out evenly. 7. Sprinkle the top of the mixture with oats, adding a delightful crunch. 8. Bake the French toast in the oven for approximately 20 minutes, or until the top turns golden brown and crispy. Once done, remove it from the oven. 9. Divide the delicious French toast among 4 plates, serving each with 1 to 2 tablespoons of maple syrup to add a touch of sweetness.

Per Serving:
calories: 352 | fat:2 g | protein: 9g | carbs: 77g | fiber: 7g

Paradise Island Overnight Oatmeal

Prep time: 5 minutes | Cook time: 0 minutes | Serves 2

2 cups rolled oats
2 cups plant-based milk
½ cup fresh or frozen mango, diced
½ cup fresh or frozen
pineapple chunks
1 sliced banana
1 tablespoon maple syrup (optional)
1 tablespoon chia seeds

1. Combine the oats, milk, mango, pineapple, banana, and, if you prefer, maple syrup in a large bowl. Add chia seeds to the mixture. 2. Cover the bowl and refrigerate it overnight or for at least 4 hours before serving.

Per Serving:
calories: 510 | fat: 12g | protein: 14g | carbs: 93g | fiber: 15g

Tofu Rancheros

Prep time: 10 minutes | Cook time: 20 minutes | Serves 4

1 (15-ounce / 425-g) can black beans, drained and rinsed
½ teaspoon onion powder
½ teaspoon garlic powder
2½ cups water, divided
1 teaspoon extra-virgin olive oil (optional)
½ head cauliflower, cut into florets (about 2 cups)
1 red or yellow bell pepper, seeded and diced small
1 (16-ounce / 454-g) package extra firm-tofu, drained and diced small
½ teaspoon salt, plus more as
needed (optional)
1 teaspoon smoked paprika
2 medium tomatoes, cut into ½-inch pieces
2 teaspoons tomato paste
1 teaspoon chili powder
2 avocados, peeled and pitted
8 (6-inch) corn tortillas
3 tablespoons chopped fresh cilantro, for serving
2 scallions, white and green parts, thinly sliced, for serving
1 lime, cut into quarters, for serving

1. In a small saucepan over medium heat, combine the beans, onion powder, garlic powder, and ½ cup of water and cook until heated through, 5 to 7 minutes. Set aside. 2. In a large saucepan, heat the oil over medium heat. Add the cauliflower and bell pepper and cook, stirring occasionally, for 2 to 3 minutes. Add the tofu, salt (if using), and smoked paprika and cook, stirring often, for 5 minutes. 3. Add the tomatoes, tomato paste, and chili powder and cook, stirring often, until the tomatoes release their juices and the tomato paste turns dark red, 2 to 3 minutes. Add the remaining 2 cups water, stir well, and bring to a boil. Cook until the sauce is thick and the flavors meld, about 4 minutes. 4. In a small bowl, combine the avocados and a pinch of salt and mash until well mixed. 5. In a large skillet, warm the tortillas over medium-high heat, about 2 minutes on each side. Put 2 tortillas on a plate, layer with the tofu mixture, scallions, cilantro, a big dollop of mashed avocado, and a squeeze of lime juice. Put a scoop of black beans on the side and serve.

Per Serving:
calories: 590 | fat: 27g | protein: 27g | carbs: 69g | fiber: 18g

Mango, Pineapple, and Spinach Smoothie

Prep time: 5 minutes | Cook time: 0 minutes | Serves 1

1¼ cups unsweetened vanilla coconut milk (or other unsweetened milk substitute)
1 small avocado, peeled and pitted
1 cup fresh spinach
⅓ cup pineapple chunks
⅓ cup mango chunks
¼ cup almond flour
1 teaspoon maple syrup (optional)
3 ice cubes

1. Place the milk, avocado, spinach, pineapple, mango, flour, maple syrup (if using), and ice cubes in a blender and blend on high until smooth or until the desired consistency is reached. 2.

Pour the smoothie into a glass and enjoy.

Per Serving:
calories: 604 | fat: 42g | protein: 17g | carbs: 52g | fiber: 19g

Vanilla Protein Pancakes

Prep time: 5 minutes | Cook time: 15 minutes | Serves 8

1½ cups pea protein isolate
½ cup whole wheat flour
1½ cups almond milk or water
2 teaspoons baking powder
2 teaspoons vanilla extract
Optional Toppings:
Walnuts
Fresh or frozen blueberries
Shredded coconut

1. Add all ingredients to a blender and blend until smooth, scraping down the sides of the blender to prevent any lumps if necessary. 2. Put a nonstick frying pan over medium heat. 3. Pour a large tablespoon of batter into the frying pan and bake until the edges are dry and bubbles form in the pancake. 4. Flip the pancake and bake the other side until it's lightly browned. 5. Repeat the process for the remaining pancake batter. 6. Serve the pancakes with the optional toppings and enjoy! 7. Store the pancakes in an airtight container in the fridge and consume within 3 days. Alternatively, store in the freezer for a maximum of 30 days and thaw at room temperature. Use a microwave or nonstick frying pan to reheat the pancakes before serving.

Per Serving:
calories: 120 | fat: 2g | protein: 18g | carbs: 9g | fiber: 2g

Banana Almond Granola

Prep time: 10 minutes | Cook time: 50 minutes | Serves 16

8 cups rolled oats
2 cups pitted and chopped dates
2 ripe bananas, peeled and chopped
1 teaspoon almond extract
1 teaspoon salt, or to taste (optional)
1 cup slivered almonds, toasted (optional)

1. Preheat the oven to 275ºF (135ºC). 2. Add the oats to a large mixing bowl and set aside. Line two 13 × 18-inch inch baking pans with parchment paper. 3. Place the dates in a medium saucepan with 1 cup of water, bring to a boil, and cook over medium heat for 10 minutes. Add more water if needed to keep the dates from sticking to the pan. Remove from the heat and add the mixture to a blender with the bananas, almond extract, and salt (if using). Process until smooth and creamy. 4. Add the date mixture to the oats and mix well. Divide the granola between the two prepared pans and spread evenly in the pans. Bake for 40 to 50 minutes, stirring every 10 minutes, until the granola is crispy. Remove from the oven and let cool before adding the slivered almonds, if desired (the cereal will get even crispier as it cools). Store the granola in an airtight container.

Per Serving:
calories: 220 | fat: 6g | protein: 10g | carbs: 49g | fiber: 10g

Seeds, Nuts, and Fruit Baked Granola

Prep time: 10 minutes | Cook time: 40 minutes | Serves 8

7 cups old-fashioned oats (use gluten-free if desired)	1 cup coconut sugar (optional)
1 cup shredded coconut	¼ cup chia seeds
1 cup sunflower seed kernels	1 cup coconut oil (optional)
1 cup walnuts	1 cup raisins

1. Begin by preheating your oven to 300ºF (150ºC). 2. In a mixing bowl, combine all the ingredients except for the raisins. Make sure everything is well mixed. Spread the mixture out evenly in a large baking pan. 3. Bake the mixture for 40 minutes. However, every 10 minutes, take the pan out of the oven and give it a good stir before returning it to the oven. 4. After 30 minutes of baking, add the raisins to the mixture and stir everything together. Continue baking for an additional 10 minutes. 5. Once done, take the pan out of the oven and allow the granola to cool. Then, pack it into an airtight container. This delicious homemade granola will stay fresh for up to 4 weeks.

Per Serving:
calories: 566 | fat: 32g | protein: 20g | carbs: 52g | fiber: 16g

Savory Ginger Green Onion Crepes

Prep time: 5 minutes | Cook time: 20 minutes | Makes 8 crepes

⅔ cup chickpea flour	1 piece of fresh ginger, peeled and finely grated
⅔ cup buckwheat flour	
2 green onions, finely sliced	1 tablespoon sesame seeds
2 teaspoons fine sea salt (optional)	1½ cups filtered water
	Olive oil spray, for cooking
1 teaspoon chili powder	(optional)

1. Preheat the oven to 275ºF (135ºC). Place a baking sheet in the oven. 2. In a large bowl, combine the chickpea flour, buckwheat flour, sliced green onions, sea salt, if using, chili powder, grated ginger, and sesame seeds. Whisk to combine. 3. Add the filtered water to the flour mixture. Whisk the batter until all flour is incorporated. The batter should be thinner than pancake batter, dripping slowly from the edge of a spoon or spatula, but not as thin as almond milk. Add extra water, by the tablespoon, if necessary. 4. Cover the bowl with plastic wrap and allow the batter to rest for 30 minutes. 5. Heat a crepe pan over medium-high heat. If your batter has thickened and seems almost elastic when you drag a spoon through it, add a couple of tablespoons of water and lightly whisk the batter one more time. 6. Spray the hot crepe pan with olive oil, if using. Ladle about ⅓ cup of batter into the crepe pan. Holding the pan's handle with your non-ladling hand, quickly use your wrist to shake the pan in a circular motion, distributing the crepe batter into a thin, circular crepe. I lift the pan right off the stove and shake it in the air to get the batter moving. 7. Once the crepe appears dry on the surface and some holes have poked through, flip the crepe over. Cook the crepe another 45 seconds, or until lightly browned and dry on the other side. 8. Keep the cooked crepes warm on the baking sheet in the oven while you repeat this process with the remaining batter.

Per Serving: (1 crepe)
calories: 87 | fat: 2g | protein: 4g | carbs: 14g | fiber: 3g

Carrot Cake Oatmeal

Prep time: 10 minutes | Cook time: 15 minutes | Serves 2

¼ cup pecans	(optional)
1 cup finely shredded carrot	1 teaspoon ground cinnamon
½ cup old-fashioned oats	1 teaspoon ground ginger
1¼ cups unsweetened nondairy milk	¼ teaspoon ground nutmeg
	2 tablespoons chia seeds
1 tablespoon pure maple syrup	

1. In a small skillet over medium-high heat, toast the pecans for 3 to 4 minutes, stirring often, until browned and fragrant (watch closely, as they can burn quickly). Pour the pecans onto a cutting board and coarsely chop them. Set aside. 2. In an 8-quart pot over medium-high heat, combine the carrot, oats, milk, maple syrup (if using), cinnamon, ginger, and nutmeg. Bring to a boil, then reduce the heat to medium-low. Cook, uncovered, for 10 minutes, stirring occasionally. 3. Stir in the chopped pecans and chia seeds. Serve immediately.

Per Serving:
calories: 307 | fat: 17g | protein: 7g | carbs: 35g | fiber: 11g

Multi-Layered Avocado Toast

Prep time: 15 minutes | Cook time: 5 minutes | Serves 2

1 tablespoon dairy-free butter	Pinch of turmeric
4 ounces (113 g) extra-firm tofu, drained and pressed	1 avocado
	Pinch of ground black pepper
¼ teaspoon black salt (optional)	1 teaspoon lime juice
	2 slices sprouted grain bread
¼ teaspoon onion powder	

1. Add the butter to a skillet and heat over medium-high heat. Crumble tofu into the skillet. Sprinkle with the salt (if desired), onion powder, and turmeric and sauté for about 4 minutes, making sure the tofu is crumbled small. 2. In a small bowl, mash the avocado with the pepper and lime juice. 3. Toast the bread. Spread half of the prepared avocado on each piece of toast. Top with half of the prepared tofu on each piece of toast. Slice the toasts in half at an angle.

Per Serving:
calories: 374 | fat: 18g | protein: 16g | carbs: 28g | fiber: 11g

Banana-Date Shake with Oats

Prep time: 15 minutes | Cook time: 0 minutes | Serves 1

1 Medjool date

10 ounces (283 g) unsweetened vanilla almond milk

1 small banana (fresh or frozen)

2 tablespoons almond butter

¼ cup rolled oats, uncooked

3 ice cubes

Pinch ground cinnamon (optional)

1. Soak the date in hot water for 5 minutes to soften it. 2. Remove the date from the hot water, place it in a blender, and add the milk, banana, almond butter, oats, ice cubes, and cinnamon (if using). Blend until smooth. 3. Enjoy immediately.

Per Serving:

calories: 526 | fat: 22g | protein: 19g | carbs: 72g | fiber: 11g

Slow Cooker Apples and Oats

Prep time: 15 minutes | Cook time: 3 hours | Serves 2

1½ cups peeled and sliced apples

1 cup old-fashioned oats

½ cup melted dairy-free butter

½ cup coconut sugar (optional)

2 tablespoons lemon juice

2 tablespoons hempseed, toasted in shell

1 teaspoon ground cinnamon

1 cup chopped pecans

1. Put all the ingredients in the slow cooker and stir. Turn to high (it must cook on high). Cook 2 to 3 hours, depending on your preference of doneness. Serve hot, warm, or cool.

Per Serving:

calories: 587 | fat: 37g | protein: 15g | carbs: 49g | fiber: 15g

Zucchini Bread Oatmeal

Prep time: 5 minutes | Cook time: 20 minutes | Serves 4

2 cups rolled oats

1 medium zucchini, grated

4 cups water

½ cup unsweetened plant-based milk

1 tablespoon ground cinnamon

½ cup raisins

1 tablespoon maple syrup (optional)

Pinch of salt (optional)

2 medium bananas, sliced

4 tablespoons chopped walnuts (optional)

1. In a medium saucepan over medium-high, combine the oats, zucchini, and water and bring to a boil. Lower the heat to medium-low and simmer, stirring often, until the oats are soft and creamy, about 15 minutes. Remove from the heat, add the plant-based milk, cinnamon, raisins, maple syrup, and salt (if using) and stir well. 2. Divide the oatmeal among 4 bowls and top each portion with ½ sliced banana and 1 tablespoon of walnuts (if using).

Per Serving:

calories: 301 | fat: 4g | protein: 9g | carbs: 62g | fiber: 8g

Chapter 3 Beans and Grains

Whole-Grain Corn Muffins

Prep time: 5 minutes | Cook time: 20 minutes | Makes 12 muffins

1½ tablespoons ground flaxseeds	1 cup cornmeal
1 cup unsweetened plain almond milk	1 cup oat flour
½ cup unsweetened applesauce	1 teaspoon baking soda
	1 teaspoon baking powder
½ cup 100% pure maple syrup (optional)	½ teaspoon salt (optional)
	1 cup corn kernels (from about 2 ears)

1. To start, preheat your oven to 375ºF (190ºC). Prepare a 12-cup muffin pan by either lining it with paper muffin liners or using a 12-cup silicone muffin pan. 2. In a small bowl, combine the flaxseeds with the almond milk and set it aside for 5 minutes to allow it to gel and thicken. 3. In a large mixing bowl, stir together the applesauce and maple syrup (if using). Add the flaxseed-almond milk mixture to the bowl. Sift in the cornmeal, oat flour, baking soda, baking powder, and, if desired, a pinch of salt. Stir everything until well combined, being careful not to overmix the batter. Lastly, fold in the corn kernels to add a delightful texture. 4. Spoon out equal portions of the batter into the prepared muffin cups. Bake the muffins for approximately 20 minutes, or until a toothpick inserted into the center comes out clean.

Per Serving:

calories: 149 | fat: 1g | protein: 3g | carbs: 30g | fiber: 2g

BLAT (Bacon, Lettuce, Avocado and Tomato) Pitas

Prep time: 10 minutes | Cook time: 5 minutes | Makes 4 sandwiches

2 teaspoons coconut oil (optional)	2 avocados, sliced
½ cup dulse, picked through and separated	¼ cup chopped cilantro
	2 sliced scallions
Few drops liquid smoke	2 tablespoons lime juice
Salt and black pepper (optional)	4 8-inch whole wheat pitas
	4 cups greens
	4 sliced plum tomatoes

1. Begin by placing a large cast-iron skillet over medium heat. Once it's warmed up, you can add coconut oil if desired, followed by the dulse and liquid smoke. Toss everything together to combine. Cook the mixture while stirring often until the dulse turns crispy, which usually takes about 5 minutes. Once done, remove the skillet from the heat and season the dulse with pepper to your taste. 2. In a separate bowl, mash the avocado with cilantro, scallions, and lime juice. Season the avocado mixture with salt and pepper if desired. 3. Next, slice the pitas in half and lightly toast them. Gently open the toasted pitas and divide the avocado mixture equally among all 8 halves. Then, divide the greens, tomatoes, and crispy dulse evenly among the pitas.

Per Serving: (1 sandwich)

calories: 381 | fat: 19g | protein: 10g | carbs: 50g | fiber: 14g

Cabbage and Millet Pilaf

Prep time: 15 minutes | Cook time: 45 minutes | Serves 4

2¼ cups vegetable stock, or low-sodium vegetable broth	1 celery stalk, diced
¾ cup millet	2 cloves garlic, peeled and minced
1 medium leek (white and light green parts), diced and rinsed	1 teaspoon minced thyme
	1 tablespoon minced dill
	3 cups chopped cabbage
1 medium carrot, peeled and diced	Salt and freshly ground black pepper, to taste

1. In a medium saucepan, bring the vegetable stock to a boil over high heat. Add the millet and let it come back to a boil over high heat. Once boiling, reduce the heat to medium and cover the pot. Allow the millet to cook for approximately 20 minutes or until it becomes tender and absorbs all the vegetable stock. 2. Meanwhile, in a large saucepan, sauté the leek, carrot, and celery over medium heat for about 7 to 8 minutes. To prevent sticking, add water 1 to 2 tablespoons at a time. Stir in the garlic, thyme, dill, and cabbage, and continue cooking over medium heat until the cabbage becomes tender, which should take around 10 minutes. Once the cabbage is ready, add the cooked millet to the saucepan and cook for an additional 5 minutes, stirring frequently. Finally, season the mixture with salt and pepper to taste.

Per Serving:

calories: 193 | fat: 2g | protein: 5g | carbs: 39g | fiber: 6g

Red Lentil Dal

Prep time: 15 minutes | Cook time: 35 minutes | Serves 4

1 large yellow onion, peeled and diced	toasted and ground
	1 tablespoon coriander seeds, toasted and ground
2 cloves garlic, peeled and minced	½ teaspoon crushed red pepper flakes
1 bay leaf	
1 tablespoon grated ginger	2 cup red lentils, rinsed
1 teaspoon turmeric	Salt, to taste (optional)
1 tablespoon cumin seeds,	Zest of 1 lemon

1. Place the onion in a large saucepan and sauté over medium heat for 10 minutes. Add water 1 to 2 tablespoons at a time to keep the onion from sticking to the pan. Add the garlic, bay leaf, ginger, turmeric, cumin, coriander, and crushed red pepper flakes and cook for another minute. 2. Add the lentils and 4 cups of water and bring the pot to a boil over high heat. Reduce the heat to medium and cook, covered, for 20 to 25 minutes, or until the lentils are tender and have started to break down. Remove from the heat. Season with salt (if using) and add the lemon zest.

Per Serving:

calories: 379 | fat: 2g | protein: 24g | carbs: 68g | fiber: 12g

Kasha Varnishkes (Buckwheat Groats with Bow-Tie Pasta)

Prep time: 20 minutes | Cook time: 35 minutes | Serves 4

2 cups vegetable stock, or low-sodium vegetable broth
1 cup buckwheat groats
1 large yellow onion, peeled and diced small
8 ounces (227 g) button mushrooms, sliced
½ pound (227 g) whole-grain

farfalle, cooked according to package directions, drained, and kept warm
2 tablespoons finely chopped dill
Salt and freshly ground black pepper, to taste

1. In a medium saucepan, bring the vegetable stock to a boil over high heat. Add the buckwheat groats and bring the pot back to a boil. Reduce the heat to medium and cook the groats uncovered until they are tender, which should take about 12 to 15 minutes. 2. While the groats are cooking, place the onion in a large saucepan and sauté over medium heat until it becomes well browned, which usually takes around 15 minutes. To prevent sticking, add water 1 to 2 tablespoons at a time, using as little water as possible. Stir in the mushrooms and cook for an additional 5 minutes. Once done, remove the saucepan from the heat and add the cooked pasta, buckwheat groats, and dill. Season the mixture with salt and pepper to your taste.

Per Serving:
calories: 240 | fat: 1g | protein: 8g | carbs: 51g | fiber: 6g

Koshari (Lentils with Rice and Macaroni)

Prep time: 15 minutes | Cook time: 2 hours | Serves 6

1 cup green lentils, rinsed
Salt, to taste (optional)
1 cup medium-grain brown rice
1 large onion, peeled and minced
4 cloves garlic, peeled and minced
1 teaspoon ground cumin
1 teaspoon ground coriander
½ teaspoon ground allspice

½ teaspoon crushed red pepper flakes
2 tablespoons tomato paste
3 large tomatoes, diced small
1 cup whole-grain elbow macaroni, cooked according to package directions, drained, and kept warm
1 tablespoon brown rice vinegar

1. Start by adding the lentils to a medium saucepan along with 3 cups of water. Bring the pot to a boil over high heat, then reduce the heat to medium. Cook the lentils, covered, for 40 to 45 minutes, ensuring they become tender but retain their texture. Once done, drain any excess water from the lentils, season with salt if desired, and set them aside. 2. In a separate medium saucepan, combine the brown rice with 2 cups of water. Cover the pan with a tight-fitting lid and bring it to a boil over high heat. Reduce the heat to medium and let the rice cook for 45 minutes until it becomes fluffy and fully cooked. 3. While the lentils and rice are cooking, heat a large skillet over high heat. Place the onion in the skillet and sauté it over medium heat for about 15 minutes, ensuring it turns well browned and caramelized. To prevent sticking, add water 1 to 2 tablespoons at a time. Stir in the garlic and cook for an additional 3 to 4 minutes. Then, add the cumin, coriander, allspice, crushed red pepper flakes, and tomato paste, and cook for another 3 minutes. Next, add the fresh tomatoes and cook over medium heat for approximately 15 minutes, or until the tomatoes begin to break down. Season the mixture with salt if desired. 4. To serve, combine the cooked lentils, rice, tomato mixture, and cooked macaroni in a large bowl. Additionally, add the brown rice vinegar to enhance the flavors.

Per Serving:
calories: 298 | fat: 1g | protein: 13g | carbs: 59g | fiber: 6g

Slow Cooker Black Bean and Lentil Super Burritos

Prep time: 15 minutes | Cook time: 8 hours | Serves 6

2 (15 ounces / 425 g) cans diced tomatoes
¼ cup salsa
2 (15 ounces / 425 g) cans black beans, drained and rinsed
1 cup brown rice
½ cup fresh, frozen, or canned corn
2 tablespoons taco seasoning
1 teaspoon ground cumin

1 teaspoon salt (optional)
2 chipotle peppers in adobo sauce, finely chopped
2½ cups vegetable broth
½ cup lentils
12 whole wheat tortillas
Additional toppings:
Salsa
Avocado or guacamole
Black olives

1. In a slow cooker, combine the tomatoes, salsa, beans, rice, corn, taco seasoning, cumin, and, if desired, salt. Add the chipotles and broth, and give everything a good stir. Cover the slow cooker and cook on low for 6 to 8 hours or on high for 3 to 4 hours. 2. About 40 minutes before the cooking time is up, add the lentils to the slow cooker and continue cooking until the lentils become tender. The rice will also be tender, and most of the liquid will be absorbed, creating a delicious filling for the burritos. 3. Lay out the tortillas and place about ⅓ to ½ cup (for a very large burrito) of the filling in the center of each tortilla. Spread the filling evenly along the length of the tortilla. Fold each end about 1½ inches over the pointed edge of the beans and then roll up the tortilla along the long edge to form a burrito. Feel free to use your preferred rolling technique if you have one. 4. Stack up the burritos and serve them with additional salsa, avocado or guacamole, and black olives for added flavor and enjoyment.

Per Serving: (2 burritos)
calories: 464 | fat: 15g | protein: 21g | carbs: 56g | fiber: 16g

Smoky Cajun Bowl

Prep time: 20 minutes | Cook time: 25 minutes | Serves 4

2 cups cooked or canned black beans	1 tablespoon salt-free Cajun spices
1 cup dry quick-cooking brown rice	¼ cup water (optional)
1 (7-ounce / 198-g) pack smoked tofu, cubed	Optional Toppings: peeled slices
2 cups canned or fresh tomato cubes	Fresh cilantro
	Avocado slices

1. If you're using dry black beans, start by soaking and cooking ⅔ cup of them as needed. Additionally, cook the brown rice separately until it's tender and ready to use. 2. Place a nonstick deep frying pan over medium-high heat, and add the tofu cubes and tomato cubes. You may also add the optional ¼ cup of water to prevent sticking. Stir occasionally as everything cooks. 3. Once everything is cooked, add the pre-cooked black beans, cooked brown rice, and Cajun spices to the pan. Mix everything together until well combined. 4. Turn off the heat and continue stirring occasionally for about 5 minutes to ensure that everything is evenly heated through.
5. Divide the flavorful smoky Cajun beans and rice mixture between 4 bowls. You can also serve it with optional toppings to enhance the taste and presentation. 6. To store any leftovers, place the smoky Cajun beans and rice in an airtight container in the fridge, where it will remain fresh for up to 3 days. Alternatively, you can store it in the freezer for a maximum of 30 days. When ready to enjoy again, simply thaw at room temperature and use a microwave, toaster oven, or nonstick frying pan to reheat the smoky Cajun beans and rice.

Per Serving:
calories: 371 | fat: 5g | protein: 20g | carbs: 60g | fiber: 12g

Smoked Tofu and Beans Bowl

Prep time: 10 minutes | Cook time: 15 minutes | Serves 2

1 cup cooked or canned black beans	sweet corn
1 (7-ounce / 198-g) pack smoked tofu, cubed	¼ cup lemon juice
1 small Hass avocado, peeled and stoned	Optional Toppings: Jalapeño slices
2 cups cooked or canned	Fresh cilantro
	Red onion

1. If using dry beans, soak and cook ⅓ cup of dry black beans until tender and fully cooked. 2. Preheat the oven to 350°F (180°C) and line a baking sheet with parchment paper. 3. Place the tofu cubes on the prepared baking sheet and bake for approximately 10 minutes or until the tofu is lightly browned and has a dry texture. 4. Remove the tofu cubes from the oven and allow them to cool for about 5 minutes. 5. Peel the avocado and cut one half into cubes while slicing the other half into thin slices. 6. In a large salad bowl, combine the baked tofu cubes, cooked black beans, avocado cubes, and corn. Use a spatula to gently stir and mix all the ingredients until they are well combined. 7. If needed, divide the salad between two bowls. Drizzle 2 tablespoons of lemon juice over each bowl and garnish with the avocado slices. You can also add optional toppings for added flavor and texture. 8. Store any leftovers in an airtight container in the fridge and consume within 2 days. Alternatively, you can freeze the tofu and beans for up to 60 days. The tofu and beans can be served cold.

Per Serving:
calories: 401 | fat: 6g | protein: 21g | carbs: 64g | fiber: 20g

Cuban-Style Black Beans with Cilantro Rice

Prep time: 20 minutes | Cook time: 1 hour 30 minutes | Serves 4

Black Beans:	stems
1 pound (454 g) black beans, soaked overnight	2 tablespoons apple cider vinegar
2 tablespoons ground cumin	½ teaspoon freshly ground white or black pepper
1 large onion, peeled and diced	3 tablespoons chopped cilantro leaves
2 bay leaves	1 medium tomato, chopped (about 1 cup)
3 cloves garlic, peeled and minced	Salt, to taste (optional)
3 celery stalks, diced	Cilantro Rice:
3 medium carrots, peeled and diced	1 cup brown rice
1 red bell pepper, seeded and diced	1 tablespoon low-sodium light brown miso paste
2 tablespoons minced oregano	2 tablespoons finely chopped cilantro leaves
1 cup finely chopped cilantro	

Make the Black Beans: 1. In a large pot, combine the beans, cumin, onion, bay leaves, garlic, celery, carrots, red pepper, oregano, cilantro stems, and 5 cups of water. Bring the mixture to a boil, then reduce the heat to a simmer. Let it cook for 90 minutes, or until the beans become tender. Take out one-quarter of the beans, mash them in a separate bowl, and then return them to the pot. Stir in the apple cider vinegar, pepper, cilantro leaves, and tomato. Once the beans are fully cooked, season with salt if desired, and remove the bay leaves. Make the Cilantro Rice: 2. In a large saucepan, combine the rice, 2 cups of water, and the miso paste. Bring the mixture to a boil, then reduce the heat to medium and let it simmer, covered, for 20 minutes. Lower the heat to low and continue simmering for an additional 30 minutes. Finally, fluff the rice and stir in the cilantro. To Serve: 3. Divide the cilantro rice among 4 individual plates, and top each serving with the prepared black beans.

Per Serving:
calories: 432 | fat: 3g | protein: 18g | carbs: 85g | fiber: 13g

Marinated Tempeh

Prep time: 15 minutes | Cook time: 1 hour | Serves 8

16 ounces (454 g) plain tempeh

1 cup pure apple juice

1 cup freshly squeezed orange juice

¼ cup extra-virgin coconut oil

(optional)

3 tablespoons tamari

1 tablespoon raw apple cider vinegar

2 large garlic cloves

1. If you plan to bake the tempeh immediately, preheat the oven to 350°F (180°C). 2. Slice the tempeh into ¼-inch thick pieces. If using unpasteurized tempeh, you can skip this step. Otherwise, place the tempeh in a steamer basket and steam it over boiling water for about 5 minutes, or until it's heated through. While the tempeh steams, prepare the marinade: In an upright blender, blend together the apple juice, orange juice, oil, tamari, vinegar, and garlic until you have a smooth mixture. 3. Arrange the steamed tempeh slices in two 12 x 8-inch or equivalent-size baking dishes, making sure they fit snugly in a single layer. Pour the marinade over the warm tempeh, ensuring it's fully submerged. You have the option to bake the tempeh immediately, leave it aside for up to 1 hour, or refrigerate it, covered, for up to 1 day before baking. 4. To bake the tempeh, cover each baking dish with parchment paper and then foil, sealing it tightly. Bake for 30 minutes. Remove the foil and parchment paper (save the foil for another use), and continue baking for another 25 to 30 minutes until the marinade is absorbed, and the tempeh turns lightly browned. Once done, take it out of the oven and serve. Any leftover tempeh can be stored in an airtight container in the fridge for up to 4 days.

Per Serving:

calories: 252 | fat: 13g | protein: 12g | carbs: 13g | fiber: 0g

Almost Instant Ramen

Prep time: 15 minutes | Cook time: 15 minutes | Serves 6

6 cups vegetable broth

1 small yellow onion, diced

2 tablespoons wakame (optional)

1 teaspoon minced or grated fresh ginger, or more to taste

1 teaspoon toasted sesame seeds

¼ teaspoon crushed red pepper, or more to taste

2 cups broccoli florets

2 cups shredded red cabbage

2 carrots, finely chopped

½ cup kimchi

8 ounces (227 g) extra-firm tofu, cubed

2 (3 ounces / 85 g) packages gluten-free ramen or soba noodles

2 tablespoons gluten-free red miso, or more to taste

2 nori sheets, cut into strips (optional)

2 scallions, sliced thin

Chopped cilantro

1. In a large stockpot, bring the broth to a boil. Add the onion, wakame (if using), ginger, sesame seeds, and crushed red pepper. 2. Reduce the heat to medium and add the broccoli, cabbage, carrots, kimchi, and tofu. Allow the ingredients to cook for 3 minutes. 3. Next, add the noodles to the pot and increase the heat to medium-high. Cook for 5 minutes or follow the instructions on the package for the appropriate cooking time. 4. Remove the pot from the heat. Whisk in the miso to blend it well. Serve the soup, and garnish with nori, scallions, and cilantro for added flavor and presentation.

Per Serving:

calories: 135 | fat: 3g | protein: 8g | carbs: 22g | fiber: 2g

Marinated Beans

Prep time: 15 minutes | Cook time: 0 minutes | Serves 4

3 cups cooked beans, drained well

3 tablespoons extra-virgin olive oil (optional)

2 tablespoons raw apple cider vinegar, plus more to taste

½ teaspoon fine sea salt, plus more to taste (optional)

1. In a medium bowl, place the beans and add olive oil, vinegar, and salt. Stir everything together until well combined. Taste and adjust the seasoning as needed. If you have some extra time, let the flavors marry by setting the bowl aside for 30 minutes; otherwise, you can serve it immediately. Any leftover beans can be stored in a jar in the fridge for up to 4 days.

Per Serving:

calories: 116 | fat: 11g | protein: 1g | carbs: 5g | fiber: 2g

Fancy Rice

Prep time: 10 minutes | Cook time: 40 minutes | Serves 4

1 cup uncooked wild and brown rice blend, rinsed

2 teaspoons virgin olive oil (optional)

1 teaspoon apple cider vinegar

½ teaspoon ground coriander

¼ teaspoon ground sumac

¼ cup unsweetened dried

cranberries

¼ cup chopped fresh flat-leaf parsley

2 green onions, thinly sliced

Salt and pepper, to taste (optional)

¼ cup almonds, chopped, for garnish

1. In a medium saucepan, place the wild and brown rice blend, then add enough cold water to cover the rice by 1 inch. Bring the mixture to a boil, then reduce the heat to a simmer, cover the saucepan, and cook for approximately 40 minutes or until all the liquid is absorbed. Once cooked, remove from the heat and let the rice sit for 5 minutes. Use a fork to fluff the rice, and transfer it gently to a medium bowl. 2. To the cooked rice, add the olive oil, apple cider vinegar, coriander, sumac, dried cranberries, parsley, green onions, and season with salt and pepper, if desired. Toss the ingredients gently to combine. Lastly, garnish the rice with the chopped almonds for an added touch of flavor and texture. This delicious rice dish is best served warm and ready to enjoy!

Per Serving:

calories: 252 | fat: 7g | protein: 5g | carbs: 25g | fiber: 3g

Soy Mince Noodle Bowl

Prep time: 10 minutes | Cook time: 15 minutes | Serves 2

2 packs brown rice noodles
1 (7-ounce / 198-g) pack textured soy mince
2 yellow onions, minced
4 cloves garlic, minced
¼ cup low-sodium soy sauce
1½ cups water
Optional Toppings:
Sauerkraut
Chili flakes
Roasted sesame seeds

1. Begin by cooking the noodles according to the package instructions. Once cooked, drain the excess water using a strainer and set the noodles aside. 2. Place a medium pot over medium heat and add ½ cup of water, along with the soy sauce, minced onion, and garlic. 3. Add the soy mince to the pot and cook for approximately 5 minutes, stirring occasionally to prevent sticking. Allow the soy mince to cook fully and for about half of the water to evaporate. 4. Pour in the remaining water and bring the mixture to a boil while stirring occasionally. 5. Turn off the heat, and add the cooked noodles to the pot. Stir everything well until the noodles and mince are evenly mixed. 6. Divide the flavorful noodles and mince between 2 bowls. You can also add your preferred optional toppings for added taste and texture. 7. If you have any leftovers, store the noodles in an airtight container in the fridge and enjoy within 2 days. Alternatively, you can freeze them for up to 30 days and thaw at room temperature before reheating. To reheat, use a nonstick frying pan or microwave.

Per Serving:
calories: 226 | fat: 1g | protein: 25g | carbs: 26g | fiber: 9g

Red Curry "Fried" Rice

Prep time: 25 minutes | Cook time: 10 minutes | Serves 2

½ medium yellow onion, peeled and cut into ½-inch strips
2 large leeks (white and light green parts), thinly sliced and rinsed
2 cups shiitake mushrooms, trimmed and thinly sliced
2 medium carrots, peeled and cut into matchsticks
4 teaspoons Thai red curry paste
¼ cup slivered almonds, toasted (optional)
4 green onions (white and green parts), chopped
2 cups cooked brown rice, fully cooled
Salt and freshly ground black pepper, to taste

1. In a large skillet, heat it over high heat. Add the onion, leeks, mushrooms, and carrots. Cook the mixture, stirring frequently, for about 5 to 6 minutes. If needed, add water, a tablespoon or two at a time, to prevent the vegetables from sticking to the pan. 2. Stir in the curry paste and cook for an additional 30 seconds, allowing the flavors to meld. Then, add the almonds (if using), green onions, and rice to the skillet. Continue cooking until everything is heated through. Season with salt and pepper to taste.

Per Serving:
calories: 415 | fat: 9g | protein: 12g | carbs: 74g | fiber: 12g

Barley and Sweet Potato Pilaf

Prep time: 10 minutes | Cook time: 55 minutes | Serves 4

1 medium onion, peeled and chopped
2 cloves garlic, peeled and minced
3½ cups vegetable stock, or low-sodium vegetable broth
1½ cups pearled barley
1 large sweet potato (about ¾ pound / 340 g), peeled and diced small
¼ cup minced tarragon
Zest and juice of 1 lemon
Salt and freshly ground black pepper, to taste

1. In a large saucepan, place the onion and sauté over medium heat for about 6 minutes. To prevent sticking, add water, 1 to 2 tablespoons at a time. 2. Add the garlic and continue cooking for an additional 3 minutes. Pour in the vegetable stock and add the barley, bringing the pot to a boil over high heat. 3. Reduce the heat to medium, cover the saucepan, and let it simmer for 30 minutes. Then, add the sweet potato and cook for an additional 15 minutes, or until both the potato and barley are tender. 4. Remove the saucepan from the heat, and stir in the tarragon, lemon zest, and lemon juice. Season the dish with salt and pepper to taste.

Per Serving:
calories: 318 | fat: 0g | protein: 8g | carbs: 71g | fiber: 13g

Chickpea Caponata

Prep time: 25 minutes | Cook time: 30 minutes | Serves 4

1 medium yellow onion, peeled and diced
2 celery stalks, chopped
1 medium eggplant, stemmed and diced
2 ripe Roma tomatoes, diced
2 cups cooked chickpeas, or 1 (15-ounce / 425-g) can, drained and rinsed
½ cup Kalamata olives, pitted
and coarsely chopped
3 tablespoons capers
3 tablespoons red wine vinegar
¼ cup golden raisins
¼ cup pine nuts, toasted (optional)
½ cup chopped basil
Salt and freshly ground black pepper, to taste

1. Place the onion and celery in a large saucepan and sauté over medium heat for 10 minutes. Add water 1 to 2 tablespoons at a time to keep the vegetables from sticking to the pan. 2. Add the eggplant, tomatoes, and chickpeas and cook, covered, for 15 minutes, or until the vegetables are tender. Stir in the olives, capers, red wine vinegar, raisins, and pine nuts (if using) and cook for 5 minutes more. Remove from the heat and add the basil. Season with salt and pepper.

Per Serving:
calories: 301 | fat: 10g | protein: 11g | carbs: 45g | fiber: 13g

Bulgur Chickpea Pilaf

Prep time: 15 minutes | Cook time: 35 minutes | Serves 4

1 medium yellow onion, peeled and diced small
3 cloves garlic, peeled and minced
1½ tablespoons grated ginger
1½ cups bulgur
3 cups vegetable stock, or low-sodium vegetable broth
2 cups cooked chickpeas,

or 1 (15-ounce / 425-g) can, drained and rinsed
1 Roma tomato, chopped
Zest and juice of 1 lemon
Salt and freshly ground black pepper, to taste
4 green onions (white and green parts), thinly sliced

1. In a large saucepan, place the onion and sauté over medium heat for 10 minutes. To prevent sticking, add water 1 to 2 tablespoons at a time as needed. Next, stir in the garlic and ginger, cooking for about 30 seconds. Add the bulgur and vegetable stock, and bring the mixture to a boil over high heat. Once boiling, reduce the heat to medium, cover the saucepan, and let the bulgur cook until tender, approximately 15 minutes. 2. After the bulgur is cooked, stir in the chickpeas, tomato, and both lemon zest and juice. Continue to cook for an additional 5 minutes, allowing the flavors to meld. Season the dish with salt and pepper to your taste preference. Finally, when serving, garnish the bulgur and chickpeas with chopped green onions for an added burst of freshness and color.

Per Serving:
calories: 344 | fat: 2g | protein: 14g | carbs: 69g | fiber: 13g

Oil-Free Rice-and-Vegetable Stir-Fry

Prep time: 5 minutes | Cook time: 15 minutes | Serves 4

2 cups fresh or frozen green peas
2 cups fresh or frozen green beans
¼ cup vegetable broth or

water
1 teaspoon garlic powder
1 teaspoon onion powder
4 cups cooked brown rice

1. Place a medium saucepan over medium heat. 2. Add the peas, green beans, vegetable broth, garlic powder, and onion powder to the pan. Stir everything together, cover the saucepan, and cook for about 8 minutes, stirring occasionally, until the vegetables reach a crisp-tender texture. If you notice any vegetables sticking to the pan, simply stir in a few more tablespoons of vegetable broth or water to prevent sticking. 3. Remove the lid, and incorporate the cooked brown rice into the vegetable mixture. Continue to cook for an additional 5 minutes, stirring every now and then. Serve the delicious and nutritious dish immediately. If needed, add a tablespoon or two of water or broth to prevent anything from sticking to the bottom of the pan during this final cooking step. Enjoy your flavorful vegetable and brown rice medley!

Per Serving:
calories: 233 | fat: 2g | protein: 8g | carbs: 48g | fiber: 7g

Bulgur Pilaf with Walnuts and Dried Fruit

Prep time: 15 minutes | Cook time: 25 minutes | Serves 4

1 medium yellow onion, peeled and diced
2 cloves garlic, peeled and minced
2 cups bulgur
½ cup golden raisins
½ cup dried unsulfured apricots, chopped
1 cinnamon stick

2 teaspoons ground coriander
3½ cups vegetable stock, or low-sodium vegetable broth
2 green onions (white and green parts), thinly sliced
Salt and freshly ground black pepper, to taste
½ cup walnuts, toasted and coarsely chopped

1. In a large saucepan over medium-high heat, place the onion and sauté until it turns golden, which should take around 7 to 8 minutes. To avoid sticking, add water 1 to 2 tablespoons at a time as needed. 2. Add the garlic to the saucepan and cook for an additional minute. 3. Stir in the bulgur, raisins, apricots, cinnamon stick, and coriander. 4. Pour in the stock and bring the mixture to a boil over high heat. 5. Reduce the heat to medium, cover the saucepan, and let it cook for about 15 minutes, or until the bulgur becomes tender. 6. Once the bulgur is cooked, remove the cinnamon stick from the mixture and stir in the green onions. 7. Season the dish with salt and pepper according to your taste. To serve, garnish it with the chopped walnuts for an added touch of flavor and texture. Enjoy this delectable and wholesome meal!

Per Serving:
calories: 453 | fat: 10g | protein: 12g | carbs: 75g | fiber: 12g

Farro Tabbouleh

Prep time: 15 minutes | Cook time: 30 minutes | Serves 6

2½ cups water or vegetable broth
1 cup farro, soaked overnight and drained
3 scallions, sliced thin
1 English cucumber, diced
1 red or yellow bell pepper, finely diced

1 bunch flat-leaf parsley leaves, chopped
Handful mint leaves, chopped
Grated zest and juice of 2 lemons
¼ cup vegetable broth
¼ teaspoon salt (optional)
⅛ teaspoon black pepper

1. Combine the water and farro in a medium saucepan. Bring to a boil, then reduce the heat to low, cover, and cook, stirring occasionally, until the farro is al dente, about 25 minutes. 2. Allow to cool for 10 minutes, then transfer to a large bowl along with the remaining ingredients. Toss to combine and serve. (The tabbouleh can be refrigerated for up to 2 days, though the herbs will discolor.).

Per Serving:
calories: 115 | fat: 1g | protein: 4g | carbs: 26g | fiber: 5g

Mexican Quinoa Bowl

Prep time: 10 minutes | Cook time: 22 minutes | Serves 2

1 cup cooked or canned chickpeas

1 cup cooked or canned black beans

½ cup dry quinoa

2 cups vegetable stock

2 tablespoons Mexican chorizo seasoning

Optional Toppings:

lime juice

fresh cilantro

avocado slices

1. If using dry chickpeas and beans, soak and cook ⅓ cup each of chickpeas and black beans according to the package instructions. 2. Place a large pot over medium-high heat and add the vegetable stock along with the quinoa. 3. Bring the mixture to a boil, then reduce the heat to medium. 4. Cook the quinoa for approximately 15 minutes, keeping the pot uncovered, and stir occasionally. 5. Stir in the Mexican chorizo seasoning, black beans, and chickpeas, and continue cooking for another 7 minutes, stirring occasionally. 6. Turn off the heat and let the dish cool down for a minute. 7. Divide the flavorful combination between 2 bowls, garnish with optional toppings, and serve to delight in the taste! 8. For storage, place the leftovers in an airtight container in the fridge, and consume within 2 days. Alternatively, you can store it in the freezer for up to 30 days and thaw at room temperature. Enjoy this delightful bowl cold or reheat it in a saucepan or microwave for a comforting meal anytime.

Per Serving:
calories: 487 | fat: 8g | protein: 23g | carbs: 80g | fiber: 19g

Nut-Crusted Tofu

Prep time: 10 minutes | Cook time: 20 minutes | Makes 8 slices

½ cup roasted, shelled pistachios

¼ cup whole wheat bread crumbs

1 shallot, minced

1 garlic clove, minced

1 teaspoon grated lemon zest

½ teaspoon dried tarragon

Salt and black pepper (optional)

1 (16-ounce / 454-g) package sprouted or extra-firm tofu, drained and sliced lengthwise into 8 pieces

1 tablespoon Dijon mustard

1 tablespoon lemon juice

1. Preheat the oven to 375ºF (190ºC) and line a baking sheet with parchment paper. 2. Using a food processor or a knife, chop the pistachios until they are about the size of the bread crumbs. In a pie plate, combine them with the bread crumbs, shallot, garlic, lemon zest, and tarragon. Season with salt (if desired) and pepper. 3. Season the tofu with salt and pepper. In a small bowl, combine the mustard and lemon juice. 4. Spread the mustard mixture evenly over the top and sides of the tofu, then press each slice into the bread crumb mixture. 5. Place the tofu uncoated side down on the baking sheet. Sprinkle any leftover bread crumb mixture evenly on top of the slices. Bake until the tops are browned, about 20 minutes. Serve.

Per Serving: (1 slice)

calories: 114 | fat: 7g | protein: 8g | carbs: 7g | fiber: 1g

Fava Bean Ratatouille

Prep time: 30 minutes | Cook time: 38 minutes | Serves 4

1 medium red onion, peeled and thinly sliced

1 red bell pepper, seeded and diced

1 large eggplant, stemmed and cut into ½-inch dice

1 medium zucchini, diced

2 cloves garlic, peeled and

finely chopped

2 cups cooked fava beans, or 1 (15-ounce / 425-g) can, drained and rinsed

2 Roma tomatoes, chopped

¼ cup basil, finely chopped

Salt and freshly ground black pepper, to taste

1. Place the onion in a large saucepan and sauté over medium heat for 7 to 8 minutes. Add water 1 to 2 tablespoons at a time to keep the onion from sticking to the pan. 2. Add the red pepper and eggplant and cook for 10 minutes. Add the zucchini, garlic, fava beans, and tomatoes and cook for 5 minutes longer. Reduce the heat and cook, uncovered, stirring occasionally, for 15 minutes, or until the vegetables are tender. Remove from the heat. Stir in the basil and season with salt and pepper.

Per Serving:
calories: 114 | fat: 0g | protein: 7g | carbs: 24g | fiber: 9g

Mango Satay Tempeh Bowl

Prep time: 10 minutes | Cook time: 30 minutes | Serves 4

1 cup cooked or canned black beans

½ cup dry quinoa

1 (14-ounce / 397-g) pack tempeh, sliced

1 cup peanut butter

1 cup fresh or frozen mango cubes

Optional Toppings:

Chili flakes

Shredded coconut

1. When using dry beans, soak and cook ⅓ cup of dry black beans if necessary and cook the quinoa for about 15 minutes. 2. Blend the mango into a smooth purée using a blender or food processor or blender, and set it aside. 3. Add the tempeh slices and the peanut butter to an airtight container. 4. Close the lid and shake well until the tempeh slices are evenly covered with the peanut butter. 5. Preheat the oven to 375ºF (190ºC) and line a baking sheet with parchment paper. 6. Transfer the peanut butter tempeh slices onto the baking sheet and bake for about 15 minutes or until the tempeh is browned and crispy. 7. Divide the black beans, quinoa, mango purée and tempeh slices between two bowls, serve with the optional toppings and enjoy! 8. Store the mango tempeh bowl in an airtight container in the fridge, and consume within 2 days. Alternatively, store in the freezer for a maximum of 30 days and thaw at room temperature. Serve cold It's not necessary to reheat the tempeh and beans.

Per Serving:
calories: 536 | fat: 24g | protein: 30g | carbs: 55g | fiber: 7g

Green Chile Rice with Black Beans

Prep time: 20 minutes | Cook time: 1 hour | Serves 4

1 poblano chile pepper, seeded and diced small	1 medium yellow onion, peeled and diced small
1 (4-ounce / 113-g) can mild green chiles	1 teaspoon ground cumin
1 cup coarsely chopped cilantro	1 jalapeño pepper, seeded and minced
½ cup spinach	2 cups cooked black beans, or 1 (15-ounce / 425-g) can, drained and rinsed
4 cups vegetable stock, or low-sodium vegetable broth	Zest of 1 lime
1½ cups medium-grain brown rice	Salt, to taste (optional)

1. Add the poblano pepper, green chiles, cilantro, and spinach to a blender and purée. Add some of the vegetable stock, as needed, to achieve a smooth consistency. Add the mixture to a medium saucepan with the remaining vegetable stock. Add the brown rice and bring to a boil over high heat. Reduce the heat to medium and cook, covered, until the rice is tender, 45 to 50 minutes. 2. Place the onion in a large saucepan and sauté over medium heat for 7 to 8 minutes. Add water 1 to 2 tablespoons at a time to keep the onion from sticking to the pan. Add the cumin, jalapeño pepper, and black beans and cook for 5 minutes longer. Fold in the cooked rice and lime zest. Season with salt, if using.

Per Serving:
calories: 403 | fat: 2g | protein: 13g | carbs: 71g | fiber: 11g

Red Peppers with Herby Breadcrumbs

Prep time: 10 minutes | Cook time: 40 minutes | Serves 6

4 red bell peppers, cores and stems removed	2 teaspoons minced fresh thyme leaves
3 tablespoons virgin olive oil, divided (optional)	1 clove garlic, minced
Salt and pepper, to taste (optional)	½ teaspoon fresh lemon zest
2½ cups cubed stale bread	¼ teaspoon nutritional yeast
	¼ cup chopped fresh flat-leaf parsley

1. Preheat the oven to 400ºF (205ºC). Line a baking sheet with parchment paper. 2. Cut each bell pepper into 4 segments. Remove any white pith pieces from the center, and place them on the baking sheet. Toss the bell peppers with 1 tablespoon of the olive oil, if using. Spread the peppers out into a single layer, and season with salt and pepper, if using. Slide the peppers into the oven, and roast until just tender, about 25 minutes. 3. Place the cubed bread into a food processor, and pulse the machine to make coarse crumbs. 4. Heat the remaining 2 tablespoons of the olive oil in a medium sauté pan over medium heat. Add the breadcrumbs to the pan along with some salt and pepper, if using. Cook the breadcrumbs, stirring frequently, until evenly golden brown, about 10 minutes. Add the thyme, garlic, lemon zest, and nutritional yeast, and cook until fragrant, about 30 seconds. 5. Remove the breadcrumbs from the heat, and stir in the chopped parsley. 6. Arrange the roasted peppers on a platter and shower with the warm breadcrumbs. Serve warm.

Per Serving:
calories: 252 | fat: 9g | protein: 7g | carbs: 36g | fiber: 3g

Chickpea Coconut Curry

Prep time: 10 minutes | Cook time: 30 minutes | Serves 4

2 teaspoons ground coriander	1 (14-ounce / 397-g) can diced tomatoes
1 teaspoon ground cumin	1 teaspoon garam masala
½ teaspoon ground turmeric	1 (14-ounce / 397-g) can full-fat coconut milk
¼ teaspoon freshly ground black pepper	1 (15-ounce /425-g) can chickpeas, drained and rinsed
¼ teaspoon cayenne pepper	Juice of 1 lime
1 large red onion, thinly sliced	1 tablespoon chopped fresh cilantro, plus more for serving
3 tablespoons water, divided, plus more as needed	Lime wedges, for serving
3 garlic cloves, minced	
1 tablespoon grated peeled fresh ginger	

1. In a small bowl, stir together the coriander, cumin, turmeric, black pepper, and cayenne pepper. 2. In a large pan over medium-high heat, combine the red onion and 1 tablespoon of water. Cook until the water evaporates and add another 1 tablespoon of water. Continue this process for 3 to 5 minutes, or until the onion is soft and just starting to brown. 3. Reduce the heat to medium-low and add the garlic and ginger. Cook for 2 to 3 minutes, adding water as needed to prevent burning, until the onion is browned. Evenly sprinkle the spice mixture onto the cooked vegetables. Cook, stirring slowly to toast the spices, for 30 seconds. Add 1 tablespoon of water and cook for 30 seconds more. 4. Carefully pour the tomatoes and their juices into the pan and stir. Cook over medium-low heat for 5 minutes, stirring. The tomatoes should be simmering and the pieces of tomato will start to soften and break down. Evenly sprinkle the garam masala on the cooked tomatoes and stir to combine. 5. Pour in the coconut milk and chickpeas. Bring the curry to a simmer and cook for 10 minutes, stirring occasionally. 6. Stir in the lime juice and 1 tablespoon of cilantro. Serve with lime wedges for squeezing and a few pinches of cilantro.

Per Serving:
calories: 324 | fat: 21g | protein: 8g | carbs: 30g | fiber: 7g

Prep time: 15 minutes | Cook time: 35 minutes | Serves 4

1 large yellow onion, peeled and chopped
1 large fennel bulb, trimmed and thinly sliced
4 cloves garlic, peeled and minced
1 tablespoon minced oregano
1½ teaspoons ground fennel seeds

1 teaspoon crushed red pepper flakes
1 (28-ounce / 794-g) can diced tomatoes
4 cups cooked chickpeas, or 2 (15-ounce / 425-g) cans, drained and rinsed
Chopped flat-leaf Italian parsley

1. Place the onion and fennel in a large saucepan, and sauté over medium heat for 10 minutes, or until the vegetables are tender. Add water 1 to 2 tablespoons at a time to keep the vegetables from sticking to the pan. 2. Add the garlic, oregano, fennel seeds, and crushed red pepper flakes and cook for 3 minutes. Add the tomatoes and chickpeas and bring the pan to a boil over high heat. Reduce the heat to medium and cook, covered, for 20 minutes. Serve garnished with the parsley.

Per Serving:
calories: 343 | fat: 5g | protein: 17g | carbs: 61g | fiber: 19g

Pepita and Almond Squares

Prep time: 20 minutes | Cook time: 15 minutes | Makes 16 squares

1 cup almonds, coarsely chopped
1 cup old-fashioned oats
⅔ cup pepitas
⅔ cup dried cranberries
½ cup unsweetened shredded coconut
¼ cup raw shelled hempseed
⅓ cup peanut butter
⅔ cup brown rice syrup
¼ cup maple syrup (optional)
2 teaspoons vanilla extract

1. Prepare an 8-inch square baking dish by lining it with parchment paper, ensuring that the paper extends about 3 inches on opposite sides. This overhang will serve as handles to easily remove the squares from the dish. 2. In a large mixing bowl, combine the almonds, oats, pepitas, cranberries, coconut, and hemp seeds. Mix the ingredients thoroughly. Add the peanut butter and work it in evenly, using your fingers if necessary. 3. In a small saucepan, combine the brown rice syrup, and maple syrup (if desired) along with the vanilla. Bring the mixture to a boil and continue boiling until it reaches the hard ball stage, which is 260°F (127°C) on a candy thermometer. Once it reaches the desired temperature, promptly pour the hot syrup over the almond mixture and stir it in swiftly. The mixture will begin to harden rapidly. Transfer it to the prepared baking dish, pressing it down firmly and as evenly as possible. Refrigerate for at least 30 minutes to set. 4. Use the extended parchment paper as handles to lift the solidified mixture out of the dish. Place it on a cutting surface and slice it into sixteen squares for serving. Enjoy these delectable treats!

Per Serving: (2 squares)
calories: 198 | fat: 11g | protein: 12g | carbs: 22g | fiber: 4g

Great Smoky Almonds

Prep time: 2 minutes | Cook time: 10 to 12 minutes | Serves 4

1 tablespoon avocado oil (optional)
2 teaspoons liquid smoke
1 teaspoon pure maple syrup
¼ teaspoon garlic powder
(optional)
2 cups raw almonds
½ teaspoon sea salt (optional)

1. Set the oven to preheat at 350°F (180°C). Cover a baking sheet with parchment paper for easy cleanup. 2. In a medium mixing bowl, blend together the oil (if using), liquid smoke, and maple syrup (if using). Add the almonds and mix until they are thoroughly coated. Sprinkle salt (if using) and garlic powder over the almonds, stirring once more to ensure even seasoning. 3. Arrange the coated almonds on the prepared baking sheet. Bake for 10 to 12 minutes, or until the nuts are beautifully toasted. Allow them to cool completely before transferring to an airtight container for storage. Enjoy these delightful almonds as a tasty snack!

Per Serving:
calories: 450 | fat: 39g | protein: 15g | carbs: 16g | fiber: 9g

Spiced Glazed Carrots

Prep time: 10 minutes | Cook time: 2 to 3 hours | Serves 4 to 6

2 pounds (907 g) fresh baby carrots or frozen cut carrots
⅓ cup no-sugar-added apricot preserves, such as Polaner All Fruit brand
2 tablespoons orange juice
1 tablespoon balsamic vinegar
1 tablespoon maple syrup
(optional)
¼ teaspoon ground cinnamon
¼ teaspoon ground nutmeg
¼ teaspoon ground turmeric
½ teaspoon ground ginger
1 teaspoon dried thyme
1 tablespoon cornstarch
2 tablespoons water

1. Place the carrots into the slow cooker. In a measuring cup or medium bowl, combine the apricot preserves, orange juice, vinegar, maple syrup (if using), cinnamon, nutmeg, turmeric, ginger, and thyme. Pour the sauce over the carrots in the slow cooker, making sure they are well coated. Cover and cook on High for 2 to 3 hours or on Low for 4 to 6 hours. 2. During the last 30 minutes of cooking, prepare a slurry by adding cornstarch and water to a small lidded jar. Shake the jar well to create a smooth mixture, and then pour it into the slow cooker with the carrots. Stir occasionally to allow the sauce to thicken and form a delicious glaze over the carrots.

Per Serving:
calories: 175 | fat: 0g | protein: 2g | carbs: 43g | fiber: 7g

Super Seeded Kale Crisps

Prep time: 10 minutes | Cook time: 10 minutes | Makes 5 cups

1 bunch lacinato or dino kale, cut into bite-sized pieces
1 tablespoon virgin olive oil (optional)
1½ teaspoons pure maple syrup (optional)
½ teaspoon apple cider vinegar
¾ teaspoon chili powder
¼ cup mixed hemp, chia, and sesame seeds
Salt and pepper, to taste (optional)

1. Preheat your oven to 400°F (205°C) and line a large baking sheet with parchment paper. Set it aside. 2. In a large bowl, combine the kale, olive oil, maple syrup, apple cider vinegar, chili powder, seed mixture, and season with salt and pepper if desired. Massage the seasoning and seeds into the kale leaves, ensuring they are evenly coated. 3. Spread the seasoned kale onto the prepared baking sheet, arranging them in a single layer with minimal overlap. 4. Bake the kale crisps for approximately 7 to 8 minutes, rotating the baking sheet halfway through. The edges of the kale should be lightly browned and crispy. While some centers of the leaves may still appear moist, they will become crisp as they cool. Allow the crisps to cool completely before consuming. Store the cooled kale crisps in a large resealable bag at room temperature.

Per Serving: (1 cup)
calories: 111 | fat: 7g | protein: 5g | carbs: 10g | fiber: 4g

Seeded Bars

Prep time: 10 minutes | Cook time: 25 minutes | Makes 20 bars

1 cup raw sunflower seeds
1 cup raw pumpkin seeds
1 cup raw unhulled sesame seeds
2 cups unsweetened flaked dried coconut

½ teaspoon fine sea salt, plus more to taste (optional)
⅓ cup brown rice syrup or yacon syrup (optional)
1 teaspoon vanilla extract

1. Preheat the oven to 300ºF (150ºC) and prepare your pan by lining the bottom and sides with parchment paper. 2. Rinse the sunflower, pumpkin, and sesame seeds under cold running water in a large strainer. Let them drain thoroughly over a bowl while the oven heats up. 3. Spread the seeds on a rimmed baking sheet lined with parchment paper. Toast them in the oven for 15 minutes. Then, sprinkle the coconut over the seeds and return to the oven for another 8 minutes until the coconut is lightly browned, and the seeds are toasted. Transfer this mixture to a bowl, add salt if desired, and mix well. 4. Take 2 cups of the mixture and place it in a food processor. Process until smooth and liquid, scraping the sides as needed. Set this aside. If using rice syrup, simmer it in a small saucepan over medium heat, stir in the vanilla, and remove from the heat. If using yacon syrup, combine it with the vanilla in a medium bowl. Add the ground seed mixture to the syrup mixture and stir until smooth. Now, pour this combined mixture into the bowl with the remaining toasted seeds and coconut. Stir thoroughly until everything is well combined, using your hands if necessary. 5. Using clean, damp hands, press the mixture firmly and evenly into the parchment-lined pan. Place the bars in the fridge for 1 hour or in the freezer for 30 minutes until thoroughly chilled and set. 6. Once chilled, cut the bars into wedges, slices, or squares depending on the pan's shape. Store the bars in an airtight container at cool room temperature for up to 4 weeks. In warmer weather, keep them in the fridge. You can also freeze the bars for up to 3 months.

Per Serving: (1 bar)
calories: 166 | fat: 13g | protein: 5g | carbs: 9g | fiber: 2g

Choco Almond Bars

Prep time: 10 minutes | Cook time: 15 minutes | Makes 4 bars

1 cup raw and unsalted almonds
5 pitted dates
1 scoop soy protein isolate,

chocolate flavor
Optional Toppings:
Shredded coconut
Cocoa powder

1. Preheat the oven to 257ºF (125ºC) and prepare a baking sheet by lining it with parchment paper. 2. Spread the almonds on the baking sheet and roast them for approximately 10 to 15 minutes until they become fragrant. 3. While the almonds are roasting, soak the dates in a small bowl with water for about 10 minutes. After soaking, drain the dates thoroughly to remove any excess water. 4. Once the almonds are done roasting, allow them to cool

for around 5 minutes. 5. Place all the ingredients, including the almonds and soaked dates, in a food processor and blend them until you have a chunky mixture. 6. Alternatively, if you prefer, you can add all the ingredients to a medium bowl, cover it, and process the mixture using a handheld blender. 7. Line a loaf pan with parchment paper and transfer the almond mixture to the pan. Spread it out evenly and press it down firmly to achieve a thickness of about 1 inch (2.5 cm) throughout. 8. Divide the mixture in the loaf pan into 4 bars. Serve the bars cold and top them with optional toppings of your choice. 9. Store the bars in an airtight container in the fridge, and they should be consumed within 4 days. Alternatively, you can store them in the freezer for up to 90 days. When ready to eat, thaw them at room temperature.

Per Serving:
calories: 254 | fat: 18g | protein: 16g | carbs: 8g | fiber: 4g

Guacamole

Prep time: 10 minutes | Cook time: 0 minutes | Makes 2 cups

3 to 4 small avocados or 2 large avocados, diced
½ tablespoon lemon or lime juice
¼ cup finely diced red, white, or yellow onion

1 teaspoon minced garlic
¾ teaspoon ground cumin
2 tablespoons chopped cilantro
½ medium tomato, chopped
Pinch of salt (optional)
Freshly ground pepper, to taste

1. Take a medium bowl and use a fork to mash the avocados to your preferred consistency. 2. Add in the lemon (or lime) juice, onion, garlic, cumin, cilantro, tomato, and season with salt (if desired) and pepper. Mix all the ingredients together until well combined.

Per Serving:
calories: 249 | fat: 22g | protein: 4g | carbs: 15g | fiber: 10g

Greens and Beans Dip

Prep time: 10 minutes | Cook time: 0 minutes | Makes about 2 cups

1 (14-ounce / 397-g) can white beans, drained and rinsed, or 1½ cups cooked
Zest and juice of 1 lemon
1 tablespoon almond butter, tahini, or other mild nut or seed butter
1 to 2 leaves kale, rinsed and

stemmed
1 tablespoon nutritional yeast (optional)
1 to 2 teaspoons curry powder
1 to 2 teaspoons ground cumin
1 teaspoon smoked paprika
¼ teaspoon sea salt (optional)

1. Combine all the ingredients in a food processor and pulse until the mixture comes together. Alternatively, if you don't have a food processor, mash the beans and chop the kale separately, then mix them together. 2. After mixing, taste the mixture and adjust the seasoning to your preference. You can add more spices, lemon juice, or salt (if desired) to enhance the flavor.

Per Serving: (1 cup)
calories: 112 | fat: 5g | protein: 6g | carbs: 13g | fiber: 6g

Carrot Cake Two-Bite Balls

Prep time: 20 minutes | Cook time: 0 minutes | Makes 16 balls

1 cup old-fashioned oats
½ cup almond meal
½ cup pecans
⅓ cup plus 2 tablespoons unsweetened shredded coconut, divided
3 grated medium carrots
15 dates, pitted
2 tablespoons unsweetened cocoa powder
2 tablespoons almond butter
1 teaspoon ground cinnamon
½ teaspoon ground nutmeg
½ teaspoon ground ginger

1. Place oats, almond meal, pecans, ⅓ cup coconut, carrots, dates, and cocoa powder into a food processor. Process on high until the ingredients are well combined. You may need to scrape down the sides a few times to ensure the dates don't stick together. Next, add almond butter, cinnamon, nutmeg, and ginger to the mixture and process again until everything is thoroughly mixed. Scrape down the sides if necessary. 2. Transfer the mixture onto a flat surface and ensure it's evenly blended. You can use your hands if needed. Take small pieces of the dough and roll them into sixteen balls. Optionally, roll the balls in additional shredded coconut for added texture and flavor.

Per Serving: (2 balls)
calories: 194 | fat: 12g | protein: 8g | carbs: 24g | fiber: 6g

Over-the-Top Bars to Go

Prep time: 20 minutes | Cook time: 15 minutes | Makes 16 squares

1½ cups old-fashioned oats
½ cup pecans
½ cup pistachios
½ cup cashews
½ cup dried cranberries
¼ cup dates, pitted and chopped
¼ cup sunflower seed kernels
¼ cup pepitas
2 tablespoons raw shelled hempseed
½ cup peanut butter
½ cup brown rice syrup
3 tablespoons maple syrup (optional)

1. Prepare an 8-inch square baking dish by lining it with parchment paper, leaving about 3 inches of paper on opposite sides to act as handles for easy removal of the bars. 2. In a large bowl, combine all the ingredients except for the peanut butter and syrups. Mix them thoroughly using a wooden spoon. Next, add the peanut butter and incorporate it into the dry ingredients, initially using the spoon and then using your hands to ensure even distribution. 3. In a small saucepan, combine the brown rice syrup and maple syrup (if using). Bring the mixture to a boil and continue cooking until it reaches the hard ball stage, measuring 260°F (127°C) on a candy thermometer. Pour the hot syrups over the oat mixture in the large bowl, and stir well to combine. Quickly transfer and spread the mixture into the prepared baking dish. Use your fingertips or the bottom of a measuring cup to press the mixture down firmly and evenly. Let it cool rapidly by refrigerating for at least 30 minutes. 4. Once the bars have set, grab the parchment paper handles and lift the entire block of bars

out of the dish. Place it on a cutting board and slice it into sixteen squares for serving.

Per Serving: (2 squares)
calories: 352 | fat: 22g | protein: 14g | carbs: 33g | fiber: 7g

Maple-Glazed Mixed Nuts

Prep time: 5 minutes | Cook time: 15 minutes | Serves 6

1 cup walnuts
1 cup pecans
1 cup cashews
1½ cups maple syrup (optional)

1. Preheat your oven to 325°F (165°C). 2. In a medium bowl, combine the nuts with maple syrup (if using), ensuring that each nut is well coated. Spread the nuts out on a baking sheet, arranging them in a single layer, with some closeness allowed. It's okay if they touch slightly. Bake the nuts for about 7 minutes. 3. Remove the baking sheet from the oven and carefully flip the nuts with a spatula. They may overlap slightly at this point, which is fine. Return the baking sheet to the oven and bake for an additional 6 minutes, keeping a close eye on them. Be cautious, as they can quickly burn if left in the oven for too long. 4. Once done, take the baking sheet out of the oven, flip the nuts one more time, and allow them to cool completely. Enjoy them right away or store them in an airtight container. These nuts will remain fresh in your pantry for several weeks, and you can keep them in the fridge for about 2 to 3 months. If you prefer to store them longer, they can be frozen for up to 6 months.

Per Serving: (½ cup)
calories: 452 | fat: 24g | protein: 10g | carbs: 59g | fiber: 3g

Raw Date Chocolate Balls

Prep time: 20 minutes | Cook time: 0 minutes | Makes 24 balls

¾ cup sunflower seed kernels, ground
½ cup dates, pitted, chopped well
½ cup chopped walnuts
½ cup unsweetened cacao powder
½ cup maple syrup (optional)
½ cup creamy almond butter
½ cup old-fashioned oats (use gluten-free if desired)
¼ cup raw shelled hempseed
6 ounces (170 g) unsweetened coconut, for coating

1. In a large bowl, combine the sunflower seeds, dates, walnuts, cacao powder, maple syrup (if using), almond butter, oats, and hempseed. Mix all the ingredients well until they are fully combined. 2. Using your hands, pinch off portions of the dough and roll them into twenty-four balls. After shaping each ball, coat it by rolling it in shredded coconut. Once all the balls are formed and coated, place them in the refrigerator for about 30 minutes to firm up. Enjoy your delicious and nutritious energy balls!

Per Serving: (2 balls)
calories: 256 | fat: 16g | protein: 7g | carbs: 24g | fiber: 6g

Garlic Hummus

Prep time: 10 minutes | Cook time: 0 minutes | Makes 3 cups

3 garlic cloves
2 (15-ounce / 425-g) cans chickpeas, drained and rinsed
3 tablespoons extra-virgin olive oil, plus more as needed (optional)

Juice of 2 lemons
¼ cup tahini
½ teaspoon salt
½ teaspoon ground cumin
1 tablespoon sesame seeds, for garnish (optional)

1. To make the hummus, add garlic, chickpeas, olive oil, lemon juice, tahini, salt, and cumin to a blender. Blend until the mixture becomes smooth and creamy. If you prefer a thinner consistency, you can add a bit more oil or water. 2. Serve the hummus by spooning it into a bowl. Drizzle a little more olive oil on top and garnish with sesame seeds if desired. Enjoy this flavorful and delicious hummus with your favorite accompaniments!

Per Serving:

calories: 58 | fat: 4g | protein: 2g | carbs: 5g | fiber: 2g

Seeded Whole-Grain Crackers

Prep time: 15 minutes | Cook time: 40 minutes | Makes 40 crackers

1½ cups raw unhulled sesame seeds
1½ cups raw sunflower seeds
1 cup raw pumpkin seeds
⅓ cup chia seeds
1 teaspoon flaky sea salt (optional)

3 cups uncooked rolled oats
3 tablespoons psyllium husks
3 tablespoons melted extra-virgin coconut oil (optional)
2 tablespoons filtered water
1 teaspoon fine sea salt (optional)

1. Preheat your oven to 350ºF (180ºC) and place the oven rack in the middle position. Prepare two large baking sheets. 2. In a large bowl, combine the sesame, sunflower, pumpkin, and chia seeds along with the optional flaky sea salt. Mix everything together and set the bowl aside. 3. In a food processor, blend the oats, psyllium husks, oil, water, and fine sea salt until a smooth dough forms and comes together into a ball. Transfer the dough to the bowl with the seeds and use your hands to thoroughly mix them. The dough will be sticky. If it sticks heavily to your dry hands, set it aside for 10 minutes before continuing. Place a large sheet of parchment paper on your counter and crumble half of the dough onto it, shaping it into a roughly 12 x 9-inch rectangle. Cover with another sheet of parchment paper and use a rolling pin to roll out the dough to approximately ⅛ inch thick, applying extra pressure to ensure the center is not thicker than the edges. Carefully remove the top sheet of parchment paper (you can reuse it later) and transfer the dough, still on the parchment, onto a baking sheet. The dough may slightly tear, but you can press it back together. Bake for about 20 minutes or until set. 4. Remove the baking sheet from the oven, lift one side of the parchment, and flip the crackers over onto the baking sheet. Remove the parchment and continue baking for another 8 to 12 minutes, or until the crackers become fragrant and crisp. Allow them to cool on a cooling rack. Repeat the process with the remaining dough. 5. Once the crackers have cooled, break them into shards. If the center of any cracker is not yet crisp, return that portion to the oven for an additional 5 to 10 minutes. Store the crackers in an airtight container, where they will remain fresh for up to 3 weeks.

Per Serving: (1 cracker)

calories: 113 | fat: 9g | protein: 5g | carbs: 7g | fiber: 3g

White Bean Tzatziki Dip

Prep time: 10 minutes | Cook time: 1 to 2 hours | Makes about 8 cups

4 (14½-ounce / 411-g) cans white beans, drained and rinsed
8 garlic cloves, minced
1 medium onion, coarsely chopped
¼ cup store-bought low-

sodium vegetable broth, plus more as needed
Juice from one lemon, divided
2 teaspoons dried dill, divided
Salt (optional)
1 cucumber, peeled and finely diced

1. In a blender, combine the beans, garlic, onion, broth, and half of the lemon juice. Blend until smooth and creamy, about 1 minute. If needed, add up to ¼ cup of additional broth to achieve the desired consistency. 2. Transfer the creamy mixture to a slow cooker, stir in 1 teaspoon of dill, and season with salt if desired. Cover and cook on Low for 1 to 2 hours, or until heated through. 3. Meanwhile, in a medium bowl, mix the cucumber with the remaining 1 teaspoon of dill and the other half of the lemon juice. Toss to coat, and season with salt if desired. 4. When the dip is ready, spoon it into a serving bowl and top with the cucumber mixture before serving. Enjoy!

Per Serving:

calories: 59 | fat: 0g | protein: 3g | carbs: 11g | fiber: 4g

Mango Plantain Nice Cream

Prep time: 10 minutes | Cook time: 0 minutes | Serves 4

2 plantains, peeled, cut into slices, and frozen
1 cup frozen mango pieces
½ cup unsweetened nondairy milk, plus more as needed

2 pitted dates or 1 tablespoon pure maple syrup
1 teaspoon vanilla extract
Juice of 1 lime

1. In a high-speed blender or food processor, add the frozen plantains, mango, milk, dates, vanilla, and lime juice. Blend for 30 seconds until well combined. Scrape down the sides of the blender and blend again until the mixture becomes smooth. If needed, add more milk, one tablespoon at a time, to achieve the desired consistency. 2. Store any leftovers in an airtight container in the refrigerator for a smoothie-like texture. Alternatively, freeze the mixture for a firmer ice cream-like texture. If frozen, allow it to thaw slightly before serving.

Per Serving: (1 cup)

calories: 208 | fat: 1g | protein: 2g | carbs: 52g | fiber: 3g

Orange Cranberry Power Cookies

Prep time: 10 minutes | Cook time: 10 minutes | Serves 12

1 cup dairy-free butter, softened
1 cup coconut sugar (optional)
⅓ cup orange juice
2 teaspoons organic vanilla extract
1½ cups whole wheat flour
2 tablespoons protein powder
1 teaspoon baking powder
¼ teaspoon baking soda
1 cup old-fashioned oats
1 cup dairy-free chocolate chips
1 cup chopped walnuts
1 cup dried cranberries

1. Preheat your oven to 375ºF (190ºC). 2. In the bowl of a stand mixer, beat together the butter and sugar (if using) until creamy. Add the orange juice and vanilla extract, and continue mixing until well combined. 3. In a separate medium bowl, whisk together the flour, protein powder, baking powder, and baking soda. Add this dry mixture to the wet ingredients in the stand mixer. Mix on medium speed until the ingredients are thoroughly blended. Then, add the oats, chocolate chips, walnuts, and cranberries, and mix on low speed until evenly distributed throughout the dough. 4. Using heaping tablespoons of dough, drop the cookies onto an ungreased baking sheet, spacing them about 2 inches apart. Keep in mind that these cookies will spread out as they bake, reaching a diameter of 3 to 4 inches. Bake the cookies for 10 to 11 minutes, until they are lightly golden. 5. Allow the cookies to cool for a minute on the baking sheet before transferring them to a wire rack to cool completely. Enjoy your delicious, large cookies!

Per Serving: (2 cookies)

calories: 294 | fat: 21g | protein: 6g | carbs: 25g | fiber: 4g

No-Bake Chocolate Peanut Butter Cookies

Prep time: 20 minutes | Cook time: 5 minutes | Makes 24 cookies

½ cup unsweetened dairy-free milk
3 tablespoons dairy-free butter
⅓ cup coconut sugar (optional)
1 tablespoon unsweetened cocoa powder
⅓ cup dairy-free semi-sweet
chocolate chips
1 teaspoon vanilla extract
⅓ cup creamy peanut butter
Pinch of salt (optional)
2½ cups old-fashioned oats or quick-cooking oats
¼ cup raw shelled hempseed

1. Prepare a baking sheet by lining it with wax paper. 2. In a large saucepan, combine the milk, butter, sugar (if using), cocoa powder, and chocolate chips. Bring the mixture to a rolling boil and set a timer for 2 minutes. Stir occasionally to prevent the chocolate chips from sticking to the pan before they melt. After 2 minutes, remove the pan from the heat and add the vanilla, peanut butter, and salt (if using). Mix until the peanut butter is fully melted. Stir in the oats and hempseed. 3. Using a spoon, drop dollops of the batter onto the prepared baking sheet. Allow them to cool and set for about an hour. If you want to speed up the process, you can place the cookies in the refrigerator to help them cool and harden more quickly. Once set, the cookies are ready to enjoy!

Per Serving: (2 cookies)

calories: 220 | fat: 77g | protein: 7g | carbs: 29g | fiber: 5g

Spirulina-Golden Berry Power Bars

Prep time: 2 minutes | Cook time: 0 minutes | Makes 8 bars

1 cup mixed raw seeds (pumpkin, sunflower, sesame, hemp)
1 tablespoon chia seeds
1 cup Medjool dates (about 10 large), pitted
2 tablespoons chopped fresh mint
2 teaspoons spirulina powder
1 tablespoon fresh lime juice
½ cup golden berries

1. Using a food processor fitted with the S blade, combine all the ingredients, except the golden berries. 2. Process the mixture until it forms a coarse dough, which may take a couple of minutes. Check the consistency by pinching the dough between your fingers—it should stick together easily to ensure the bars hold their shape. If the dough appears too dry, add small amounts of water, about ½ teaspoon at a time, and blend again until the desired stickiness is achieved. 3. Add the golden berries to the dough and pulse several times to coarsely chop them, giving the bars a delightful texture. 4. Prepare a flat surface with a large sheet of parchment paper. Transfer the dough onto the parchment and gather it into a solid mass at the center. Fold the parchment paper over the dough and use a rolling pin to flatten it to about ¼ inch (6 mm) thickness. 5. Place the flattened dough in the freezer for a few hours to firm up. Then, carefully use a knife or cookie cutter to cut the bars into your preferred shapes. 6. Store the bars in an airtight glass container for 2 to 3 weeks or keep them in the freezer for up to 3 months. Enjoy these healthy and delicious treats!

Per Serving:

calories: 186 | fat: 8g | protein: 6g | carbs: 26g | fiber: 3g

Basic Oil-Free Hummus

Prep time: 10 minutes | Cook time: 0 minutes | Makes 1½ cups

1 (15-ounce / 425-g) can chickpeas, drained and rinsed
1 tablespoon tahini
¼ teaspoon garlic powder
¼ teaspoon ground cumin
¼ cup lemon juice
1/16 teaspoon cayenne
¼ teaspoon za'atar

1. Using a food processor, blend together the chickpeas, tahini, garlic powder, cumin, lemon juice, cayenne, and za'atar until the mixture becomes smooth and creamy.

Per Serving:

calories: 136 | fat: 6g | protein: 3g | carbs: 21g | fiber: 3g

Berry Chia Energy Gel

Prep time: 2 minutes | Cook time: 0 minutes | Serves 3 to 4

1 small beet, peeled and chopped	1 tablespoon raw agave nectar (optional)
1 cup fresh or frozen blueberries	¼ teaspoon ground turmeric
1 tablespoon fresh lime juice	Pinch of sea salt (optional)
	2 tablespoons chia seeds

1. Using a blender or food processor, blend together all the ingredients except for the chia seeds until the mixture becomes smooth. Transfer the mixture to a bowl and stir in the chia seeds. Cover the bowl with a plate or lid and refrigerate for at least 20 minutes. 2. When you're ready to use it, portion the gel into small ziplock plastic bags or reusable gel containers. 3. The gel can be stored in the refrigerator for up to 3 days, but it's best enjoyed fresh.

Per Serving:
calories: 56 | fat: 1g | protein: 1g | carbs: 9g | fiber: 3g

Emerald Green Gem

Prep time: 15 minutes | Cook time: 0 minutes | Serves 1

1 cup fresh spinach	½ banana, peeled
½ cup water	¼ avocado, peeled
1 orange, peeled	½ cup frozen peaches

1. In a high-powered blender, combine the spinach, water, and orange until a smooth and juice-like consistency is achieved. Next, add the banana, avocado, and peaches, and blend again until well combined. 2. Optionally, serve the smoothie over ice for a refreshing and chilled experience. Enjoy your nutritious green smoothie!

Per Serving:
calories: 235 | fat: 8g | protein: 4g | carbs: 42g | fiber: 10g

Broccoli Veggie Dippers

Prep time: 10 minutes | Cook time: 25 minutes | Makes 12 patties

¾ cup lentils	¼ teaspoon ground black pepper
2 cups fresh broccoli florets	
1 tablespoon ground chia seeds	¼ teaspoon onion powder
½ cup shredded carrots	¼ teaspoon dried oregano
¼ teaspoon garlic powder	¼ teaspoon dried basil
¼ teaspoon dried parsley	¾ cup bread crumbs, divided
½ teaspoon salt (optional)	1 tablespoon extra virgin olive oil (optional)

1. Rinse and drain the lentils. Place them in a medium-large saucepan and add ½ cup of water. Bring the pan to a boil over high heat, then reduce to medium-high and cook for 20 minutes or until the lentils are tender and all the water is absorbed. Set aside. 2. In the meantime, fill a medium saucepan with water and bring it to a boil. Place a steamer insert in the pan and add the broccoli. Steam the broccoli over the boiling water for 10 minutes. Remove from the steamer and set aside. 3. In a small bowl, mix ground chia seeds with 3 tablespoons of water. 4. Put all the ingredients, except for ¼ cup of bread crumbs, into a food processor. Process until well combined and crumbly. Divide the mixture into twelve pieces, shaping each piece into a ball and then flattening them into patties. Coat each patty on both sides with the remaining bread crumbs. 5. If desired, heat oil in a medium skillet over medium-high heat. Brown the patties for 3 minutes on each side. 6. Serve the patties with dairy-free chipotle mayonnaise or any other spicy dipping sauce of your choice.

Per Serving: (2 patties)
calories: 92 | fat: 3g | protein: 5g | carbs: 14g | fiber: 2g

Protein Power Pistachio Bites

Prep time: 15 minutes | Cook time: 0 minutes | Makes 18 balls

½ cup old-fashioned oats	⅓ cup flaxseed meal
½ cup almond butter	⅓ cup pistachios, ground
¼ cup maple syrup (optional)	1 tablespoon raw shelled hempseed
⅓ cup oat bran	

1. Combine all the ingredients in a large bowl and thoroughly mix them together. 2. Shape the mixture into eighteen evenly-sized balls.

Per Serving: (2 balls)
calories: 188 | fat: 12g | protein: 7g | carbs: 17g | fiber: 5g

No-Bake Cereal Date Bars

Prep time: 15 minutes | Cook time: 15 minutes | Makes 16 bars

2 cups granola cereal	½ cup dates, chopped small
2 tablespoons flaxseed meal	½ cup almond butter
2 tablespoons protein powder	½ cup brown rice syrup
½ cup chopped peanuts	¼ cup maple syrup (optional)

1. Line an 8-inch square baking dish with parchment paper and come up about 3 inches on opposite sides. This will act as a handle to remove the bars from the pan. 2. Combine the cereal, flaxseed meal, protein powder, peanuts, and dates in a large bowl. 3. In a small saucepan, add the almond butter and both syrups. Bring to a boil and cook to the hard ball stage, 260°F (127°C), on a candy thermometer. Quickly stir into the cereal mixture and then spread into the prepared dish. It will cool quickly, so you can use your fingertips to press down into the dish as evenly as possible. Refrigerate for at least 30 minutes. 4. Grab the "handles" of the parchment paper and lift out of the dish. Place on a cutting board and slice into sixteen squares.

Per Serving: (2 bars)
calories: 232 | fat: 13g | protein: 9g | carbs: 28g | fiber: 5g

Packed Peanut Oatmeal Cookies

Prep time: 15 minutes | Cook time: 11 minutes | Serves 12

1 tablespoon chia seeds or ground chia seeds
1 cups whole wheat flour
1 teaspoon baking powder
1½ cups old-fashioned oats
2 tablespoons vanilla protein powder
½ cup dairy-free butter
1 cup coconut sugar (optional)
½ cup softened dairy-free cream cheese
1 teaspoon vanilla extract
1 banana
1 cup chopped peanuts

1. Preheat the oven to 400ºF (205ºC). Cut parchment paper to fit on a baking sheet. Set aside. 2. Mix the chia seeds with 3 tablespoons water and set aside. 3. Add the flour, baking powder, oats, and protein powder to a large bowl. Set aside. 4. Add the butter and sugar (if desired) to the bowl of a stand mixer. Cream on medium-low speed for 5 minutes. Add the cream cheese and mix well. Turn off the beater and add the prepared chia seed mixture, vanilla, and banana. Mix well on medium speed. Add the dry ingredients and peanuts and keep mixing until just combined. 5. Spoon dollops on a cookie sheet 2 inches apart and flatten with the bottom of a glass to about ½-inch thick. Bake for 11 minutes. 6. Cool on a wire rack.

Per Serving: (2 squares)

calories: 233 | fat: 14g | protein: 9g | carbs: 22g | fiber: 6g

Baked Vegetable Chips

Prep time: 20 minutes | Cook time: 35 minutes | Serves 2

1 pound (454 g) starchy root vegetables, such as russet potato, sweet potato, rutabaga, parsnip, red or golden beet, or taro
1 pound (454 g) high-water vegetables, such as zucchini or summer squash
Kosher salt, for absorbing
moisture
1 teaspoon garlic powder
1 teaspoon paprika
½ teaspoon onion powder
½ teaspoon freshly ground black pepper
1 teaspoon avocado oil or other oil (optional)

1. Preheat your oven to 300ºF (150ºC) and line two baking sheets with parchment paper. Set them aside. 2. Thoroughly scrub the root vegetables to remove any dirt. Wash and dry the high-water vegetables. 3. Using a mandoline or a sharp kitchen knife, slice all the vegetables into thin slices, about ⅛-inch thick. Remember, the thinner the slices, the crispier they will become. 4. Place the sliced high-water vegetables on a clean kitchen towel or paper towel. Sprinkle them generously with kosher salt to draw out moisture. This step is crucial for achieving crispy chips. Allow the vegetables to sit for 15 minutes, then use a paper towel to dab off any excess moisture and salt. 5. In a small bowl, mix together garlic powder, paprika, onion powder, and pepper. 6. Transfer all the sliced vegetables onto the prepared baking sheets, arranging them in a single layer. If desired, brush the vegetables with oil. Sprinkle the spice mix evenly over the vegetables. 7. Bake the chips for 15 minutes. Then, switch the baking sheets between the oven racks and continue baking for an additional 20 minutes, or until the vegetables turn darker in color and become crispy around the edges. 8. Using a spatula, carefully transfer the chips to a wire rack to cool. As they cool, the chips will become even more crispy within a few minutes.

Per Serving:

calories: 250 | fat: 3g | protein: 8g | carbs: 51g | fiber: 6g

Kale Chips

Prep time: 5 minutes | Cook time: 20 minutes | Serves 4

¼ cup vegetable broth
1 tablespoon nutritional yeast
½ teaspoon garlic powder
½ teaspoon onion powder
6 ounces (170 g) kale, stemmed and cut into 2- to 3-inch pieces

1. Preheat your oven to 300ºF (150ºC) and prepare a baking sheet by lining it with parchment paper. 2. In a small bowl, combine the broth, nutritional yeast, garlic powder, and onion powder. 3. Take a large bowl and place the kale in it. Pour the broth mixture over the kale and toss it well to ensure that the kale is thoroughly coated. 4. Arrange the kale pieces in a single layer on the prepared baking sheet. Bake for approximately 20 minutes, or until the kale turns crispy, remembering to flip the kale halfway through the baking process.

Per Serving:

calories: 41 | fat: 0g | protein: 4g | carbs: 7g | fiber: 2g

Oatmeal Granola Bar Bites

Prep time: 5 minutes | Cook time: 25 minutes | Serves 12

1½ cups rolled oats
⅓ cup unsweetened applesauce
¼ cup unsweetened natural peanut butter
2 tablespoons pure maple syrup
2 tablespoons ground flaxseed
1 tablespoon finely chopped pecans
1 tablespoon sliced almonds
1 tablespoon unsweetened raisins
1 tablespoon mini vegan chocolate chips

1. Preheat the oven to 350ºF (180ºC). Line an 8-by-8-inch baking dish and a baking sheet with parchment paper. 2. In a large bowl, using a wooden spoon or rubber spatula, mix together the oats, applesauce, peanut butter, maple syrup, flaxseed, pecans, almonds, raisins, and chocolate chips. 3. Using the back of a measuring cup, firmly press the mixture into the prepared baking dish. 4. Lift the pressed mixture out, and cut into 12 equal pieces. 5. Place the cut pieces in single layer on the prepared baking sheet. 6. Transfer the baking sheet to the oven, and bake for 20 to 25 minutes, flipping halfway through, or until the bars are golden brown. Remove from the oven.

Per Serving:

calories: 98 | fat: 5g | protein: 3g | carbs: 12g | fiber: 2g

Mexikale Crisps

Prep time: 10 minutes | Cook time: 15 minutes | Serves 2

8 cups large kale leaves, chopped	1 teaspoon ground cumin
2 tablespoons avocado oil (optional)	½ teaspoon chili powder
	1 teaspoon dried oregano
2 tablespoons nutritional yeast	1 teaspoon dried cilantro
1 teaspoon garlic powder	Salt and pepper to taste (optional)

1. Preheat your oven to 350ºF (180ºC) and prepare a baking tray by lining it with parchment paper. Set it aside. 2. Use paper towels to absorb any excess water from the chopped kale leaves. Transfer the chopped leaves to a large bowl and add avocado oil, nutritional yeast, and seasonings. Mix and shake well, adding more yeast and extra seasonings if desired. Ensure all the ingredients are thoroughly combined.
3. Spread out the seasoned kale chips on the prepared baking tray. Bake them in the oven for 10 to 15 minutes, checking every minute after the 10-minute mark until they reach your preferred level of crispiness. Once done, remove the tray from the oven and set it aside to cool down. 4. Serve and enjoy your homemade kale chips immediately, or store them in an airtight container for later consumption.

Per Serving:
calories: 313 | fat: 14g | protein: 12g | carbs: 33g | fiber: 7g

Thai Sweet Chili Tofu Stacks

Prep time: 30 minutes | Cook time: 15 minutes | Serves 6

1 tablespoon cornstarch	½ teaspoon chopped parsley
½ cup rice vinegar	¼ teaspoon cayenne pepper
½ cup coconut sugar (optional)	8 ounces (227 g) extra-firm tofu, drained, pressed, and cut into 1-inch cubes
1 chili pepper, chopped fine	
2 cloves garlic, chopped fine	1 (8-ounce / 227-g) can sliced pineapple
2 teaspoons tamari	

1. In a small bowl, mix the cornstarch with 1 tablespoon of water until smooth. Set it aside. 2. In a food processor, combine rice vinegar, ⅔ cup water, sugar (if desired), chili pepper, garlic, tamari, parsley, and cayenne pepper. Process until well blended and the chili pepper is finely broken down. 3. Transfer the mixture to a small saucepan and bring it to a boil, stirring until the sugar is dissolved. Reduce the heat and simmer for 5 minutes. Add the cornstarch mixture and continue stirring occasionally for about 5 minutes or until the sauce thickens slightly. Remove from heat and let it cool. 4. Place the tofu cubes in a bowl and pour the cooled sweet chili sauce over them. Allow the tofu to marinate for approximately 30 minutes. 5. Drain the pineapple slices and cut them into wedges, about 1 to 1¼ inches thick. 6. Take a plate and place a slice of pineapple on it. Put a marinated tofu cube in the center of the pineapple slice. Top it with another slice of pineapple and secure the stack with a toothpick.

Per Serving: (4 stacks)
calories: 105 | fat: 2g | protein: 9g | carbs: 14g | fiber: 1g

Strawberry Shortcake Rice Bites

Prep time: 20 minutes | Cook time: 25 minutes | Makes 8 balls

3 cups water	½ teaspoon vanilla extract
3 cups white sushi rice	2 cups strawberries, hulled and quartered
½ cup coconut sugar (optional)	
	3 tablespoons chia seeds
3 tablespoons fresh lemon juice	Salt (optional)

1. In a large saucepan, bring water to a boil. Reduce the heat to medium-low and add the rice. Stir occasionally and cook for about 15 to 20 minutes until the rice is soft and tender. It should be moist, sticky, but not overly soggy. 2. Transfer the cooked rice to a large bowl. Add the sugar, lemon juice, and vanilla. Mix well until thoroughly combined. Allow the mixture to cool slightly. 3. Prepare a sushi mat or silicone liner by covering it with plastic wrap. Spread 1 cup of the rice evenly on top of the plastic wrap using wet hands. Press the rice down firmly to create a uniform layer that is about ½-inch thick. 4. Arrange a row of strawberries end to end, about 1 inch from the bottom edge of the rice. Sprinkle 1 teaspoon of chia seeds over the strawberries. Starting from the edge closest to you, tightly roll the rice into a cylinder shape, using the plastic wrap and mat to assist you. Make sure to pull the plastic wrap and mat away from the rice as you roll. Repeat this process with the remaining ingredients. 5. If desired, sprinkle the outside of the rolls with salt to taste. Let the rolls sit for 5 minutes, then use a sharp knife to slice each roll into 8 to 10 pieces. For easy portability, wrap the individual pieces tightly in parchment paper and plastic wrap. You can refrigerate the rolls for up to 2 days or freeze them for up to 3 months. If frozen, allow them to thaw overnight before consuming.

Per Serving:
calories: 385 | fat: 2g | protein: 9g | carbs: 87g | fiber: 5g

Protein Peanut Butter Balls

Prep time: 20 minutes | Cook time: 0 minutes | Makes 24 balls

½ cup creamy peanut butter	¼ cup flaxseed meal
½ cup maple syrup (optional)	½ cup coconut flour
½ cup powdered soy milk, non-GMO	¼ cup peanuts, chopped fine

1. Place the peanut butter and maple syrup (if desired) in a medium bowl. Mix well. Add the powdered soy milk, flaxseed meal, and coconut flour. Mix well and roll into 24 balls. Lightly roll each ball in the chopped peanuts. 2. Store in the refrigerator for up to 2 weeks.

Per Serving: (2 balls)
calories: 133 | fat: 8g | protein: 10g | carbs: 12g | fiber: 2g

Crispy Baked Puffed Tofu with Teriyaki Sauce

Prep time: 10 minutes | Cook time: 40 minutes | Serves 6

Puffed Tofu:
7 ounces (198 g) extra-firm tofu, drained and pressed
½ cup vegetable broth
2 tablespoons hot sauce
¼ cup cornstarch
Dipping Sauce:

2 tablespoons tamari
2 teaspoons cornstarch
2 tablespoons maple syrup (optional)
¼ teaspoon garlic powder
¼ teaspoon ground ginger

Make Puffed Tofu: 1. Turn the tofu on its side and cut through the center to make two rectangles. Flip them onto their flat sides and stack. Cut through the center, and without separating the halves, cut those two halves twice each. Make two equal-size cuts lengthwise. There are now twenty-four cubes. Place the cubes in a small flat casserole dish or other container in which all the cubes will fit on one level. 2. Mix together the vegetable broth and hot sauce. Pour over the tofu. Marinate for an hour. 3. Preheat the oven to 350°F (180°C). 4. Place ¼ cup cornstarch in a medium bowl. Remove the tofu from the marinade and place on the cornstarch. Toss and then place the tofu on a baking sheet. Bake for 30 to 40 minutes. Toss with a spatula every 10 minutes until golden and puffed. Make Dipping Sauce: 5. To a small saucepan, add ½ cup water, tamari, and cornstarch and heat on medium high. Stir until the cornstarch is dissolved. Add the remaining ingredients and bring to a boil. Turn down heat to medium and cook, stirring until desired thickness. Place the tofu on a platter with toothpicks and dip into the sauce.

Per Serving: (4 pieces)
calories: 78 | fat: 2g | protein: 8g | carbs: 11g | fiber: 1g

Slow Cooker Chipotle Tacos

Prep time: 15 minutes | Cook time: 4 hours | Serves 4

2 (15 ounces / 425 g) cans pinto beans, drained and rinsed
1 cup fresh, frozen, or canned corn
3 ounces (85 g) chipotle pepper in adobo sauce (about 2 peppers), chopped
6 ounces (170 g) tomato paste
¾ cup Thai sweet chili sauce
1 tablespoon unsweetened

cocoa powder
1½ teaspoons taco seasoning
8 white corn taco shells or tortillas
Favorite toppings:
Spinach
Lettuce
Black olives
Lime
Avocado
Peppers

1. Put everything in the crockpot except the taco shells and toppings. Cook on low for 3 to 4 hours or on high for 1½ to 2 hours. 2. Spread quite a bit of the filling on your taco shells, hard or soft. Add your favorite toppings.

Per Serving: (2 tacos)
calories: 484 | fat: 8g | protein: 20g | carbs: 65g | fiber: 19g

Tamari Toasted Almonds

Prep time: 2 minutes | Cook time: 8 minutes | Makes ½ cup

½ cup raw almonds or sunflower seeds
2 tablespoons tamari or soy

sauce
1 teaspoon toasted sesame oil (optional)

1. Begin by heating a dry skillet over medium-high heat. Add the almonds, ensuring to stir them frequently to prevent burning. 2. Toast the almonds for about 7 to 8 minutes (or 3 to 4 minutes for sunflower seeds) until they are nicely toasted. Once done, pour the tamari over the toasted almonds and, if using, add the sesame oil. Stir well to coat the nuts evenly with the mixture. 3. Turn off the heat and let the almonds cool. As they cool, the tamari mixture will cling to the nuts and dry, creating a flavorful coating.

Per Serving: (1 tablespoon)
calories: 164 | fat: 13g | protein: 6g | carbs: 5g | fiber: 3g

Homemade Hummus

Prep time: 10 minutes | Cook time: 0 minutes | Makes 2 cups

1 (15-ounce / 425-g) can chickpeas, drained and rinsed
2 cloves garlic
¼ cup tahini

2 tablespoons lemon juice
3 tablespoons water
1 teaspoon ground cumin
Salt, to taste (optional)

1. In a food processor or blender, blend all the ingredients on high until completely smooth.

Per Serving: (½ cup)
calories: 183 | fat: 10g | protein: 8g | carbs: 19g | fiber: 6g

Salsa with Mushrooms and Olives

Prep time: 30 minutes | Cook time: 0 minutes | Serves 3

½ cup finely chopped white button mushrooms
1 tablespoon chopped fresh parsley
1 tablespoon chopped fresh basil
2 Roma tomatoes, finely chopped

1 tablespoon finely chopped scallions
⅓ cup chopped marinated artichoke hearts
½ cup chopped olives
1 tablespoon balsamic vinegar
3 slices sourdough toast

1. Combine the mushrooms, parsley, basil, tomatoes, scallions, artichoke hearts, and olives in a medium mixing bowl. 2. Dress with the balsamic vinegar. Let marinate at room temperature about 20 minutes to blend flavors. Alternatively, refrigerate until serving time. 3. Serve the salsa with the slices of sourdough toast.

Per Serving:
calories: 205 | fat: 3g | protein: 9g | carbs: 41g | fiber: 4g

Nori Snack Rolls

Prep time: 5 minutes | Cook time: 8 to 10 minutes | Makes 4 rolls

2 tablespoons almond, cashew, peanut, or other nut butter
2 tablespoons tamari or soy sauce
4 standard nori sheets
1 mushroom, sliced
1 tablespoon pickled ginger
½ cup grated carrots

1. Preheat the oven to 350ºF (180ºC). 2. Mix together the nut butter and tamari until smooth and very thick. Lay out a nori sheet, rough side up, the long way. Spread a thin line of the tamari mixture on the far end of the nori sheet, from side to side. Lay the mushroom slices, ginger, and carrots in a line at the other end (the end closest to you). Fold the vegetables inside the nori, rolling toward the tahini mixture, which will seal the roll. 3. Repeat to make 4 rolls. 4. Put on a baking sheet and bake for 8 to 10 minutes, or until the rolls are slightly browned and crispy at the ends. Let the rolls cool for a few minutes, then slice each roll into 3 smaller pieces.

Per Serving: (1 roll)
calories: 62 | fat: 4g | protein: 2g | carbs: 3g | fiber: 1g

Endurance Snack Mix

Prep time: 5 minutes | Cook time: 0 minutes | Makes 3 cups

½ cup raw pistachios
1 cup raw pumpkin seeds
½ cup unsweetened large coconut flakes
¼ cup raisins
¼ cup goji berries
½ cup dried mulberries
Handful of dried dulse, or 1 sheet nori, cut into bite-sized pieces

1. In a medium-sized bowl, combine all the ingredients and toss well. 2. Portion into several servings in either snack-sized paper bags, reusable bags or small glass jars. You can then keep them in your backpack, purse, gym bag, car or any other place that's convenient. 3. They will keep for several weeks in the fridge or freezer.

Per Serving:
calories: 236 | fat: 17g | protein: 9g | carbs: 12g | fiber: 3g

Pressure Cooker Thai Nuggets

Prep time: 10 minutes | Cook time: 5 minutes | Serves 4

¾ cup plus 3 tablespoons vital wheat gluten
¼ cup chickpea flour
½ teaspoon ground ginger
½ teaspoon salt (optional)
¼ teaspoon garlic powder
¼ teaspoon paprika
¾ cup vegetable broth
2 teaspoons tamari, divided
4 teaspoons red curry paste, divided
1½ cups vegetable broth, divided

1. Add the gluten, flour, ginger, salt (if desired), garlic powder, and paprika to a large bowl. 2. Mix ¾ cup vegetable broth, 1 teaspoon tamari, and 2 teaspoons red curry paste in a small bowl. Pour the wet mixture into the dry ingredients. 3. Mix and then knead for about 2 to 3 minutes or until elastic. It's a very wet dough but you will see it is still elastic. It should be mildly stretchy and pull back but still pliable. Pinch off pieces of seitan dough into very small balls, about 1 to 1½ inches in diameter. They will fatten up when cooking. 4. Place in an electric pressure cooker. 5. Add 1½ cups vegetable broth, 1½ cups water, and 2 teaspoons red curry paste to a bowl and stir well. Pour over the nuggets in the pressure cooker. Close the lid, make sure the top knob is turned to sealing. Press Manual on the front of the pot. Push button to 4 (meaning 4 minutes). The pressure cooker will make a click and start to build pressure. It will take about 15 minutes to build pressure and cook. Leave the nuggets in the pot to set. They will cook more as the pressure is naturally releasing. Don't vent. 6. After about an hour, go ahead and vent. It may already have cooled completely, but vent to make sure the pressure has released and then open the lid. 7. Remove the nuggets from the liquid and set aside to cool. You can eat them right away, add to a recipe, or keep in the fridge overnight. They are great the next day. You can also freeze them.

Per Serving:
calories: 155 | fat: 2g | protein: 26g | carbs: 11g | fiber: 2g

Coco-Mango Performance Bars

Prep time: 2 minutes | Cook time: 0 minutes | Makes 6 bars

1 cup soft Medjool dates (about 10), pitted
1 cup shredded unsweetened coconut
½ cup raw macadamia nuts or cashews
¼ cup fresh or frozen mango
1 tablespoon chia seeds
2 teaspoons maca powder
2 tablespoons cacao nibs
2 tablespoons raw nuts/seeds (your favorite kind)

1. In a food processor, grind together all the ingredients, except the 2 tablespoons of nuts/seeds, until a coarse dough has formed (this process may take a couple of minutes). 2. Stop the machine and check the consistency—pinch the dough between 2 fingers and make sure it sticks together easily, so that your bars don't end up crumbly. If the dough is too dry, add a small amount of water—about ½ teaspoon at a time—and blend again until your desired stickiness is achieved. Then, add the 2 tablespoons of nuts/seeds and pulse several times until coarsely chopped, to give the bars a nice texture. 3. To shape into bars: Turn out the mixture onto a clean work surface. Flatten with your hands. Place a sheet of parchment paper on top, then roll out with a rolling pin to your desired thickness. Cut into bars. 4. Alternatively, form the mixture into a brick, then cut into slices. Or press the mixture into a parchment paper-lined baking dish or brownie pan, refrigerate for about 5 hours, then slice into bars. 5. As the bars dry in the fridge, they become easier to handle and slice. 6. Store in an airtight glass container for 1 week or in the freezer for up to 1 month.

Per Serving:
calories: 282 | fat: 16g | protein: 3g | carbs: 37g | fiber: 6g

Pita Chips

Prep time: 5 minutes | Cook time: 20 minutes | Serves 2 to 4

4 to 6 whole-grain pita breads, cut into triangles

1. Spread the pita triangles out in a single layer on a parchment-lined baking sheet. 2. Transfer the baking sheet to a cold oven, and heat to 350°F (180°C). 3. When the oven reaches temperature, flip the pitas over. Bake for another 10 to 15 minutes, or until crispy.
Per Serving:
calories: 150 | fat: 1g | protein: 11g | carbs: 32g | fiber: 6g

Carrot Cake Date Balls

Prep time: 10 minutes | Cook time: 0 minutes | Makes 24 balls

1 cup shredded carrots
1 cup pitted dates
½ cup walnut pieces
¼ cup rolled oats
1 tablespoon coconut flakes

½ teaspoon ground cinnamon
¼ teaspoon ground ginger
⅛ teaspoon ground cloves
⅛ teaspoon ground nutmeg

1. Line a plate with parchment paper. 2. In a food processor, combine the carrots, dates, walnuts, oats, coconut flakes, ginger, cloves, and nutmeg. Process until a paste forms. 3. Using a 1-tablespoon scoop, form the paste into balls. 4. Place the balls in a single layer on the prepared plate. Serve immediately, or refrigerate in an airtight container for up to 5 days.
Per Serving:
calories: 43 | fat: 2g | protein: 1g | carbs: 7g | fiber: 1g

Carrot Cake Balls

Prep time: 10 minutes | Cook time: 0 minutes | Makes 30 balls

2 cups unsweetened coconut flakes
1 carrot, coarsely chopped
2 cups old-fashioned oats
½ cup smooth natural peanut butter
½ cup pure maple syrup (optional)

¼ cup coarsely chopped pecans
1 teaspoon ground cinnamon
½ teaspoon vanilla extract
½ teaspoon ground ginger

1. In a sauté pan or skillet over medium-high heat, toast the coconut for 3 to 6 minutes, stirring or flipping occasionally, until lightly browned. Remove from the heat. 2. In a food processor, pulse the carrot until finely chopped but not puréed. Transfer the carrot to a bowl and set aside. 3. In the food processor (it is okay if there is a little carrot in the bowl from the previous step), combine the toasted coconut flakes and oats. Pulse until coarsely ground but not until the ingredients become a flour. 4. Return the carrots to the processor and add the peanut butter, maple syrup (if using), pecans, cinnamon, vanilla, and ginger. Pulse until the dough starts to form a ball. Divide the dough into 30 portions. Using your clean hands, press and form each portion into a ball. 5. Refrigerate in a sealable bag or airtight container for up to 2 weeks.
Per Serving: (2 balls)
calories: 203 | fat: 13g | protein: 4g | carbs: 19g | fiber: 4g

Chapter 5

Vegetables and Sides

Provençal Potato Gratin

Prep time: 10 minutes | Cook time: 40 minutes | Makes 1 gratin

¼ cup vegetable broth
2 yellow onions, thinly sliced
1 tablespoon fresh thyme leaves
3 garlic cloves, minced
¼ teaspoon salt, plus more to taste (optional)

2 pounds (907 g) waxy potatoes, sliced ¼ inch thick
1 (14½-ounce / 411-g) can diced tomatoes with juice
½ cup pitted Kalamata olives, chopped
¼ teaspoon pepper

1. Preheat the oven to 400ºF (205ºC). 2. Place a large skillet over medium heat. Add the broth, then add the onions and thyme and sauté until they brown slightly, about 5 minutes. Add the garlic, season with salt (if desired) to taste, and remove from the heat. 3. Layer half of the onion mixture in a medium baking dish; top with the potatoes, tomatoes with their juice, and olives; then season with the ¼ teaspoon salt (if desired) and ¼ teaspoon pepper. Top with the remaining onion mixture. 4. Bake, covered, for 20 minutes. Remove the lid and continue to bake until the potatoes are fully cooked and the edges start to brown, 15 to 20 minutes. Serve warm or at room temperature.

Per Serving: (¼ gratin)
calories: 238 | fat: 2g | protein: 6g | carbs: 51g | fiber: 9g

Garlicky Winter Vegetable and White Bean Mash

Prep time: 20 minutes | Cook time: 25 minutes | Serves 4

Vegetable and Bean Mash:
2 cups peeled and diced celery root
2 cups chopped cauliflower
1 cup chopped parsnips
5 cloves garlic, peeled
1 cup cooked and drained white beans, such as navy or cannellini
¾ cup unsweetened almond milk
1 teaspoon virgin olive oil (optional)
Salt and pepper, to taste (optional)
Mushroom Miso Gravy:

1 tablespoon virgin olive oil (optional)
5 cups sliced mushrooms
2 teaspoons chopped fresh thyme leaves
4 cloves garlic, minced
Salt and pepper, to taste (optional)
2 teaspoons balsamic vinegar
1¼ cups vegetable stock
1 tablespoon mellow or light miso
2 teaspoons arrowroot powder
Freshly ground black pepper, for serving (optional)

1. To make the Vegetable and Bean Mash, place the diced celery root, cauliflower, parsnips, and garlic cloves in a medium saucepan. Cover the vegetables with cold water and place the pot over medium heat. Bring it to a boil and simmer until the vegetables are tender, approximately 15 minutes. 2. Drain the cooked vegetables and transfer them to the bowl of a food processor. Add the white beans and pulse a few times to lightly chop them. Then, add almond milk, olive oil, salt, and pepper if desired. Run the food processor on high speed until you achieve a creamy and smooth mixture. Keep it warm. 3. For the Mushroom Miso Gravy, heat olive oil in a large sauté pan over medium heat. Add the mushrooms and let them sit for 2 full minutes without stirring. Stir them up and let them sear for another full minute. Add thyme and garlic, and stir. Once the mushrooms start to glisten slightly, season them with salt and pepper if desired. Add balsamic vinegar and stir. 4. In a small bowl, whisk together vegetable stock, miso, and arrowroot powder until no lumps remain. Pour this mixture into the pan with the mushrooms and stir. 5. Bring the gravy to a light simmer and cook until it thickens slightly. 6. Serve the Mushroom Miso Gravy hot on top of the vegetable mash. You can sprinkle freshly ground black pepper on top if desired.

Per Serving:
calories: 225 | fat: 6g | protein: 10g | carbs: 36g | fiber: 8g

Millet-Stuffed Portobello Mushrooms

Prep time: 20 minutes | Cook time: 1 hour 5 minutes | Serves 4

4 large portobello mushrooms, stemmed
2 tablespoons low-sodium soy sauce
3 cloves garlic, peeled and minced
Freshly ground black pepper, to taste
Filling:
2 cups low-sodium vegetable stock

⅔ cup millet
1 small yellow onion, peeled and diced small
1 medium red bell pepper, seeded and diced small
1 fennel bulb, trimmed and diced
3 cloves garlic, peeled and minced
2 sage leaves, minced
Salt, to taste (optional)

1. Prepare a baking dish and place the mushrooms, stem side up, in it. Set aside.
2. In a small bowl, combine soy sauce, garlic, and black pepper to make the marinade. Brush each mushroom with some of the marinade. Set the mushrooms aside while you prepare the filling. Make the Filling:
3. In a medium saucepan, bring vegetable stock to a boil. Add millet and return the pot to a boil. Reduce the heat to medium and cook, covered, for 15 minutes or until the millet is tender. 4. Preheat your oven to 350ºF (180ºC). 5. In a large saucepan, sauté onion, red pepper, and fennel over medium heat for 10 minutes. If needed, add water 1 to 2 tablespoons at a time to prevent sticking. Add garlic and sage leaves, cooking for an additional 2 minutes. Stir in the cooked millet, mixing well, and season with salt and pepper. Remove from heat. 6. Divide the millet mixture among the 4 mushrooms. Arrange the stuffed mushrooms in the baking dish, cover with aluminum foil, and bake for 25 minutes. Remove the foil and bake for another 10 minutes.

Per Serving:
calories: 179 | fat: 1g | protein: 7g | carbs: 35g | fiber: 6g

Grilled Vegetable Kabobs

Prep time: 25 minutes | Cook time: 15 minutes | Serves 6

½ cup balsamic vinegar
3 cloves garlic, peeled and minced
1½ tablespoons minced rosemary
1½ tablespoons minced thyme
Salt and freshly ground black pepper, to taste
1 green bell pepper, seeded and cut into 1-inch pieces

1 red bell pepper, seeded and cut into 1-inch pieces
1 pint cherry tomatoes
1 medium zucchini, cut into 1-inch rounds
1 medium yellow squash, cut into 1-inch rounds
1 medium red onion, peeled and cut into large chunks

1. Get the grill ready for cooking. 2. Soak 12 bamboo skewers in water for 30 minutes to prevent them from burning on the grill. 3. In a small bowl, combine balsamic vinegar, garlic, rosemary, thyme, salt, and pepper. 4. Thread the vegetables onto the soaked skewers, alternating between different-colored vegetables for an appealing presentation. Place the skewers on the grill and cook, brushing the vegetables with the vinegar mixture and turning every 4 to 5 minutes. Continue grilling until the vegetables are tender and start to char, which usually takes about 12 to 15 minutes.

Per Serving:
calories: 50 | fat: 0g | protein: 1g | carbs: 10g | fiber: 2g

Mustard-Roasted Broccoli Pâté

Prep time: 15 minutes | Cook time: 20 minutes | Makes 2 cups

3 cups broccoli florets
1 leek, white and light-green parts only, rough-chopped
⅓ cup plus 2 tablespoons virgin olive oil, divided (optional)
1½ tablespoons grainy mustard, divided
2 teaspoons fresh thyme leaves
Salt and pepper, to taste (optional)

2 teaspoons lemon zest
1½ tablespoons fresh lemon juice
2 tablespoons nutritional yeast
Flaky sea salt, to taste (optional)
Serve:
Sliced bread
Olives
Pickles
Vegetables

1. Preheat the oven to 400ºF (205ºC). Line a baking sheet with parchment paper. 2. Toss the broccoli florets and leeks with 1 tablespoon of the olive oil, 1 tablespoon of the grainy mustard, and the thyme leaves, salt, and pepper, if using. After everything is coated, spread the mixture out on the lined baking sheet. Roast the vegetables until lightly browned and tender, about 15 to 18 minutes. 3. When they have slightly cooled, transfer the roasted vegetables to a food processor. Pulse the mixture until the broccoli is somewhat chopped. Set aside a spoonful of the chopped broccoli for garnish. 4. To the food processor, add the remaining ½ tablespoon of the grainy mustard and the lemon zest, lemon juice, salt, pepper, and nutritional yeast. Pulse until everything is combined. With the food processor running on low, drizzle in ⅓ cup of the olive oil through the feed tube. Continue to mix until you have a smooth, lightly chunky paste. Remove the bowl from the food processor, check the seasoning, and adjust if necessary. 5. Scrape the pâté mixture into a 2-cup nonreactive serving vessel, and scatter the reserved chopped broccoli over the top. Pour the remaining 1 tablespoon of the olive oil on top. Cover and place the pâté in the fridge for at least 2 hours or until the top oil layer has solidified a little bit. 6. Sprinkle the flaky sea salt, if using, over the pâté before you serve it with sliced bread, olives, pickles, and vegetables.

Per Serving: (½ cup)
calories: 200 | fat: 18g | protein: 4g | carbs: 7g | fiber: 2g

Loaded Frijoles

Prep time: 10 minutes | Cook time: 20 minutes | Serves 6

1 tablespoon avocado oil (optional)
1 yellow onion, finely chopped
3 garlic cloves, minced
2 teaspoons chili powder

1 teaspoon ground cumin
2 (15-ounce / 425-g) cans pinto beans, undrained
¼ cup tomato sauce
Sea salt, to taste (optional)

1. Heat avocado oil (if using) in a 4-quart pan over medium-high heat. Add the onion and sauté for 5 minutes. 2. Stir in the garlic and cook for 30 seconds, then add the chili powder and cumin. Cook for an additional 30 seconds. 3. Add the beans and tomato sauce to the pan. Taste and add salt if needed. 4. Mash the beans with a fork or use an immersion blender to puree them until you reach your desired consistency. Cook over medium-low heat for 15 minutes, or until the beans thicken. If the beans become too thick, you can add a little water. 5. Transfer the bean mixture to an airtight container and store it in the refrigerator for up to 1 week or in the freezer for several months.

Per Serving:
calories: 142 | fat: 3g | protein: 7g | carbs: 22g | fiber: 6g

Savory Sweet Potato Casserole

Prep time: 15 minutes | Cook time: 30 minutes | Serves 6

8 cooked sweet potatoes
½ cup vegetable broth
1 tablespoon dried sage

1 teaspoon dried thyme
1 teaspoon dried rosemary

1. Preheat your oven to 375ºF (190ºC). 2. Peel the cooked sweet potatoes and place them in a baking dish. Mash the sweet potatoes using a fork or potato masher, then add the broth, sage, thyme, and rosemary. Stir everything together until well combined. 3. Bake the sweet potato mixture in the preheated oven for 30 minutes. Once done, remove from the oven and serve.

Per Serving:
calories: 154 | fat: 0g | protein: 3g | carbs: 35g | fiber: 6g

Cauliflower and Pine Nut "Ricotta" Toasts

Prep time: 15 minutes | Cook time: 15 minutes | Makes 1½ cups

3 cups chopped cauliflower
1 teaspoon fresh thyme leaves
¼ cup raw pine nuts, soaked for at least 4 hours
2 tablespoons virgin olive oil (optional)
1 teaspoon lemon zest
1 tablespoon fresh lemon juice
½ teaspoon nutritional yeast
½ teaspoon sea salt (optional)
Serve:
Toasted baguette slices
Fruit
Good quality balsamic vinegar

1. Place a steamer basket over a large pot of simmering water. Add the chopped cauliflower to the basket and cover the pot with a tight-fitting lid. Steam the cauliflower for about 15 minutes or until it becomes tender. 2. Remove the steamed cauliflower from the pot and carefully transfer the florets to the bowl of a food processor. Add thyme, pine nuts, olive oil, lemon zest, lemon juice, nutritional yeast, and sea salt if desired. 3. Pulse the ingredients a few times to break up the cauliflower and nuts. Then, run the food processor on high until you achieve a smooth, almost purée-like texture. You may need to stop and scrape down the sides of the bowl a couple of times. 4. Transfer the cauliflower ricotta to a small bowl and cover it with plastic wrap. Chill in the refrigerator for at least 30 minutes before serving. Enjoy with toasted baguette slices and fruit.

Per Serving: (½ cup)
calories: 186 | fat: 17g | protein: 4g | carbs: 8g | fiber: 3g

Fennel and Green Cabbage Kraut

Prep time: 10 minutes | Cook time: 0 minutes | Makes 8 cups

1 medium green cabbage, cored and thinly sliced with 1 leaf reserved
1 large fennel bulb, trimmed, cored, and shaved on a
mandoline or thinly sliced
5 teaspoons fine sea salt (optional)
2 teaspoons fennel seeds

1. In a large bowl, combine the cabbage, shaved or sliced fennel, salt (if desired), and fennel seeds. Mix the vegetables together using clean hands, squeezing and softening them until they become juicy and wilted. Transfer a handful of the mixture to a wide-mouthed jar or fermentation crock. Press it down firmly with your fist. Repeat this process with the remaining mixture, adding any liquid left in the bowl. The liquid should completely cover the vegetables. If not, continue pressing the mixture down until it does. Leave at least 3 inches of headspace above the vegetables. Clean the edges of the jar or crock from any stray vegetable pieces. 2. Place a reserved cabbage leaf on top of the vegetables. Use a weight, such as a small glass jar filled with water, a flat glass plate or lid, or a fermentation weight, to keep the vegetables submerged. Seal the jar or crock tightly. Label and date it, then store it in a cool, dark place for 10 days. 3. After 10 days, carefully remove the lid, as it may pop off due to

built-up gases. Take out the weight and cabbage leaf. Use a clean fork to taste a little bit of the kraut. If the level of tanginess and flavor complexity is to your liking, transfer the jar or crock to the refrigerator. Alternatively, you can transfer the kraut to smaller jars and refrigerate. If the flavor is not yet satisfactory, replace the leaf and weight, tighten the lid, and set it aside for a few more days. Taste again. Usually, 2 to 3 weeks of fermentation results in a good flavor. The kraut will keep in the fridge for months, and its flavor will continue to develop, albeit at a slower rate.

Per Serving: (1 cup)
calories: 39 | fat: 0g | protein: 2g | carbs: 9g | fiber: 4g

Radish Turmeric Pickle

Prep time: 5 minutes | Cook time: 0 minutes | Serves 6

1 pound (454 g) medium radishes
6 tablespoons raw apple cider vinegar
1 teaspoon fine sea salt, or more to taste (optional)
1 (2-inch) piece fresh turmeric

1. Begin by trimming the tail ends of the radishes. Using a mandoline, thinly slice the radishes while holding them by their greens. Alternatively, you can use a sharp knife to slice them into paper-thin slices. Place the sliced radishes in a medium bowl and add vinegar and salt if desired. Mix well until the radishes are thoroughly coated. 2. Peel the turmeric and finely grate it. Stir the grated turmeric into the bowl with the radishes and season with additional salt if needed. You can serve the dish immediately or transfer it to a jar, cover it, and store it in the refrigerator for up to 2 weeks. After an hour or two, invert the jar to ensure that all the radishes are evenly combined with the liquid and have absorbed the vibrant color from the turmeric.

Per Serving:
calories: 20 | fat: 0g | protein: 1g | carbs: 4g | fiber: 2g

Baby Potatoes with Dill, Chives, and Garlic

Prep time: 5 minutes | Cook time: 20 minutes | Serves 2

2 cups water
12 baby potatoes
2 garlic cloves, minced
2 tablespoons chopped fresh dill
2 tablespoons chopped fresh chives
Pinch freshly ground black pepper (optional)

1. Combine the water and potatoes in a medium saucepan and bring to a boil over medium-high heat. Cook for 20 minutes or until the potatoes are soft when pierced with a fork. 2. Drain the liquid and add the garlic; then mix well. 3. Serve warm and top each portion with 1 tablespoon of dill, 1 tablespoon of chives, and pepper (if using).

Per Serving:
calories: 155 | fat: 1g | protein: 4g | carbs: 34g | fiber: 6g

Creamy Curried Potatoes and Peas

Prep time: 15 minutes | Cook time: 30 minutes | Serves 4

1 tablespoon extra-virgin olive oil (optional)	2 cups water
8 small red potatoes (about 1 pound / 454 g), diced small	1 cup frozen peas
3 garlic cloves, minced	3 tablespoons tomato paste
1 (2-inch) piece fresh ginger, peeled and minced	1 teaspoon salt, plus more as needed (optional)
1 small yellow onion, cut into ¼-inch pieces	Black pepper
	Red pepper flakes (optional)
3 teaspoons curry powder	¼ cup chopped fresh cilantro, for garnish

1. In a large saucepan or wok, heat the oil over medium heat. Add the potatoes and cook, stirring often, until they start to brown, about 10 minutes. Push the potatoes to one side of the pan, then add the garlic, ginger, and onion and cook, stirring occasionally, until very fragrant, about 5 minutes. Stir the onion mixture with the potatoes until combined. 2. Add the curry powder and water and stir until combined. Raise the heat to high and bring to a boil. Lower the heat to medium and cook, stirring occasionally, until the potatoes are fork-tender, 10 to 15 minutes. 3. Stir in the peas, tomato paste, and salt (if using) and cook, stirring occasionally, until the liquid reduces to a creamy sauce, 4 to 5 minutes. 4. Taste and season with salt (if using) and black pepper. Sprinkle with red pepper flakes (if using) and the cilantro.

Per Serving:

calories: 323 | fat: 4g | protein: 9g | carbs: 65g | fiber: 9g

Vegan Goulash

Prep time: 20 minutes | Cook time: 50 minutes | Serves 5

5 tablespoons olive oil (optional)	½ cup dry red wine
12 medium onions, finely chopped	3 to 6 cups vegetable broth
1 head garlic, minced	10 medium potatoes, skinned, cubed
4 red bell peppers, cored and chopped	1 (7-ounce / 198-g) pack tempeh
10 small tomatoes, cubed	Salt and pepper to taste (optional)
4 tablespoons paprika powder	¼ cup fresh parsley, chopped

1. Heat olive oil in a large pot over medium heat. Sauté the onions until they turn brown. Add minced garlic and stir for 1 minute. Next, add chopped bell peppers and cook for another 3 minutes while stirring. Blend in tomatoes, paprika powder, salt (if desired), pepper, and dry red wine. Stir well and let the mixture cook for an additional 2 minutes. Add vegetable broth and potato cubes to the pot, stirring to combine all ingredients. Cover the pot with a lid and allow the goulash to cook for 5 more minutes. 2. Reduce the heat to low and continue gently cooking the goulash for 15 minutes. The goulash will thicken, and the potatoes will cook properly. Add tempeh and taste to

adjust seasoning with salt and pepper if needed. Let the goulash cook for another 15 minutes. Check the potatoes' tenderness by piercing them with a fork. If they are still hard, cook for a few more minutes. Once the potatoes are soft, add parsley, stir, and remove the goulash from the heat. 3. Allow the goulash to cool for about 10 minutes before serving, or let it cool longer if storing for later use.

Per Serving:

calories: 591 | fat: 18g | protein: 16g | carbs: 74g | fiber: 14g

Garlic Toast

Prep time: 5 minutes | Cook time: 5 minutes | Makes 1 slice

1 teaspoon coconut oil or olive oil (optional)	yeast
Pinch sea salt (optional)	1 small garlic clove, pressed, or ¼ teaspoon garlic powder
1 to 2 teaspoons nutritional	1 slice whole-grain bread

1. In a small bowl, combine the oil, salt (if desired), nutritional yeast, and garlic. 2. There are two options for preparing the bread: a) Toast the bread first and then spread the seasoned oil mixture on top. b) Brush the oil mixture onto the bread and bake it in a toaster oven for 5 minutes. If using fresh garlic, it is recommended to spread it onto the bread before baking.

Per Serving:

calories: 134 | fat: 5g | protein: 4g | carbs: 16g | fiber: 2g

Tangy Cabbage, Apples, and Potatoes

Prep time: 15 minutes | Cook time: 3 to 4 hours | Serves 4 to 6

6 red or yellow potatoes (about 2 pounds / 907 g), unpeeled and cut into 1½-inch chunks	½ cup apple juice, apple cider, or hard apple cider
½ medium onion, diced	2 tablespoons apple cider vinegar
2 apples, peeled, cored, and diced	2 teaspoons ground mustard, or 1 tablespoon spicy brown mustard
½ teaspoon ground cinnamon	1 teaspoon fennel seeds
½ medium head green cabbage, sliced	1 bay leaf
1 cup store-bought low-sodium vegetable broth	Ground black pepper
	Salt (optional)

1. Begin by layering the potatoes, onion, and apples in the slow cooker, in that order. Sprinkle cinnamon over the apples, and then top everything with the cabbage. 2. In a small bowl, whisk together the broth, apple juice, vinegar, mustard, fennel, bay leaf, pepper, and salt (if desired). Pour this mixture over the cabbage in the slow cooker. 3. Cover the slow cooker and cook on High for 3 to 4 hours or on Low for 6 to 8 hours. Once done, remove and discard the bay leaf. Serve and enjoy!

Per Serving:

calories: 266 | fat: 1g | protein: 7g | carbs: 62g | fiber: 10g

Oven-Roasted Dijon Veggies

Prep time: 5 minutes | Cook time: 20 minutes | Serves 4

½ large head cauliflower, cut into florets (about 2 cups)
½ large head broccoli, cut into florets (about 2 cups)
1 red or yellow bell pepper, seeded and cut into 2-inch-thick slices

2 carrots, peeled and cut into 1-inch rounds
1 teaspoon extra-virgin olive oil (optional)
1 teaspoon Dijon mustard
½ teaspoon salt (optional)

1. Preheat your oven to 425ºF (220ºC). 2. In a large bowl, combine the cauliflower, broccoli, bell pepper, carrots, olive oil, Dijon mustard, and salt if desired. Toss the vegetables until they are well coated with the seasonings. 3. Transfer the seasoned vegetables to a sheet pan and bake them in the preheated oven for 10 minutes. After 10 minutes, use a spatula to turn the veggies, ensuring even cooking. Continue baking for another 10 minutes or until the vegetables are browned and slightly crispy on the outside, while remaining tender inside. Oven temperatures can vary, so if the vegetables are not yet done, continue baking in 5-minute increments until they reach your desired level of doneness.

Per Serving:
calories: 64 | fat: 1g | protein: 3g | carbs: 13g | fiber: 4g

Fluffy Mashed Potatoes with Gravy

Prep time: 10 minutes | Cook time: 15 minutes | Serves 6

Mashed Potatoes:
8 red or Yukon Gold potatoes, cut into 1-inch cubes
½ cup plant-based milk (here or here)
1 teaspoon garlic powder
1 teaspoon onion powder
Gravy:
2 cups vegetable broth,

divided
¼ cup gluten-free or whole-wheat flour
½ teaspoon garlic powder
½ teaspoon onion powder
¼ teaspoon freshly ground black pepper
¼ teaspoon dried thyme
¼ teaspoon dried sage

Make Mashed Potatoes: 1. Fill a large stockpot with water and bring it to a boil over high heat. Carefully add the potatoes to the boiling water, cover the pot, and reduce the heat to medium. Boil the potatoes for about 15 minutes or until they can be easily pierced with a fork. 2. Drain the water from the pot and return the potatoes to it. Use a potato masher or a large mixing spoon to mash the potatoes until they are smooth. 3. Stir in the milk, garlic powder, and onion powder to the mashed potatoes. Make Gravy: 1. In a medium saucepan, whisk together ½ cup of broth and the flour until no dry flour remains. Then, whisk in the remaining 1½ cups of broth. 2. Stir in the garlic powder, onion powder, pepper, thyme, and sage. Bring the gravy to a boil over medium-high heat, then reduce the heat to low. 3. Simmer the gravy for 10 minutes, stirring every other minute. Serve the gravy with the mashed potatoes.

Per Serving:
calories: 260 | fat: 1g | protein: 8g | carbs: 56g | fiber: 4g

Roasted Carrots with Ginger Maple Cream

Prep time: 10 minutes | Cook time: 25 minutes | Serves 6

Carrots:
1 pound (454 g) medium carrots, cut into ½-inch batons
1 teaspoon minced fresh thyme leaves
2 teaspoons virgin olive oil (optional)
Salt and pepper, to taste (optional)
Ginger Maple Cream:

2 tablespoons raw cashew butter
1½ tablespoons filtered water
1 tablespoon pure maple syrup (optional)
1½ teaspoons fresh lemon juice
1 piece of fresh ginger, peeled and finely grated
Salt, to taste (optional)

1. Preheat your oven to 400ºF (205ºC) and line a baking sheet with parchment paper. 2. Prepare the Carrots: Spread the carrots evenly on the prepared baking sheet. Toss them with thyme, olive oil, salt, and pepper if desired. Arrange the carrots in a single layer on the baking sheet and place it in the preheated oven. Roast the carrots for approximately 25 minutes or until they are just tender. Flip and toss the carrots halfway through the cooking time. 3. Make the Ginger Maple Cream: In a medium bowl, combine cashew butter and water. Stir until there are no large chunks of cashew butter remaining. Press the cashew butter against the side of the bowl and gradually incorporate it into the water. Whisk in maple syrup, lemon juice, and grated ginger. Season the cream with salt if desired. 4. Arrange the roasted carrots on a serving platter. Drizzle the Ginger Maple Cream over the carrots and serve them warm.

Per Serving:
calories: 85 | fat: 4g | protein: 2g | carbs: 11g | fiber: 2g

Baked Sweet Potato Fries

Prep time: 5 minutes | Cook time: 30 to 45 minutes | Serves 2

1 medium sweet potato
1 teaspoon olive oil or 1 tablespoon vegetable broth

¼ teaspoon sea salt (optional)
1 teaspoon dried basil
½ teaspoon dried oregano

1. Preheat your oven to 350ºF (180ºC). 2. Peel the sweet potato and cut it into stick shapes. In a bowl, rub the sweet potato sticks with oil, salt if desired, basil, and oregano, making sure they are evenly coated. 3. Arrange the seasoned sweet potato sticks on a large baking sheet. Roast them in the preheated oven for 30 to 45 minutes, or until they become soft. Remember to flip the sticks halfway through the cooking time to ensure even browning.

Per Serving:
calories: 77 | fat: 2g | protein: 1g | carbs: 13g | fiber: 2g

Delicata Squash Boats

Prep time: 20 minutes | Cook time: 1 hour 20 minutes | Serves 4

2 delicata squash, halved and seeded
Salt and freshly ground black pepper, to taste
1 shallot, peeled and minced
½ red bell pepper, seeded and diced small
6 cups chopped spinach
2 cloves garlic, peeled and minced
1 tablespoon minced sage

2 cups cooked cannellini beans, or 1 (15-ounce / 425-g) can, drained and rinsed
¾ cup whole-grain bread crumbs
3 tablespoons nutritional yeast (optional)
3 tablespoons pine nuts, toasted
Zest of 1 lemon

1. Preheat your oven to 350ºF (180ºC) and line a baking sheet with parchment paper. 2. Season the cut sides of the squash with salt and pepper. Place the squash halves, cut sides down, on the prepared baking sheet. Bake them in the preheated oven for about 45 minutes or until the squash becomes tender. 3. In a large saucepan, sauté the shallot and red pepper over medium heat for 2 to 3 minutes. Add water, 1 to 2 tablespoons at a time, to prevent sticking. Stir in the spinach, garlic, and sage, cooking until the spinach wilts, about 4 to 5 minutes. Add the beans and season with salt and pepper. Cook for an additional 2 to 3 minutes. Remove the pan from heat and stir in the bread crumbs, nutritional yeast if desired, pine nuts, and lemon zest. Mix well. 4. Divide the bean mixture among the baked squash halves. Place the stuffed squash halves in a baking dish and cover with aluminum foil. Bake for 15 to 20 minutes, or until heated through.

Per Serving:
calories: 194 | fat: 5g | protein: 10g | carbs: 29g | fiber: 7g

Stir-Fried Vegetables with Miso and Sake

Prep time: 25 minutes | Cook time: 10 minutes | Serves 4

¼ cup mellow white miso
½ cup vegetable stock, or low-sodium vegetable broth
¼ cup sake
1 medium yellow onion, peeled and thinly sliced
1 large carrot, peeled, cut in half lengthwise, and then cut into half-moons on the diagonal
1 medium red bell pepper, seeded and cut into ½-inch

strips
1 large head broccoli, cut into florets
½ pound (227 g) snow peas, trimmed
2 cloves garlic, peeled and minced
½ cup chopped cilantro (optional)
Salt and freshly ground black pepper, to taste

1. In a small bowl, whisk together the miso, vegetable stock, and sake. Set aside.
2. Heat a large skillet over high heat. Add the onion, carrot, red pepper, and broccoli. Stir-fry the vegetables for 4 to 5 minutes. If needed, add water 1 to 2 tablespoons at a time to prevent sticking. Add the snow peas and continue stir-frying for another 4 minutes. Add the garlic and cook for an additional 30 seconds. 3. Pour in the miso mixture and cook until heated through. Remove the skillet from the heat and stir in the cilantro if desired. Season with salt and pepper to taste.

Per Serving:
calories: 135 | fat: 1g | protein: 7g | carbs: 24g | fiber: 7g

Teriyaki Mushrooms

Prep time: 15 minutes | Cook time: 2 hours | Serves 4 to 6

2 (8-ounce / 227-g) packages whole cremini mushrooms
½ cup low-sodium soy sauce, tamari, or coconut aminos
¼ cup maple syrup (optional)
2 tablespoons rice vinegar
2 garlic cloves, minced

1 piece (1-inch) fresh ginger, peeled and minced, or 1 teaspoon ground ginger
2 tablespoons sesame seeds, divided
2 scallions, green and white parts, chopped, for serving

1. Put the mushrooms in the slow cooker. 2. In a measuring cup or medium bowl, combine the soy sauce, maple syrup (if using), rice vinegar, garlic, and ginger. Pour the sauce over the mushrooms and sprinkle with 1 tablespoon of sesame seeds. Cover and cook on High for 2 hours or on Low for 4 hours. 3. Serve the mushrooms garnished with the scallions and the remaining 1 tablespoon of sesame seeds.

Per Serving:
calories: 129 | fat: 3g | protein: 7g | carbs: 21g | fiber: 2g

Lemony Steamed Kale with Olives

Prep time: 10 minutes | Cook time: 20 minutes | Serves 4

1 bunch kale, leaves chopped and stems minced
½ cup celery leaves, roughly chopped
½ bunch flat-leaf parsley, stems and leaves roughly chopped

4 garlic cloves, chopped
2 tablespoons vegetable broth
¼ cup pitted Kalamata olives, chopped
Grated zest and juice of 1 lemon
Salt and pepper (optional)

1. Place the kale, celery leaves, parsley, and garlic in a steamer basket set over a medium saucepan. Steam over medium-high heat, covered, for 15 minutes. Remove from the heat and squeeze out any excess moisture. 2. Place a large skillet over medium heat. Add the broth, then add the kale mixture to the skillet. Cook, stirring often, for 5 minutes. 3. Remove from the heat and add the olives and lemon zest and juice. Season with salt (if desired) and pepper and serve.

Per Serving:
calories: 41 | fat: 1g | protein: 2g | carbs: 7g | fiber: 2g

Beet Sushi and Avocado Poke Bowls

Prep time: 20 minutes | Cook time: 20 minutes | Serves 2

2 red beets, trimmed and peeled
3 cups water
2 teaspoons low-sodium soy sauce or gluten-free tamari
½ teaspoon wasabi paste (optional)
1 tablespoon maple syrup (optional)
1 teaspoon sesame oil (optional)
1 teaspoon rice vinegar
1 cup frozen shelled edamame
1 cup cooked brown rice
1 cucumber, peeled and cut into matchsticks
2 carrots, cut into matchsticks
1 avocado, peeled, pitted, and sliced
1 scallion, green and white parts, chopped small, for garnish
2 tablespoons sesame seeds, for garnish (optional)

1. In a medium saucepan, combine the beets and water. Bring to a boil over high heat, then reduce the heat to medium and cook until the beets are tender but still firm, approximately 15 minutes. Drain, rinse, and set aside to cool. 2. In a small bowl, prepare the dressing by mixing together soy sauce, wasabi if desired, maple syrup, sesame oil, and rice vinegar. Set the dressing aside. 3. Once the beets have cooled, remove the skins by sliding them off. Using a sharp knife, thinly slice the beets to resemble tuna sashimi. Place the beet slices in a small bowl and drizzle with 1 teaspoon of the prepared dressing. Allow the beets to marinate. 4. Place the edamame in a microwave-safe bowl, add enough water to cover them, and cook in the microwave for 1 minute. Drain the edamame and set aside. 5. To assemble the bowls, divide the rice between two bowls. Top each bowl with sliced beets, cucumbers, carrots, edamame, and avocado. Drizzle the remaining dressing over the ingredients. Garnish with scallions and sesame seeds if desired.

Per Serving:

calories: 488 | fat: 22g | protein: 16g | carbs: 63g | fiber: 18g

Ratatouille

Prep time: 30 minutes | Cook time: 25 minutes | Serves 4

1 medium red onion, peeled and diced
1 medium red bell pepper, seeded and diced
1 medium eggplant, about 1 pound / 454 g, stemmed and diced
1 small zucchini, diced
4 cloves garlic, peeled and minced
½ cup chopped basil
1 large tomato, diced
Salt and freshly ground black pepper, to taste

1. In a medium saucepan, sauté the onion over medium heat for 10 minutes. Add water, 1 to 2 tablespoons at a time, to prevent sticking. Add the red pepper, eggplant, zucchini, and garlic. Cook, covered, for 15 minutes, stirring occasionally. 2. Stir in the basil and tomatoes, and season with salt and pepper.

Per Serving:

calories: 34 | fat: 0g | protein: 1g | carbs: 7g | fiber: 2g

Baked Spaghetti Squash with Spicy Lentil Sauce

Prep time: 15 minutes | Cook time: 55 minutes | Serves 4

2 small spaghetti squash (about 1 pound / 454 g each), halved
Salt and freshly ground black pepper, to taste
1 medium yellow onion, peeled and diced small
3 cloves garlic, peeled and minced
2 teaspoons crushed red pepper flakes, or to taste
¼ cup tomato paste
1 cup cooked green lentils
1 cup vegetable stock, or low-sodium vegetable broth, plus more as needed
Chopped parsley

1. Preheat the oven to 350°F (180°C). 2. Season the cut sides of the squash with salt and pepper. Place the squash halves, cut side down, on a baking sheet, and bake them for 45 to 55 minutes, or until the squash is very tender (it is done when it can be easily pierced with a knife). 3. While the squash bakes, place the onion in a large saucepan and sauté over medium heat for 5 minutes. Add water 1 to 2 tablespoons at a time to keep the onion from sticking to the pan. Add the garlic, crushed red pepper flakes, tomato paste, and ½ cup of water and cook for 5 minutes. Add the lentils to the pan and cook until heated through. Season with additional salt. Purée the lentil mixture using an immersion blender or in a blender with a tight-fitting lid, covered with a towel, until smooth and creamy. Add some of the vegetable stock, as needed, to make a creamy sauce. 4. To serve, scoop the flesh from the spaghetti squash (it should come away looking like noodles) and divide it among 4 plates. Top with some of the lentil sauce and garnish with the parsley.

Per Serving:

calories: 94 | fat: 0g | protein: 6g | carbs: 18g | fiber: 5g

Blackened Sprouts

Prep time: 10 minutes | Cook time: 20 minutes | Serves 4

1 pound (454 g) fresh Brussels sprouts, trimmed and halved
2 tablespoons avocado oil (optional)
Sea salt and ground black
pepper, to taste
1 cup walnut halves
1 tablespoon pure maple syrup (optional)

1. Preheat oven to 425°F (220°C). Line a baking sheet with parchment paper, or grease it well. 2. In a medium bowl, toss the sprouts with the oil (if using). Season well with salt and pepper to taste. Arrange in a single layer on the prepared baking sheet. 3. Roast for 20 minutes, or until the edges start to blacken. 4. Meanwhile, place the walnuts in a bowl and drizzle with the maple syrup (if using). Toss until well coated. During the last 3 minutes of roasting time, place the coated walnuts on the same baking sheet as the sprouts to toast and caramelize. 5. Let cool slightly before serving.

Per Serving:

calories: 254 | fat: 20g | protein: 6g | carbs: 16g | fiber: 5g

Lemony Roasted Cauliflower with Coriander

Prep time: 15 minutes | Cook time: 50 minutes | Serves 6

1 medium cauliflower, cut into 1-inch florets
¼ cup raw cashew butter
2 tablespoons filtered water
Grated zest of 1 lemon
2 tablespoons freshly squeezed lemon juice
2 tablespoons melted extra-

virgin coconut oil (optional)
2 teaspoons ground coriander
1 teaspoon fine sea salt (optional)
1 large garlic clove, grated or pressed
¼ teaspoon ground turmeric

1. Preheat the oven to 400ºF (205ºC). Line a rimmed baking sheet with parchment paper and set aside. 2. Set up a steamer and fill the pot with about 1 inch of filtered water. Bring to a boil over high heat and set the steamer basket in place. Arrange the cauliflower evenly in the basket and steam for 5 minutes, or until a knife slides easily into a floret. Transfer to a bowl and set aside. 3. Combine the cashew butter, water, lemon zest, and lemon juice in a small bowl and stir until smooth. Add the coconut oil, coriander, salt, if using, garlic, and turmeric and stir to combine. Pour over the cauliflower and use your hands to gently and thoroughly mix, making sure every floret is thoroughly coated. 4. Spread the cauliflower out on the parchment-lined baking sheet and roast for 20 to 25 minutes, until browned on the bottom. Remove from the oven and turn each piece over, then roast for another 10 to 15 minutes, until golden brown. Serve warm. This is best served right away, but any leftovers can be stored in an airtight container in the fridge for 2 to 3 days.

Per Serving:
calories: 130 | fat: 10g | protein: 4g | carbs: 9g | fiber: 2g

Glowing, Fermented Vegetable Tangle

Prep time: 15 minutes | Cook time: 0 minutes |Makes 2 quarts

1 fennel bulb, cored
1 head green cabbage, quartered cored and save the flexible outer leaves
6 medium carrots, shredded
2 medium beets, shredded
2 apples, peeled, cored and shredded
1 (2-inch) piece of fresh

ginger, peeled and finely grated
1 (2-inch) piece of fresh turmeric root, peeled and finely grated or 2 teaspoons turmeric powder
2 teaspoons cumin seeds
2 teaspoons chili flakes
Sea salt, to taste (optional)

1. Using a mandoline, thinly shave the fennel into a large bowl. Repeat the process with the cabbage, shaving it over the same

bowl. 2. Add the carrots, beets, apples, ginger, turmeric, cumin seeds, and chili flakes to the bowl. If desired, season everything generously with sea salt. Massage the vegetables for about 5 minutes or until you notice liquid pooling at the bottom of the bowl. It is recommended to wear gloves to prevent turmeric stains on your hands. 3. Pack the vegetable mixture tightly into jars with tight-fitting lids, pressing down with your hands or a spatula to ensure the liquid covers the surface. Leave about 1 inch of empty space at the top of each jar. Place a flexible cabbage leaf on top of the mixture in each jar and press down once more. Secure the lids tightly. 4. To prevent any potential staining from the liquid, consider placing the jars in plastic bags and tying knots at the top. Put the bagged jars in a large bowl in a convenient location, such as a basement. Make a note on your calendar to check the jars in 3 weeks. The vegetables should have a lightly sour and tangy taste, with a bit of texture when bitten. 5. If the vegetables have reached your desired flavor, remove the cabbage leaf toppers and store the jars in the refrigerator.

Per Serving: (½ quart)
calories: 187 | fat: 1g | protein: 6g | carbs: 44g | fiber: 14g

Spicy Butternut Squash Bisque

Prep time: 10 minutes | Cook time: 30 minutes | Serves 4

Olive oil cooking spray
1 large butternut squash, peeled, seeded and cut into 1-inch cubes (about 3 cups)
2 garlic cloves, peeled
1 teaspoon smoked paprika
½ teaspoon salt (optional)
4 cups unsweetened plant-based milk

2 tablespoons nutritional yeast
2 tablespoons tomato paste
1 teaspoon sriracha
4 tablespoons chopped cilantro leaves, for garnish
4 tablespoons plain plant-based yogurt, for garnish
4 tablespoons pepitas, for garnish (optional)

1. Preheat the oven to 400ºF (205ºC). Spray a sheet pan with olive oil cooking spray. 2. Combine the squash, garlic, smoked paprika, and salt (if using) on the sheet pan and toss until evenly coated. Bake for 10 minutes. Using a spatula, turn the squash and continue to bake for another 10 minutes, or until cooked through. 3. Transfer the squash and garlic to a blender. Add the plant-based milk, nutritional yeast, tomato paste, and sriracha and purée until smooth and creamy. Pour the mixture into a large saucepan and cook over medium heat until warm. Taste and adjust the seasonings, if desired. 4. Portion the soup into 4 bowls, garnish each with 1 tablespoon each of cilantro, yogurt, pepitas, and serve.

Per Serving:
calories: 141 | fat: 3g | protein: 8g | carbs: 24g | fiber: 3g

Chapter 6

Stews and Soups

Hearty Potato, Tomato, and Green Beans Stufato

Prep time: 10 minutes | Cook time: 3 to 4 hours | Serves 4 to 6

1 large onion, chopped
4 garlic cloves, minced
3 red or yellow potatoes (about 1 pound / 454 g), unpeeled and cut into 1- to 2-inch chunks
1 pound (454 g) fresh or frozen green beans, cut into bite-size pieces
1 (28-ounce / 794-g) can no-

salt-added crushed tomatoes
2 teaspoons dried oregano
2 teaspoons dried basil
1 teaspoon dried rosemary
½ teaspoon red pepper flakes (optional)
Ground black pepper
Salt (optional)
Chopped fresh parsley, for garnish (optional)

1. Place the onion, garlic, potatoes, green beans, tomatoes, oregano, basil, rosemary, red pepper flakes (if desired), pepper, and salt (if desired) into the slow cooker. 2. Cover the slow cooker and cook on High for 3 to 4 hours or on Low for 6 to 7 hours, until the potatoes are tender when pierced with a fork. Serve the dish garnished with parsley if desired.

Per Serving:
calories: 197 | fat: 1g | protein: 8g | carbs: 40g | fiber: 9g

Lemony Herbed Lentil Soup

Prep time: 10 minutes | Cook time: 35 minutes | Serves 2

1 cup dried brown or green lentils, rinsed
4 cups water
1 teaspoon extra-virgin olive oil (optional)
½ small yellow onion, chopped
2 garlic cloves, minced
1 celery stalk, minced
2 carrots, sliced

1 potato, peeled and diced
1 zucchini, diced
1 (15-ounce / 425-g) can crushed tomatoes
1 teaspoon Italian seasoning
½ teaspoon smoked paprika
2 cups baby spinach
Juice of 1 lemon
1 teaspoon salt, plus more as needed (optional)

1. In a large saucepan, bring lentils and water to a boil over high heat. Reduce the heat to medium and cook for about 25 minutes or until the lentils are soft. 2. Meanwhile, in a large skillet, heat olive oil over medium heat. Add onion and garlic, cooking until fragrant for about 5 minutes. Add celery, carrots, and potato, and cook for an additional 5 minutes. Transfer this mixture to the cooked lentils and stir to combine. 3. Stir in zucchini, tomatoes, Italian seasoning, and smoked paprika. Bring the mixture to a boil over medium-high heat, then reduce the heat to medium and simmer for about 10 minutes to allow the flavors to meld together. 4. Add spinach to the pot, stirring until wilted. Stir in lemon juice and salt if desired, adjusting the amount of salt according to taste.

Per Serving:
calories: 546 | fat: 5g | protein: 31g | carbs: 102g | fiber: 21g

Vegetable Goulash

Prep time: 5 minutes | Cook time: 25 minutes | Serves 4 to 6

4 cups vegetable broth
4 cups diced (½-inch) yellow potatoes
2 cups frozen carrots
2 tablespoons tomato paste
½ cup chopped water-packed roasted red pepper
¼ cup sweet paprika
1 teaspoon whole caraway

seeds
3 strips dried porcini mushrooms, chopped (about 2 tablespoons)
1 tablespoon onion powder
½ teaspoon garlic powder
2 teaspoons dried parsley
½ teaspoon smoked paprika
1 bay leaf

1. In a large Dutch oven or saucepan, combine the broth, potatoes, carrots, tomato paste, roasted red pepper, sweet paprika, caraway, mushrooms, onion powder, garlic powder, parsley, smoked paprika, and bay leaf. Bring the mixture to a boil over high heat. 2. Reduce the heat to low, cover the pot, and simmer for 15 to 20 minutes, or until the potatoes are tender and can be easily pierced with a knife. Remove the pot from the heat. 3. Discard the bay leaf and serve the soup.

Per Serving:
calories: 295 | fat: 2g | protein: 14g | carbs: 55g | fiber: 10g

Kale White Bean Soup

Prep time: 20 minutes | Cook time: 2 hours | Serves 6

1 pound (454 g) navy beans
1 tablespoon coconut oil (optional)
½ cup coarsely chopped onions
1 clove garlic, minced
¼ cup nutritional yeast
1 diced red bell pepper
4 chopped Roma tomatoes

2 cups sliced carrots
5 cups vegetable broth
1 teaspoon Italian seasoning
2 teaspoons salt (optional)
½ teaspoon ground black pepper
1 pound (454 g) kale, de-stemmed and coarsely chopped

1. In a large stockpot, place the beans and cover them with water by about 3 inches. Let the beans sit overnight to allow them to expand. Alternatively, for a quick method, cover the beans with water by 2 inches in the stockpot. Cover with a lid and bring to a boil. Remove from heat and let it stand, uncovered, for 1 hour. Drain the beans in a colander and set aside. 2. If desired, add oil to the same stockpot and heat over medium heat. Add onions and sauté for about 10 to 15 minutes until they become soft and translucent. Stir in garlic and cook for 1 minute. Add 4 cups of water, the soaked beans, nutritional yeast, bell pepper, tomatoes, carrots, broth, Italian seasoning, salt (if desired), and pepper. Cover the pot and bring it to a boil. Then, uncover and reduce the heat to a simmer. Cook until the beans are tender, approximately 1 to 1½ hours. 3. Stir in kale and 2 cups of water. Simmer the mixture, uncovered, until the kale becomes tender, which usually takes about 12 to 15 minutes.

Per Serving:
calories: 131 | fat: 4g | protein: 14g | carbs: 20g | fiber: 7g

Coconut Watercress Soup

Prep time: 10 minutes | Cook time: 15 minutes | Makes 4 bowls

1 teaspoon coconut oil (optional)
1 onion, diced
2 cups fresh or frozen peas
4 cups water or vegetable stock
1 cup fresh watercress,
chopped
1 tablespoon fresh mint, chopped
Pinch sea salt (optional)
Pinch freshly ground black pepper
¾ cup coconut milk

1. Heat the coconut oil (if using) in a large pot over medium-high heat. Add the onion and cook until it becomes soft, approximately 5 minutes. Then, add the peas and water to the pot. 2. Bring the mixture to a boil, then reduce the heat. Add the watercress, mint, salt (if desired), and pepper. Cover the pot and let it simmer for 5 minutes. 3. Stir in the coconut milk, then use a blender or an immersion blender to puree the soup until it becomes smooth.

Per Serving: (1 bowl)
calories: 155 | fat: 12g | protein: 3g | carbs: 10g | fiber: 3g

"Don't Waste the Good Stuff" Squash Soup

Prep time: 15 minutes | Cook time: 30 minutes | Serves 6

2 (2-pound / 907-g) butternut squash
Salt and black pepper (optional)
1 large yellow onion, peeled and quartered
2 carrots, roughly chopped
1 celery rib, roughly chopped
3 garlic cloves, chopped
2 bay leaves
2 tablespoons fresh sage,
chopped
3 sprigs fresh thyme, leaves stripped and stems discarded
2 sprigs fresh rosemary, leaves stripped and chopped fine, stems discarded
6 cups water
2 cups cooked white beans
2 tablespoons gluten-free mild white miso

1. Preheat the oven to 425°F (220°C) and line a baking sheet with parchment paper. 2. Cut the squash in half, remove the seeds and innards, and transfer them to a large stockpot. Season the squash halves with salt (if desired) and pepper, then place them cut side down on the prepared baking sheet. 3. Bake the squash in the oven for about 25 minutes or until it becomes fork-tender. Once done, remove from the oven and flip the halves cut side up to cool faster. 4. While the squash is baking, add onion, carrots, celery, garlic, bay leaves, sage, thyme, rosemary, and water to the stockpot with the squash innards and seeds. Bring the mixture to a boil, then reduce the heat to medium-low. Cook uncovered until the squash finishes baking. Remove from heat and discard the bay leaves. 5. Scoop the flesh of the baked squash into a blender. Add the contents of the stockpot, including the white beans (you may need to do this in batches). Blend until smooth, then return the soup to the stockpot. 6. Whisk in the miso, season

with salt and pepper according to taste, and serve.
Per Serving:
calories: 243 | fat: 1g | protein: 10g | carbs: 54g | fiber: 11g

Savory Squash Soup

Prep time: 20 minutes | Cook time: 27 minutes | Serves 4

2½ cups butternut squash, peeled, halved, seeded, and diced (from about 1 medium)
1 large russet potato, diced (about 1 cup)
1 medium yellow onion, peeled and chopped (about ½ cup)
1 clove garlic, peeled and chopped
¼ teaspoon dried Italian herb mix, or a pinch each of oregano, basil, rosemary, and thyme
Pinch freshly ground black pepper, or to taste
¼ cup green peas
¼ teaspoon fresh lime juice
Finely chopped parsley

1. In a large pot, bring 3 cups of water to a boil over high heat. Add the squash, potato, onion, garlic, herb mix, and pepper. Reduce the heat to medium and cook, covered, for about 20 minutes or until the vegetables are tender. 2. Using an immersion blender or a regular blender with a tight-fitting lid (covered with a towel), puree the soup until smooth. Return the soup to the pot and add the green peas and lime juice. Cook for an additional 5 to 7 minutes, or until the peas are tender. Serve the soup hot, garnished with parsley.
Per Serving:
calories: 137 | fat: 0g | protein: 4g | carbs: 32g | fiber: 4g

Deconstructed Stuffed Pepper Stew

Prep time: 15 minutes | Cook time: 4 to 5 hours | Serves 6 to 8

1 medium onion, diced
1 medium red bell pepper, diced
1 medium green bell pepper, diced
2 celery stalks, diced
1 cup brown rice
1 cup dried green or brown lentils, rinsed and sorted
1 (14½-ounce / 411-g) can no-
salt-added diced tomatoes
1 (8-ounce / 227-g) can tomato sauce
4 cups store-bought low-sodium vegetable broth
1 tablespoon maple syrup or date syrup (optional)
1 tablespoon Italian seasoning
Ground black pepper
Salt (optional)

1. Place the onion, red bell pepper, green bell pepper, celery, rice, lentils, tomatoes, tomato sauce, broth, syrup (if using), Italian seasoning, black pepper, and salt (if using) in the slow cooker. Stir well to combine, then cover and cook on Low for 4 to 5 hours. 2. After 2 hours, stir the mixture to prevent sticking. Continue to stir every 30 minutes until the rice and lentils are fully cooked.
Per Serving:
calories: 284 | fat: 2g | protein: 11g | carbs: 59g | fiber: 18g

Miso Split Pea Soup

Prep time: 15 minutes | Cook time: 20 minutes | Serves 8

3 tablespoons water	peas
1 cup diced red, white, or yellow onion	6 cups vegetable broth
1 teaspoon minced garlic	2 tablespoons yellow or white miso
1 cup diced carrot	1 bay leaf
¾ cup diced celery	Salt and pepper, to taste (optional)
2 batches cooked green split	

1. Heat water in a large pot over medium-high heat. 2. Add onion, garlic, carrot, and celery to the pot and sauté for 3 to 4 minutes. 3. Stir in split peas, broth, miso, and bay leaf. Cook for 15 minutes or until the vegetables are tender. 4. Remove the pot from heat. Season with salt (if desired) and pepper.

Per Serving:

calories: 52 | fat: 1g | protein: 3g | carbs: 10g | fiber: 3g

Indian Red Split Lentil Soup

Prep time: 5 minutes | Cook time: 50 minutes | Makes 4 bowls

1 cup red split lentils	potato
2 cups water	1 cup sliced zucchini
1 teaspoon curry powder plus 1 tablespoon, divided, or 5 coriander seeds (optional)	Freshly ground black pepper, to taste
	Sea salt, to taste (optional)
1 teaspoon coconut oil, or 1 tablespoon water or vegetable broth	3 to 4 cups vegetable stock or water
	1 to 2 teaspoons toasted sesame oil (optional)
1 red onion, diced	
1 tablespoon minced fresh ginger	1 bunch spinach, chopped
	Toasted sesame seeds
2 cups peeled and cubed sweet	

1. Place lentils in a large pot with 2 cups of water and 1 teaspoon of curry powder. Bring to a boil, then reduce heat and simmer covered for about 10 minutes until lentils are soft. 2. In the meantime, heat a large pot over medium heat. If using, add coconut oil and sauté onion and ginger until soft, approximately 5 minutes. Add sweet potato and cook for about 10 minutes to slightly soften, then add zucchini and cook until it becomes shiny, around 5 minutes. Stir in remaining 1 tablespoon of curry powder, pepper, and salt (if desired), ensuring vegetables are coated. 3. Add vegetable stock, bring to a boil, then reduce to simmer and cover. Allow vegetables to cook slowly for 20 to 30 minutes or until sweet potato is tender. 4. Add fully cooked lentils to the soup. Season with another pinch of salt, toasted sesame oil (if using), and spinach. Stir, allowing the spinach to wilt before removing the pot from the heat. 5. Serve garnished with toasted sesame seeds.

Per Serving: (1 bowl)

calories: 238 | fat: 3g | protein: 15g | carbs: 38g | fiber: 9g

Tuscan Bean Stew

Prep time: 25 minutes | Cook time: 40 minutes | Serves 6

3 large leeks (white and light green parts), diced and rinsed	minced
	3 cups cooked cannellini beans
2 celery stalks, diced	
2 medium carrots, peeled and diced	6 cups vegetable stock, or low-sodium vegetable broth
2 cups chopped green cabbage	½ cup chopped basil
1 large russet potato, peeled and diced	Salt and freshly ground black pepper, to taste
6 cloves garlic, peeled and	

1. In a large saucepan, sauté the leeks, celery, and carrots over medium heat for 10 minutes. Add 1 to 2 tablespoons of water at a time to prevent the vegetables from sticking to the pan. 2. Add the cabbage, potato, garlic, beans, and vegetable stock to the saucepan and bring the soup to a boil over high heat. Reduce the heat to medium and cook, uncovered, for 30 minutes or until the potatoes are tender. Stir in the basil and season the soup with salt and pepper.

Per Serving:

calories: 128 | fat: 0g | protein: 3g | carbs: 29g | fiber: 4g

Sweet Potato Stew

Prep time: 15 minutes | Cook time: 1 hour | Serves 4

1 cup dried split peas	5 cups water
1 (7-ounce / 198-g) pack smoked tofu, cubed	2 stalks celery, sliced
	Optional Toppings:
2 small cubed sweet potatoes	Green peppercorns
6 tablespoons salt-free Cajun spices	Fresh cilantro

1. Heat a large pot over medium-high heat and add water, split peas, and 2 tablespoons of Cajun spices. 2. Bring the water to a boil, then reduce the heat to medium. 3. Cook the split peas uncovered for approximately 25 minutes, removing any foam that forms and stirring occasionally. 4. Add sweet potato cubes, celery stalk slices, and the remaining Cajun spices. Simmer for about 15 minutes. 5. Cover the pot with a lid and simmer for an additional 10 minutes, stirring occasionally. 6. Stir in tofu cubes and let it simmer for another 10 minutes. 7. Turn off the heat and allow the soup to cool for 5 minutes. 8. Divide the soup into two bowls, optionally garnish with toppings, and enjoy! 9. Store the soup in an airtight container in the refrigerator and consume within 2 days. Alternatively, freeze for up to 60 days and thaw at room temperature. Reheat the soup in a pot or microwave before serving.

Per Serving:

calories: 165 | fat: 4g | protein: 21g | carbs: 11g | fiber: 16g

Roasted Potato and Cauliflower Soup

Prep time: 20 minutes | Cook time: 30 minutes | Serves 6

8 garlic cloves, peeled
1 large cauliflower head, cut into small florets
2 russet potatoes, peeled and chopped into 1-inch pieces
1 yellow onion, coarsely chopped
1 celery stalk, coarsely chopped
1 tablespoon water, plus more

as needed
6 cups no-sodium vegetable broth
2 thyme sprigs
2 teaspoons paprika
¼ teaspoon freshly ground black pepper
1 tablespoon chopped fresh rosemary leaves

1. Preheat the oven to 450°F (235°C) and line a baking sheet with parchment paper. 2. Wrap the garlic cloves in aluminum foil or place them in a garlic roaster. 3. Spread the cauliflower and potatoes evenly on the prepared baking sheet. Place the wrapped garlic on the same sheet. 4. Roast for 15 to 20 minutes, or until the cauliflower is lightly browned. 5. In an 8-quart pot over high heat, sauté the onion and celery for 4 to 5 minutes. Add water, 1 tablespoon at a time, to prevent burning, until the onion starts to brown. 6. Pour in the vegetable broth and bring the soup to a simmer. 7. Add the roasted vegetables and garlic, along with thyme, paprika, and pepper. Simmer the soup, cover the pot, and cook for 10 minutes. 8. Remove and discard the thyme. Use an immersion blender to purée the soup until smooth. If the soup is too thick, add water as needed to achieve the desired consistency. Stir in the rosemary.

Per Serving:
calories: 120 | fat: 1g | protein: 5g | carbs: 26g | fiber: 5g

Chickpea Vegetable Soup

Prep time: 15 minutes | Cook time: 30 minutes | Serves 4

1 yellow onion, coarsely chopped
2 carrots, coarsely chopped
2 celery stalks, coarsely chopped
1 red bell pepper, coarsely chopped
3 garlic cloves, minced
1 tablespoon water, plus more as needed
2 teaspoons grated peeled fresh ginger
1 small cauliflower head, cut

into small florets
1 teaspoon ground turmeric
1 teaspoon Hungarian sweet paprika
6 cups no-sodium vegetable broth
2 cups chopped kale
1 (15-ounce /425-g) can chickpeas, rinsed and drained
Freshly ground black pepper, to taste
Chopped scallions, green parts only, for garnish

1. Heat a large pot over medium-high heat and add the onion, carrots, celery, bell pepper, and garlic. Cook, stirring occasionally, for 5 minutes until the onion is translucent but not browned. If needed, add water, 1 tablespoon at a time, to prevent the onion and garlic from cooking too quickly. 2. Stir in the ginger and cook for 30 seconds. 3. Add the cauliflower, turmeric, and paprika, stirring well to coat the cauliflower evenly with the spices. 4. Pour in the vegetable broth and bring the liquid to a simmer. Reduce the heat to medium-low, cover the pot, and cook for 10 minutes. 5. Add the kale and chickpeas, cooking for an additional 5 minutes to soften the kale leaves. Season with pepper and garnish with scallions. 6. Store any leftovers in an airtight container in the refrigerator for up to 1 week or freeze for up to 1 month.

Per Serving:
calories: 173 | fat: 3g | protein: 8g | carbs: 32g | fiber: 9g

Minestrone Soup

Prep time: 15 minutes | Cook time: 25 minutes | Serves 8

3 tablespoons water
½ cup diced red, white, or yellow onion
1 teaspoon minced garlic
2 carrots, thinly sliced
2 ribs celery, thinly sliced
1 (14½-ounce / 411-g) can diced tomatoes with their juices

5 cups vegetable broth
2 (15-ounce / 425-g) cans kidney beans, drained and rinsed
1 teaspoon dried oregano
1 teaspoon ground cumin
1½ cups shaped pasta
Salt and pepper, to taste (optional)

1. Heat water in a large pot over medium-high heat. 2. Add onion, garlic, carrots, and celery to the pot. Sauté for 3 minutes or until the onion becomes tender and translucent. 3. Stir in tomatoes, broth, beans, oregano, and cumin. Cook for 5 minutes. 4. Add pasta and cook for the recommended time mentioned on the package. 5. Remove from heat. Season with salt (if desired) and pepper.

Per Serving:
calories: 144 | fat: 1g | protein: 7g | carbs: 28g | fiber: 7g

Chickpea "Polenta" Stew

Prep time: 5 minutes | Cook time: 35 minutes | Serves 4

¼ cup vegetable broth
2 tablespoons spice blend, such as Harissa
1 yellow onion, chopped
2 cups water

1 cup chickpea flour, soaked in water overnight
1 (28-ounce / 794-g) can diced tomatoes with juice

1. Place a medium stockpot over medium heat. Add broth and the spice blend and cook until fragrant, about 1 minute. Add the onion and cook until beginning to soften, about 3 minutes. 2. Add the water and flour, then the tomatoes with their juice. Stir to combine, cover, and cook for 30 minutes, stirring every 10 minutes. 3. Remove from the heat and let sit for 10 minutes before serving.

Per Serving:
calories: 160 | fat: 5g | protein: 7g | carbs: 24g | fiber: 8g

Cauliflower, Chickpea, Quinoa, and Coconut Curry

Prep time: 15 minutes | Cook time: 3 to 4 hours | Serves 5 to 7

1 head cauliflower, cut into bite-size pieces (about 4 cups)
1 medium onion, diced
3 garlic cloves, minced
1 medium sweet potato (about ⅓ pound / 136 g), peeled and diced
1 (14½-ounce / 411-g) can chickpeas, drained and rinsed
1 (28-ounce / 794-g) can no-salt-added diced tomatoes
¼ cup store-bought low-sodium vegetable broth
¼ cup quinoa, rinsed
2 (15-ounce / 425-g) cans full-fat coconut milk
1 (1-inch) piece fresh ginger, peeled and minced
2 teaspoons ground turmeric
2 teaspoons garam masala
1 teaspoon ground cumin
1 teaspoon curry powder
Ground black pepper
Salt (optional)
½ bunch cilantro, coarsely chopped (optional)

1. Place cauliflower, onion, garlic, sweet potato, chickpeas, tomatoes, broth, quinoa, coconut milk, ginger, turmeric, garam masala, cumin, curry powder, pepper, and salt (if desired) in the slow cooker. 2. Cover and cook on High for 3 to 4 hours or on Low for 7 to 8 hours. Stir in cilantro (if desired) at the end of cooking, reserving a couple of tablespoons for garnish on each dish.

Per Serving:
calories: 503 | fat: 32g | protein: 11g | carbs: 48g | fiber: 12g

Black-Eyed Pea and Collard Stew with Spicy Tahini

Prep time: 20 minutes | Cook time: 40 minutes | Serves 6

Stew:
2 tablespoons olive oil (optional)
1 large yellow onion, chopped
1 large green bell pepper, chopped
2 small carrots, chopped
1 large celery rib, chopped
1 teaspoon dried thyme
1 bay leaf
¼ teaspoon cayenne pepper or crushed red pepper
3 garlic cloves, minced
1 (14½-ounce / 411-g) can fire-roasted tomatoes with juice
1 cup pearled barley, soaked
1 teaspoon reduced-sodium tamari
2 cups water
1 cup vegetable broth
1 bunch collard greens, stemmed and chopped
2 cups cooked black-eyed peas
1 tablespoon fresh lemon juice
Salt and black pepper (optional)
Spicy Tahini:
2 tablespoons nutritional yeast
1 to 2 tablespoons Sriracha sauce
1 teaspoon fresh lemon juice
1 teaspoon maple syrup (optional)
¼ teaspoon liquid smoke
¼ cup tahini
¼ to ½ cup water
Sliced scallions

1. To prepare the stew, heat oil (if using) in a Dutch oven over medium-high heat. Add onion, bell pepper, carrots, and celery, stirring to coat them thoroughly. Cook for 2 minutes, then reduce heat to medium, cover, and gently cook the vegetables for 5 minutes, stirring occasionally. 2. Stir in thyme, bay leaf, cayenne, and garlic. Cook for an additional 2 minutes. 3. Add tomatoes with their juice, barley, and tamari. Cook, stirring often, until the moisture has evaporated, about 3 minutes. 4. Pour in water, broth, and collards. Increase heat to high and bring to a boil, then reduce heat to medium-low. Cover and cook for 15 minutes. 5. Stir in black-eyed peas. Remove from heat and let it sit for 15 minutes. Discard the bay leaf. Stir in lemon juice and season with salt (if desired) and pepper to taste. 6. While the stew is resting, prepare the sauce. Combine nutritional yeast, Sriracha, lemon juice, maple syrup (if desired), liquid smoke, and tahini in a jar with a tight-fitting lid. Gradually add water, shaking to mix, until the sauce reaches a pourable consistency that sticks to a spoon. Refrigerate until ready to serve. 7. Serve the stew topped with the sauce and scallions.

Per Serving:
calories: 354 | fat: 11g | protein: 14g | carbs: 54g | fiber: 15g

Fiesta Soup

Prep time: 15 minutes | Cook time: 30 minutes | Serves 6

1 tablespoon avocado oil (optional)
1 yellow onion, diced
1 red bell pepper, diced
1 zucchini, diced
3 garlic cloves, minced
2 tablespoons taco seasoning
4 cups vegetable stock
1 (15-ounce / 425-g) can black beans, drained and rinsed
1 (15-ounce / 425-g) can pinto beans, drained and rinsed
1 (15-ounce / 425-g) can organic diced tomatoes, undrained
1 (7-ounce / 198-g) can diced green chiles
1 cup organic frozen corn
2 tablespoons fresh lime juice (from 1 lime)
¼ cup fresh cilantro, chopped
Sea salt and ground black pepper, to taste
For Serving:
½ cup organic corn tortilla strips
3 ripe avocados, diced
½ cup fresh cilantro, roughly chopped
1 lime, cut into wedges

1. Heat a large pot over medium-high heat. If using, add the oil and let it warm for 30 seconds. Then, add the onion and bell pepper. Cook, stirring frequently, for 5 minutes until the bell peppers start to brown and the onions become translucent. Add the zucchini and garlic, cooking for an additional minute until fragrant. Stir in the taco seasoning and cook, stirring constantly, for a bit longer to toast the spices. 2. Add the stock, beans, tomatoes, and chiles. Stir well. Bring the mixture just to a boil, then reduce the heat to low and simmer for 20 minutes until the flavors blend and the veggies become tender. Stir in the corn, lime juice, and cilantro. Season with salt and black pepper. Remove from the heat. Ladle the soup into bowls and top with some of the tortilla strips, avocado, and cilantro. Serve with a lime wedge.

Per Serving:
calories: 330 | fat: 18g | protein: 8g | carbs: 38g | fiber: 14g

Minty Beet and Sweet Potato Soup

Prep time: 10 minutes | Cook time: 40 minutes | Makes 6 bowls

5 cups water, or salt-free vegetable broth (if salted, omit the sea salt below)
1 to 2 teaspoons olive oil or vegetable broth
1 cup chopped onion
3 garlic cloves, minced
1 tablespoon thyme, fresh or dried
1 to 2 teaspoons paprika
2 cups peeled and chopped beets

2 cups peeled and chopped sweet potato
2 cups peeled and chopped parsnips
½ teaspoon sea salt (optional)
1 cup fresh mint, chopped
½ avocado, or 2 tablespoons nut or seed butter (optional)
2 tablespoons balsamic vinegar (optional)
2 tablespoons pumpkin seeds

1. Boil the water in a large pot. 2. In another large pot, heat the olive oil (if using) and sauté the onion and garlic until they become soft, which usually takes about 5 minutes. 3. Add the thyme, paprika, beets, sweet potato, and parsnips to the pot, along with the boiling water and salt (if using). Cover the pot and let the mixture gently boil for approximately 30 minutes, or until the vegetables become tender. 4. Reserve a small amount of mint for garnishing, and add the remaining mint to the pot along with the avocado (if using). Stir everything together until well combined. 5. Transfer the soup to a blender or use an immersion blender to puree it, adding the balsamic vinegar (if using). 6. Serve the soup topped with fresh mint, pumpkin seeds, and optionally, chunks of the remaining half of the avocado if you included it in the recipe.

Per Serving: (1 bowl)

calories: 157 | fat: 5g | protein: 3g | carbs: 26g | fiber: 6g

Chestnut Soup

Prep time: 15 minutes | Cook time: 25 minutes | Serves 4

1 medium yellow onion, peeled and finely chopped
1 stalk celery, finely chopped
1 medium carrot, peeled and finely chopped
1½ tablespoons minced sage
1 tablespoon minced thyme
1 bay leaf
⅛ teaspoon ground cloves

4 to 5 cups vegetable stock, or low-sodium vegetable broth
1 (15-ounce / 425-g) can chestnut purée
Salt and freshly ground black pepper, to taste
2 tablespoons finely chopped parsley

1. In a large saucepan, sauté the onion, celery, and carrot over medium heat for about 15 minutes, or until the onion becomes tender and starts to brown. Add 1 to 2 tablespoons of water at a time to prevent the vegetables from sticking to the pan. 2. Stir in the sage, thyme, bay leaf, cloves, and vegetable stock. Bring the mixture to a boil over high heat and whisk in the chestnut purée. Season with salt and pepper and continue cooking for an additional 5 minutes. Serve the dish garnished with chopped parsley.

Per Serving:

calories: 158 | fat: 1g | protein: 2g | carbs: 32g | fiber: 7g

Indian Zuppa with Tomatoes and Fava Beans

Prep time: 20 minutes | Cook time: 20 minutes | Serves 4

1½ cups cooked fava beans
½ cup uncooked quinoa
Pinch fenugreek seeds
½ cup leeks (white and light green parts), finely chopped and rinsed
½ clove garlic, peeled and minced

2 medium tomatoes, chopped
⅛ teaspoon turmeric
¼ teaspoon ground cumin
¼ teaspoon salt, or to taste (optional)
½ cup spinach
Freshly ground black pepper, to taste

1. Add the fava beans, quinoa, and fenugreek seeds to a pot with 3 cups of water and bring to a boil over high heat. Add the leeks and garlic and cook on medium heat for 10 to 15 minutes. Add 1½ cups of water, the tomatoes, turmeric, cumin, and salt (if using) and cook for another 5 to 7 minutes on medium heat, or until the quinoa and fava beans are tender. 2. Add the spinach and season with black pepper. Serve hot.

Per Serving:

calories: 115 | fat: 1g | protein: 4g | carbs: 21g | fiber: 4g

Moroccan Chickpea Soup

Prep time: 15 minutes | Cook time: 20 minutes | Serves 4

3 cups cooked or canned chickpeas
1 medium onion, minced
1 clove garlic, minced
2 cups canned or fresh tomato cubes

2 tablespoons Ras El Hanout
2 cups water
Optional Toppings:
Lemon slices
Fresh cilantro
Cranberries

1. If using dry chickpeas, soak and cook 1 cup of dry chickpeas. 2. Heat a large pot over medium-high heat and add water, minced onions, and garlic to the pot. 3. Bring the water to a boil, then reduce the heat to medium. 4. Add the chickpeas and Ras El Hanout spices to the pot and continue cooking for approximately 5 minutes, stirring occasionally. 5. After 5 minutes, reduce the heat to a simmer. 6. Stir in the tomato cubes, cover the pot with a lid, and let it simmer for another 10 minutes. 7. Turn off the heat and allow the stew to cool down for 5 minutes. 8. Divide the stew between two bowls, serve with optional toppings, and enjoy! 9. Store any remaining soup in an airtight container in the refrigerator and consume within 2 days. Alternatively, you can store it in the freezer for up to 60 days. To thaw, leave it at room temperature. Reheat the stew in a pot or microwave before serving.

Per Serving:

calories: 260 | fat: 2g | protein: 15g | carbs: 44g | fiber: 17g

Caribbean Coconut Collards and Sweet Potatoes

Prep time: 20 minutes | Cook time: 35 minutes | Serves 4

1 tablespoon coconut oil (optional)	1 (15-ounce / 425-g) can red kidney beans or chickpeas, drained and rinsed
1 yellow onion, diced	1 (14½-ounce / 411-g) can diced tomatoes with juice
3 garlic cloves, chopped	
½ teaspoon crushed red pepper	1½ cups water
2 bunches collard greens, stemmed, leaves chopped into 1-inch squares	½ cup light or full-fat coconut milk
1 large sweet potato, peeled and diced	Salt and black pepper (optional)

1. If desired, melt the oil in a large, deep skillet over medium heat. Add the onion, garlic, and crushed red pepper. Cook for 3 minutes over medium heat, then add the collards and sweet potato. Stir in the beans, tomatoes with their juice, water, and coconut milk. 2. Bring the mixture to a gentle boil, then reduce the heat to medium-low. Cover the skillet and cook until the collards and sweet potato become tender, which usually takes about 30 minutes. 3. Season with salt and pepper if desired, and serve.

Per Serving:
calories: 300 | fat: 12g | protein: 12g | carbs: 40g | fiber: 11g

Tom Yum Goong (Thai Hot-and-Sour Soup)

Prep time: 30 minutes | Cook time: 30 minutes | Serves 4

4 cups vegetable stock, or low-sodium vegetable broth	3 shallots, peeled and thinly sliced
4 thin slices fresh ginger	2 Roma tomatoes, chopped
1 stalk lemongrass, cut into 1-inch pieces	1 head baby bok choy, thinly sliced
2 tablespoons Thai red curry paste	1 small carrot, peeled and cut into matchsticks
3 tablespoons low-sodium soy sauce	1 cup mung bean sprouts
	¼ cup chopped Thai basil
Zest and juice of 2 limes	2 Thai red chiles, sliced into thin rounds
1 (14-ounce / 397-g) can lite coconut milk	Cilantro sprigs

1. In a large saucepan, add the vegetable stock, ginger, lemongrass, curry paste, soy sauce, lime zest and juice, and coconut milk. Bring the pot to a boil over high heat. Stir in the shallots, tomatoes, bok choy, and carrot. Reduce the heat to medium-low and simmer until the vegetables are tender, about 25 minutes. 2. Remove the ginger and lemongrass and add the mung bean sprouts, basil, and chiles. Serve garnished with cilantro.

Per Serving:

calories: 332 | fat: 26g | protein: 8g | carbs: 24g | fiber: 8g

Mushroom Barley Soup

Prep time: 10 minutes | Cook time: 40 minutes | Serves 4

1 cup pearled barley	diced small
4 cups water	1 celery stalk, minced
2 teaspoons extra-virgin olive oil, divided (optional)	8 ounces (227 g) white mushrooms, thinly sliced
1 small yellow onion, diced small	1 teaspoon salt (optional)
3 garlic cloves, minced	¼ teaspoon dried thyme
2 large carrots, peeled and	½ teaspoon smoked paprika

1. In a large pot, combine the barley and water and bring to a boil over high heat. Lower the heat to medium-low and cook until tender, about 40 minutes. 2. While the barley is cooking, in a large skillet, heat 1 teaspoon of olive oil over medium heat. Add the onion, garlic, carrots, and celery and cook, stirring often, until the vegetables are tender, about 8 minutes. Add the mixture to the barley. 3. Wipe out the skillet with a paper towel. Heat the remaining 1 teaspoon oil over medium heat. Add the mushrooms and cook, stirring occasionally, until they are browned, about 8 minutes. 4. Add the mushrooms, salt (if using), thyme, and paprika to the barley and vegetables and cook over medium heat, stirring often, until the mixture is well combined and barley is soft, about more 20 minutes. Spoon into bowls and serve hot.

Per Serving:
calories: 235 | fat: 3g | protein: 7g | carbs: 47g | fiber: 10g

Curried Cauliflower Bisque

Prep time: 15 minutes | Cook time: 1 hour | Serves 4

1 large onion, peeled and diced	1 large head cauliflower, cut into florets
2 teaspoons grated ginger	4 cups vegetable stock, or low-sodium vegetable broth
1 jalapeño pepper, minced (for less heat, remove the seeds)	¼ cup chopped cilantro
2 cloves garlic, peeled and minced	4 green onions (white and green parts), thinly sliced
1½ teaspoons curry powder	

1. Place the onion in a large saucepan and sauté over medium heat for 10 minutes. Add water 1 to 2 tablespoons at a time to keep the onion from sticking to the pan. Add the ginger, jalapeño pepper, garlic, and curry powder and cook for 30 seconds. Add the cauliflower and vegetable stock and bring the pot to a boil over high heat. Reduce the heat to medium and cook, covered, for 20 to 25 minutes, or until the cauliflower is tender. 2. Purée the soup using an immersion blender or in batches in a blender with a tight-fitting lid, covered with a towel to avoid splatter. Return to the pot and season with salt and pepper. Serve garnished with the cilantro and green onions.

Per Serving:
calories: 58 | fat: 0g | protein: 2g | carbs: 13g | fiber: 3g

Tofu Noodle Soup with Coconut Lemongrass Broth

Prep time: 15 minutes | Cook time: 10 minutes | Serves 6

4 cups vegetable stock
2 stalks fresh lemongrass, chopped
1 cup full-fat coconut milk
1 cup tightly packed fresh cilantro leaves
Salt and pepper, to taste
1 tablespoon virgin coconut oil (optional)
1 medium shallot, small diced
1 small green chili pepper, seeded and minced
1 (2-inch) piece fresh ginger,
peeled and minced
1 cup snow peas
1½ cups small broccoli florets
1 block (14 ounces / 397 g) extra-firm tofu, drained and cut into ½-inch cubes
1 teaspoon gluten-free tamari soy sauce
2 tablespoons fresh lime juice
Serve:
Cooked rice or rice noodles
Lime wedges

1. In a large pot, bring the vegetable stock and chopped lemongrass to a boil. Remove from the heat and allow the lemongrass to steep for 10 minutes. Strain the steeped broth. Discard the lemongrass. 2. Transfer the broth to a blender. Add the coconut milk, cilantro, salt, and pepper, if using. Blend the mixture on high until completely smooth. Set aside. 3. In the same large pot, heat the coconut oil over medium heat. Add the shallots, chili, and ginger. Stir and sauté until the onions are translucent and slightly soft, about 2 minutes. 4. Add the snow peas and broccoli florets and stir. Season the vegetables with salt and pepper, if using. Add the tofu and stir. Pour the coconut lemongrass broth and tamari into the pot, and stir to combine. Taste the broth for seasoning and adjust if necessary. 5. Bring the soup to a boil. Lower the heat to a simmer and cook, uncovered, until broccoli is tender, about 4 minutes. Stir in the lime juice. 6. Serve the soup hot with cooked rice or rice noodles and lime wedges on the side.

Per Serving:

calories: 204 | fat: 16g | protein: 10g | carbs: 9g | fiber: 2g

Italian Lentil Soup

Prep time: 10 minutes | Cook time: 3 to 4 hours | Serves 6 to 8

1 medium onion, diced
3 garlic cloves, minced
2 carrots, diced
2 celery stalks, diced
1 pound (454 g, about 2⅓ cups) dried green or brown lentils, rinsed and sorted
1 (28-ounce / 794-g) can no-salt-added crushed tomatoes
8 cups store-bought low-sodium vegetable broth
1 tablespoon Italian seasoning
Ground black pepper
Salt (optional)

1. In the slow cooker, combine the onion, garlic, carrots, celery, lentils, tomatoes, broth, Italian seasoning, pepper, and salt (if using). 2. Cover the slow cooker and cook on High for 3 to 4 hours or on Low for 7 to 8 hours.

Per Serving:

calories: 354 | fat: 1g | protein: 20g | carbs: 67g | fiber: 34g

Creamy Pumpkin and Toasted Walnut Soup

Prep time: 15 minutes | Cook time: 30 minutes | Makes 4 bowls

1 small pie pumpkin, peeled, seeded, and chopped (about 6 cups)
1 teaspoon olive oil (optional)
¼ teaspoon sea salt (optional)
1 onion, diced
4 cups water or vegetable stock
2 to 3 teaspoons ground sage
2 to 3 tablespoons nutritional yeast
1 cup nondairy milk, or 1 tablespoon nut or seed butter plus 1 cup water or stock
¼ cup toasted walnuts
Freshly ground black pepper, to taste

1. Heat a large saucepan over medium heat and sauté the pumpkin in oil, seasoning with salt (if desired), until slightly softened, about 10 minutes. Add the onion to the pot and sauté for an additional 5 minutes until slightly softened. 2. Pour in water and bring to a boil. Reduce heat to a simmer, cover, and cook for 15 to 20 minutes until the pumpkin is tender when pierced with a fork. 3. Stir in sage, nutritional yeast, and nondairy milk. Use an immersion blender or regular blender to purée the soup until smooth. 4. Garnish with toasted walnuts and pepper before serving.

Per Serving: (1 bowl)

calories: 140 | fat: 5g | protein: 7g | carbs: 20g | fiber: 3g

Quick Creamy Herbed Tomato Soup

Prep time: 5 minutes | Cook time: 15 minutes | Serves 4

2 teaspoons extra-virgin olive oil (optional)
4 garlic cloves, roughly chopped
2 (15-ounce / 425-g) cans crushed tomatoes
½ teaspoon maple syrup (optional)
2 cups plain unsweetened plant-based milk
1 teaspoon Italian seasoning
2 tablespoons roughly chopped fresh mint
½ teaspoon salt (optional)
Black pepper

1. In a medium saucepan, heat the oil over medium heat. Add the garlic and cook it until it is fragrant and beginning to turn golden, about 2 minutes. Remove from the heat and let cool. 2. In a blender or food processor, combine the tomatoes, maple syrup, plant-based milk, Italian seasoning, mint, salt (if using), and cooled garlic and blend until smooth. 3. Return the mixture to the saucepan and bring to a boil over high heat. Lower the heat to medium-low and simmer, stirring occasionally, for 5 minutes. Ladle into bowls, sprinkle with black pepper, and serve.

Per Serving:

calories: 126 | fat: 5g | protein: 6g | carbs: 17g | fiber: 5g

Smoky Saffron Chickpea, Chard, and Rice Soup

Prep time: 15 minutes | Cook time: 35 minutes | Serves 6

2 teaspoons virgin olive oil (optional)
1 medium yellow onion, small diced
1 stalk celery, small diced
3 cloves garlic, minced
1½ teaspoons smoked paprika
¼ cup tomato paste
1 medium zucchini, chopped into ½-inch pieces
1½ cups cooked chickpeas
⅓ cup medium-grain brown rice, rinsed
Salt and pepper, to taste (optional)
Pinch of saffron threads
5 to 6 cups vegetable stock
1 bunch chard, leaves chopped
¼ cup chopped fresh flat-leaf parsley
1 tablespoon fresh lemon juice

1. Heat the olive oil in a large soup pot over medium heat. Add the onions and celery. Stir and sauté until the onions are quite soft and translucent, about 5 minutes. 2. Add the garlic, smoked paprika, and tomato paste, and stir. Add the zucchini, chickpeas, and rice. Season with salt and pepper, if using. Add the saffron and vegetable stock, stir, and cover. Bring to a boil and then reduce the heat to a simmer. Cook, covered, until the rice is just cooked through, about 25 minutes. Add the chopped chard to the pot and continue to cook until it has just wilted, about 3 minutes. 3. Stir in the parsley and lemon juice and serve immediately.

Per Serving:

calories: 155 | fat: 3g | protein: 6g | carbs: 27g | fiber: 5g

Miso Noodle Soup with Shiitake Mushrooms

Prep time: 5 minutes | Cook time: 25 minutes | Serves 4 to 6

1 (8-ounce / 227-g) package brown rice noodles
4 cups vegetable broth
2 cups water
1 (5-ounce / 142-g) package shiitake mushrooms, cut into ¼-inch-thick slices
3 scallions, green and white parts, thinly sliced on a bias (about ½ cup)
3 garlic cloves, sliced
3 or 4 (¼-inch) slices unpeeled fresh ginger
8 ounces (227 g) bok choy
2 tablespoons red miso paste
1 tablespoon soy sauce

1. Cook the noodles for about 5 minutes. 2. Meanwhile, in a large Dutch oven or saucepan, combine the broth, water, mushrooms, scallions, garlic, and ginger. Cover, and bring to a boil over high heat. 3. Reduce the heat to low. Cover, and simmer for 15 minutes. 4. Uncover, and increase the heat to medium. Add the bok choy, and simmer for 3 minutes, or until the bok choy is crisp-tender. 5. Add the noodles, and heat through. Remove from the heat. 6. Add the miso and soy sauce. Stir until the miso has dissolved. 7. Remove the ginger, and serve.

Per Serving:

calories: 396 | fat: 3g | protein: 13g | carbs: 80g | fiber: 8g

Sweet Potato Bisque

Prep time: 20 minutes | Cook time: 40 minutes | Serves 6

1 large onion, peeled and diced
2 cloves garlic, peeled and minced
1 tablespoon grated ginger
1 tablespoon thyme
½ teaspoon ground nutmeg
1 teaspoon ground cinnamon
3 large sweet potatoes, peeled
and diced
6 cups vegetable stock, or low-sodium vegetable broth
Zest and juice of 1 orange
1½ cups unsweetened plain almond milk
Salt and freshly ground black pepper, to taste

1. Place the onion in a large saucepan and sauté over medium heat for 10 minutes. Add water 1 to 2 tablespoons at a time to keep the onion from sticking to the pan. Add the garlic, ginger, thyme, nutmeg, and cinnamon and cook for 1 minute. Add the sweet potatoes, vegetable stock, and orange zest and juice and bring the pot to a boil over high heat. Reduce the heat to medium and cook, covered, for 25 minutes, or until the sweet potatoes are tender. 2. Purée the soup using an immersion blender or in batches in a blender with a tight-fitting lid, covered with a towel. Return the soup to the pot and add the almond milk. Cook for an additional 5 minutes, or until heated through, and season with salt and pepper.

Per Serving:

calories: 110 | fat: 0g | protein: 3g | carbs: 24g | fiber: 3g

Lentil Mushroom Soup

Prep time: 10 minutes | Cook time: 30 minutes | Serves 4

⅔ cup dried green lentils
2 cups button mushrooms, sliced
1 red bell pepper
4 cups vegetable stock
¼ cup dried thyme
Optional Toppings:
Black pepper
Sun-dried tomatoes

1. Put a large pot over medium-high heat and add the vegetable stock along with the green lentils. 2. Bring the water to a boil and turn the heat down to medium. 3. Cook the lentils for about 15 minutes, without covering the pot, remove any foam produced by the lentils and stir occasionally. 4. Add the mushrooms and thyme to the pot, bring the heat down to a simmer, cover the pot with a lid and let it simmer for another 10 minutes. 5. Remove the stem, seeds and placenta of the bell pepper and dice the flesh. 6. Add the bell pepper to the pot, then make sure to stir well and let it simmer for another 5 minutes. 7. Turn the heat off and let the soup cool down for 5 minutes. 8. Divide between two bowls, serve with the optional toppings and enjoy! 1. Store the soup in an airtight container in the fridge, and consume within 2 days. Alternatively, store in the freezer for a maximum of 60 days and thaw at room temperature. The soup can be reheated in a pot or the microwave.

Per Serving:

calories: 146 | fat: 1g | protein: 10g | carbs: 24g | fiber: 12g

Chipotle Pumpkin Chili with Tempeh and Beer

Prep time: 15 minutes | Cook time: 35 minutes | Serves 6

1 tablespoon virgin olive oil (optional)
1 large onion, chopped
3 cloves garlic, minced
3 to 5 canned chipotles in adobo, chopped
2 teaspoons ground cumin
2 teaspoons chili powder
1 teaspoon ground coriander
1 tablespoon unsweetened cocoa powder
1 cup beer or vegetable stock or water
2 cups peeled and chopped
pumpkin or butternut squash or sweet potatoes
2 cups cooked black beans
1 block (8 ounces / 227 g) tempeh, finely chopped or crumbled
1 can (28 ounces / 794 g) crushed tomatoes
Salt and pepper, to taste (optional)
Serve:
Chopped fresh cilantro leaves
Diced ripe avocado

1. Heat the olive oil in a large pot over medium heat. Add the onions and sauté until translucent, about 3 minutes. 2. Add the garlic, chipotles, cumin, chili powder, coriander, and cocoa powder to the pot and stir. Keep stirring until the garlic is very fragrant, about 30 seconds. The pot should look quite dry. 3. Pour the beer into the pot, and start scraping up any bits from the bottom. Add the chopped pumpkin, black beans, tempeh, and tomatoes. Stir to combine. Season the chili liberally with salt and pepper, if using. Stir one more time. 4. Cover and bring to a boil. Lower the heat to a simmer. Cook the chili, covered, for 30 to 35 minutes or until the pieces of pumpkin are tender. Stir the chili occasionally. 5. Serve the chili hot with chopped cilantro and diced avocado

Per Serving:
calories: 233 | fat: 7g | protein: 14g | carbs: 32g | fiber: 8g

Savory Pumpkin Bisque

Prep time: 0 minutes | Cook time: 20 minutes | Serves 4

2 (15-ounce / 425-g) cans pumpkin purée
3 cups vegetable broth
2 tablespoons nutritional yeast
2 tablespoons apple cider vinegar
1 tablespoon onion powder
1 tablespoon soy sauce
2 teaspoons pure maple syrup
½ teaspoon dried thyme
½ teaspoon freshly ground black pepper
¼ teaspoon garlic powder
2 bay leaves

1. In a Dutch oven or saucepan, combine the pumpkin purée, broth, nutritional yeast, vinegar, onion powder, soy sauce, maple syrup, thyme, pepper, garlic powder, and bay leaves. Bring to a simmer over medium-high heat. Cover, and cook for 20 minutes, or until the soup is fragrant and heated through. Remove from the heat. 2. Remove the bay leaves, and serve.

Per Serving:
calories: 133 | fat: 2g | protein: 9g | carbs: 23g | fiber: 8g

Roasted Eggplant and Lentil Stew

Prep time: 20 minutes | Cook time: 1 hour 10 minutes | Serves 8

1 large eggplant
4 carrots, coarsely chopped
4 cups no-sodium vegetable broth
1 cup dried brown or green lentils
1 large yellow onion, diced
1 bunch chopped scallions, white and green parts, divided
3 garlic cloves, diced
1 tablespoon water, plus more as needed
1 (14-ounce / 397-g) can full-fat coconut milk
1 tablespoon red miso paste
1 tablespoon low-sodium soy sauce
1 (28-ounce / 794-g) can diced tomatoes
4 teaspoons ground cumin
1 teaspoon adobo chili powder or smoked paprika
1 celery stalk, coarsely chopped
Fresh cilantro leaves, for serving

1. Preheat the oven to 350ºF (180ºC). 2. Halve the eggplant lengthwise and place it on a baking sheet, flesh-side up. Spread the carrots around the eggplant on the same baking sheet. 3. Roast for 30 minutes, or until the eggplant and carrots are lightly browned or caramel colored and the carrots are fork-tender. 4. Set the carrots aside. Let the eggplant cool before handling it. Scoop out as much flesh as possible without scooping into the skin and set aside in a bowl. 5. In an 8-quart pot over high heat, bring the vegetable broth to a boil. Lower the heat to maintain a simmer and add the lentils. Cover the pot and cook for 20 to 30 minutes, or until the lentils are soft yet retain their shape. 6. While the lentils cook, in a small sauté pan or skillet over medium heat, cook the onion, white parts of the scallion, and garlic for 7 to 10 minutes, adding water, 1 tablespoon at a time, to prevent burning, until darkly browned. 7. In a blender, combine the roasted eggplant and onion mixture with the coconut milk, miso paste, and soy sauce. Purée for 2 to 3 minutes until smooth. 8. Once the lentils are finished cooking, add the tomatoes, cumin, chili powder, and celery. Bring the mixture to a simmer. Pour in the eggplant sauce and add the roasted carrots. Cook until warmed to your liking. 9. This stew is best served with a few fresh cilantro leaves and scallion greens on top.

Per Serving:
calories: 259 | fat: 10g | protein: 10g | carbs: 35g | fiber: 9g

Prep time: 20 minutes | Cook time: 35 minutes | Serves 4

1 large yellow onion, peeled and diced small

4 cloves garlic, peeled and minced

1 medium butternut squash (about 1 pound / 454 g), peeled, halved, seeded, and cut into ½-inch pieces

2 cups cooked pinto beans, or 1 (15-ounce / 425-g) can, drained

and rinsed

6 ears corn, kernels removed (about 3½ cups)

Salt and freshly ground black pepper, to taste

1 cup finely chopped basil

1. Place the onion in a large saucepan and sauté over medium heat for 10 minutes. Add water 1 to 2 tablespoons at a time to keep the onion from sticking to the pan. 2. Add the garlic, squash, beans, corn, and 2 cups of water and cook for 25 minutes, or until the squash is tender. Season with salt and pepper and stir in the basil.

Per Serving:

calories: 305 | fat: 2g | protein: 15g | carbs: 65g | fiber: 14g

Prep time: 5 minutes | Cook time: 30 minutes | Serves 6

1 (28-ounce / 794-g) can crushed tomatoes

1 (15-ounce / 425-g) can low-sodium black beans

1 (15-ounce / 425-g) can low-sodium cannellini beans

1 (15-ounce / 425-g) can low-sodium chickpeas

1 tablespoon chili powder

1 teaspoon garlic powder

1 teaspoon onion powder

½ teaspoon ground cumin

½ teaspoon red pepper flakes (optional)

1. In a large stockpot, combine the tomatoes, black beans, cannellini beans, and chickpeas and their liquids with the chili powder, garlic powder, onion powder, cumin, and red pepper flakes, if using. Bring the chili to a boil over medium-high heat. 2. Cover, reduce the heat to medium-low, simmer for 25 minutes, and serve.

Per Serving:

calories: 185 | fat: 1g | protein: 11g | carbs: 33g | fiber: 13g

Chapter

7

Salads

Creamy Chickpea and Avocado Salad

Prep time: 20 minutes | Cook time: 0 minutes | Serves 2

1 (15-ounce / 425-g) can chickpeas, drained and rinsed
1 avocado, peeled and pitted
2 tablespoons slivered almonds
1 celery stalk, minced
1 large carrot, peeled and grated or minced

3 cherry tomatoes, diced small
6 Kalamata olives, pitted and chopped
Juice of 1 lemon
2 tablespoons chopped fresh parsley
½ teaspoon salt (optional)

1. In a medium bowl, mash the chickpeas and avocados together using a fork until the avocado is smooth and the chickpeas are mostly broken but still chunky. 2. Add the almonds, celery, carrot, tomatoes, olives, lemon juice, parsley, and salt to the bowl. Mix everything together until well combined. Serve immediately.

Per Serving:
calories: 396 | fat: 22g | protein: 12g | carbs: 43g | fiber: 17g

Broccoli Caesar with Smoky Tempeh Bits

Prep time: 20 minutes | Cook time: 10 minutes | Serves 4

Creamy Cashew Caesar Dressing:
2 tablespoons raw cashew butter
2 tablespoons filtered water
1½ tablespoons fresh lemon juice
salt and pepper, to taste (optional)
3 cloves garlic, grated
1 teaspoon Dijon mustard
1 teaspoon minced capers
1 tablespoon nutritional yeast
3 tablespoons virgin olive oil (optional)
Salad:
Pinch of salt (optional)

1 bunch broccoli, cut into florets
1 teaspoon sweet paprika
1 teaspoon smoked paprika
1 teaspoon pure maple syrup (optional)
1 teaspoon apple cider vinegar
½ teaspoon gluten-free tamari soy sauce
2 teaspoons virgin olive oil (optional)
½ block (4 ounces / 113 g) tempeh, crumbled
Garnishes:
2 teaspoons nutritional yeast
Freshly ground black pepper

1. Prepare the Creamy Cashew Caesar Dressing: In a jar with a tight-fitting lid, combine cashew butter, water, lemon juice, salt, and pepper (if desired). Stir the mixture with a spoon or small spatula until the cashew butter is broken up. Mash any remaining chunks against the sides of the jar to integrate them. Add garlic, Dijon mustard, capers, nutritional yeast, and olive oil (if desired). Secure the lid tightly and shake the jar vigorously until the dressing reaches a smooth and creamy consistency. Set aside. 2. Assemble the Salad: Bring a large saucepan of water to a boil over medium-high heat. Add a pinch of salt and the broccoli florets. Simmer for about 4 minutes, until the broccoli is tender and bright green. Drain the broccoli and rinse it under cold water to halt the cooking process. Set aside. 3. In a small bowl, stir together paprika, smoked paprika, maple syrup (if desired), apple cider vinegar, and tamari. Set aside. 4. Dry the saucepan and return it to the stove over medium heat. Add oil and let it heat until slightly shimmering. Add crumbled tempeh, spreading it out in a single layer. Let it brown undisturbed for 2 minutes, then stir and let it sit for another minute. Pour the paprika mixture into the pan; it should sizzle. Stir to coat all of the tempeh. Remove from heat. 5. Place the broccoli on a serving platter. Drizzle the Creamy Cashew Caesar Dressing over the top. Scatter the smoky tempeh bits over the broccoli. Garnish with nutritional yeast and freshly ground black pepper. Serve immediately.

Per Serving:
calories: 204 | fat: 19g | protein: 9g | carbs: 10g | fiber: 2g

Quinoa Tabouli

Prep time: 10 minutes | Cook time: 25 minutes | Serves 3

½ cup quinoa, uncooked
1¼ cups water
2 Persian cucumbers, diced
2 medium tomatoes, diced
½ medium red onion, diced

½ cup chopped fresh parsley
½ cup chopped fresh mint
2 ounces (57 g) freshly squeezed lemon juice

1. Rinse the quinoa under cold running water using a strainer, making sure to shake off any excess water. In a medium pot, combine the quinoa and water. Bring it to a boil, then cover with a lid and reduce the heat to a simmer. Continue cooking until all the water is absorbed, which usually takes about 15 to 20 minutes. The quinoa will become soft and translucent, with a visible germ ring along the outside edge of the grain when done. 2. Transfer the cooked quinoa to a bowl and let it chill in the refrigerator for 10 minutes. 3. Add the cucumbers, tomatoes, onions, parsley, mint, and lemon juice to the chilled quinoa. Toss everything together to combine.

Per Serving:
calories: 156 | fat: 2g | protein: 6g | carbs: 30g | fiber: 5g

Vegan "Toona" Salad

Prep time: 10 minutes | Cook time: 0 minutes | Serves 4

3 cups cooked chickpeas
1 avocado, peeled and pitted
½ cup chopped red onion
¼ cup chopped celery
2 tablespoons Dijon mustard

1½ tablespoons freshly squeezed lemon juice
½ tablespoon maple syrup (optional)
1 teaspoon garlic powder

1. In a large bowl, combine the chickpeas and the avocado. Using a fork or a potato masher, smash them down until the majority of the chickpeas have been broken apart. 2. Stir in the onion, celery, mustard, lemon juice, maple syrup (if desired), and garlic powder, making sure everything is thoroughly combined, and serve.

Per Serving:
calories: 298 | fat: 10g | protein: 13g | carbs: 42g | fiber: 13g

Wedge Salad with Avocado Citrus Dressing

Prep time: 20 minutes | Cook time: 0 minutes | Serves 6

Dressing:
¼ cup filtered water
3 tablespoons fresh orange juice
3 tablespoons fresh lemon juice
2 tablespoons fresh lime juice
1 tablespoon apple cider vinegar
2 tablespoons raw agave nectar
3 tablespoons coconut oil (optional)
1 small jalapeño pepper, seeded and chopped
1 medium, ripe avocado,

peeled and pitted
3 tablespoons chopped fresh dill
Salt and pepper, to taste (optional)
Salad:
3 romaine hearts, cut into wedges
1 head radicchio, cut into wedges
1 head Boston or Bibb lettuce, cut into wedges
Salt and pepper, to taste (optional)
2 cups cherry tomatoes, halved
Chopped fresh dill, for garnish

1. Prepare the Dressing: In a blender, combine water, orange juice, lemon juice, lime juice, apple cider vinegar, agave nectar, coconut oil, jalapeño, avocado, dill, and salt and pepper (if desired). Blend on high speed until the mixture has a smooth and creamy consistency, which usually takes about 1 minute. Set the dressing aside. 2. Assemble the Salad: Arrange wedges of romaine, radicchio, and Boston or Bibb lettuce on a platter or individual plates. Sprinkle the wedges with salt and pepper (if desired). Drizzle the prepared dressing evenly over the lettuce wedges. Garnish with halved cherry tomatoes and chopped dill. Serve immediately.

Per Serving:
calories: 167 | fat: 12g | protein: 3g | carbs: 15g | fiber: 4g

Rice Salad with Fennel, Orange and Chickpeas

Prep time: 15 minutes | Cook time: 50 minutes | Serves 4

1½ cups brown basmati rice
2 cups cooked chickpeas, or 1 (15-ounce / 425-g) can, drained and rinsed
1 fennel bulb, trimmed and diced
1 orange, zested, peeled, and

segmented (zest and segments reserved)
¼ cup plus 2 tablespoons white wine vinegar
½ teaspoon crushed red pepper flakes
¼ cup finely chopped parsley

1. Rinse the rice under cold water and drain it. In a pot, combine the rice with 3 cups of cold water. Bring it to a boil over high heat, then reduce the heat to medium and cover the pot. Cook the rice for 45 to 50 minutes, or until it becomes tender. 2. While the rice is cooking, mix together the chickpeas, fennel, orange zest and segments, white wine vinegar, crushed red pepper flakes,

and parsley in a large bowl. Once the rice is done, add it to the bowl and mix everything well.

Per Serving:
calories: 317 | fat: 11g | protein: 14g | carbs: 54g | fiber: 18g

Smoky Potato Salad over Greens

Prep time: 25 minutes | Cook time: 15 minutes | Serves 6

2 pounds (907 g) waxy potatoes
¼ cup apple cider vinegar
2 scallions, sliced
1 teaspoon maple syrup (optional)
1 teaspoon tomato paste
½ teaspoon gluten-free Dijon

mustard
½ teaspoon salt (optional)
½ teaspoon smoked paprika
¼ teaspoon black pepper
2 drops liquid smoke
12 ounces (340 g) baby greens
¼ cup unsalted, roasted almonds, chopped

1. Cook the potatoes by steaming or boiling them in a large pot over medium-high heat until they become fork-tender, which usually takes about 15 minutes. Drain the potatoes and allow them to cool in a single layer. 2. In the meantime, whisk together the vinegar, scallions, maple syrup, tomato paste, mustard, salt (if desired), paprika, pepper, and liquid smoke in a large bowl. 3. Chop the cooled potatoes into bite-size pieces and add them to the bowl with the dressing. Gently toss the potatoes with the dressing to coat them. If serving immediately, serve the potato salad over the greens and top it with almonds. If not serving immediately, refrigerate the salad for up to 5 days. However, if using an oil-free version with avocado, it will only last for a day. Combine the refrigerated salad with the greens and almonds before eating.

Per Serving:
calories: 179 | fat: 3g | protein: 5g | carbs: 34g | fiber: 6g

Orange, Fennel and White Bean Salad

Prep time: 15 minutes | Cook time: 0 minutes | Serves 4

6 large oranges, peeled and segmented
2 tablespoons fresh lemon juice
2 tablespoons balsamic vinegar
1 medium fennel bulb, trimmed and thinly sliced

2 tablespoons minced fresh fennel fronds
2 cups cooked navy beans, or 1 (15-ounce / 425-g) can, drained and rinsed
Salt, to taste (optional)
Cayenne pepper, to taste
4 cups arugula

1. In a large bowl, combine orange sections, lemon juice, balsamic vinegar, fennel bulb and fronds, beans, salt (if desired), and cayenne pepper. Mix everything together well. Allow the mixture to sit for 1 hour before serving. 2. To serve, divide the arugula evenly among 4 individual plates. Spoon the salad on top of the greens, distributing it evenly among the plates.

Per Serving:
calories: 267 | fat: 1g | protein: 10g | carbs: 56g | fiber: 18g

Zingy Melon and Mango Salad

Prep time: 5 minutes | Cook time: 0 minutes | Serves 2

1 large mango, peeled, pitted, and cut into 1-inch pieces (about 1 cup)
½ small cantaloupe or watermelon, peeled and cut
into 1-inch pieces (about 2 cups)
Juice of 1 lime
¼ cup chopped fresh cilantro
1 teaspoon chili powder

1. In a large bowl, mix together the mango and cantaloupe. Add the lime juice and cilantro, then gently toss until well combined. To serve, spoon the mixture into bowls and sprinkle with chili powder.

Per Serving:

calories: 171 | fat: 1g | protein: 3g | carbs: 42g | fiber: 5g

Bean and Corn Salad

Prep time: 15 minutes | Cook time: 0 minutes | Serves 6

1 (15-ounce / 425-g) can pinto beans, drained and rinsed
1 (15-ounce / 425-g) can black beans, drained and rinsed
1 (15-ounce / 425-g) can chickpeas, drained and rinsed
1 (15-ounce / 425-g) can
unsalted corn, drained and rinsed
¾ cup diced tomato
¼ cup chopped cilantro
3 to 4 tablespoons lemon or lime juice
Salt, to taste (optional)

1. Combine all the ingredients in a large bowl and mix well. The salad can be served chilled or at room temperature.

Per Serving:

calories: 200 | fat: 30g | protein: 10g | carbs: 38g | fiber: 9g

Beet, Cabbage, and Black Bean Salad

Prep time: 2 minutes | Cook time: 20 minutes | Serves 4 to 6

3 or 4 medium beets, peeled and cut into ½-inch dice
½ cup water
1 (15-ounce / 425-g) can black beans, drained and rinsed
1 cup shredded cabbage
1 cup shredded spinach
1 cup halved grape tomatoes
2 scallions, green and white
parts, thinly sliced
½ cup seasoned rice vinegar
¼ teaspoon freshly ground black pepper
4 to 6 cups cooked brown rice
1 ripe avocado, pitted, peeled, and diced
Fresh cilantro, for garnish

1. In a sauté pan or skillet, combine the beets and water. Bring it to a simmer over high heat. 2. Reduce the heat to medium-low, cover the pan, and cook for 10 to 15 minutes until the beets are slightly tender. Remove from heat. 3. Stir in the beans, cabbage, spinach, tomatoes, scallions, vinegar, and pepper. 4. Serve the vegetable mixture over rice. 5. Top with avocado and garnish with cilantro.

Per Serving:

calories: 179 | fat: 7g | protein: 7g | carbs: 26g | fiber: 10g

Warm Sweet Potato and Brussels Sprout Salad

Prep time: 20 minutes | Cook time: 30 minutes | Serves 4

3 sweet potatoes, peeled and cut into ¼-inch dice
1 teaspoon dried thyme
1 teaspoon garlic powder
½ teaspoon onion powder
1 pound (454 g) Brussels sprouts
1 cup walnuts, chopped
¼ cup reduced-sugar dried cranberries
2 tablespoons balsamic vinegar
Freshly ground black pepper, to taste

1. Preheat the oven to 450ºF (235ºC) and line a baking sheet with parchment paper. 2. Rinse the sweet potatoes in a colander and shake off any excess water. Sprinkle them with thyme, garlic powder, and onion powder while they are still damp. Toss to evenly coat the sweet potatoes with the spices. Transfer them to the prepared baking sheet and spread them out in a single layer. 3. Bake for 20 minutes. Flip the sweet potatoes and bake for an additional 10 minutes, or until they are fork-tender. 4. While the sweet potatoes are roasting, wash the Brussels sprouts and remove any tough or discolored outer leaves. Cut them in half lengthwise, then thinly slice the sprouts crosswise into thin shreds. Discard the root end and separate the shreds. 5. In a large bowl, combine the Brussels sprouts, roasted sweet potatoes, walnuts, and cranberries. Drizzle with vinegar and season with pepper. Toss everything together until well mixed.

Per Serving:

calories: 360 | fat: 20g | protein: 10g | carbs: 44g | fiber: 12g

Lentil Cranberry Salad

Prep time: 10 minutes | Cook time: 0 minutes | Serves 2

2 cups cooked or canned green lentils
1 small red onion, minced
½ cubed cucumber
¼ cup lemon juice
¼ cup dried cranberries
Optional Toppings:
Black pepper
Tahini

1. When using dry lentils, soak and cook ⅔ cup of dry lentils if necessary. 2. Transfer the lentils to a large bowl, and add the minced red onion, cucumber cubes, lemon juice and cranberries. 3. Stir thoroughly using a spatula and make sure everything is mixed evenly. 4. Divide the lentil salad between two bowls, garnish with the optional toppings, serve and enjoy! 5. Store the salad in an airtight container in the fridge, and consume within 2 days. Alternatively, store in the freezer for a maximum of 30 days and thaw at room temperature. The salad can be served cold.

Per Serving:

calories: 268 | fat: 1g | protein: 19g | carbs: 46g | fiber: 17g

Sweet Potato, Kale, and Red Cabbage Salad

Prep time: 10 minutes | Cook time: 20 minutes | Serves 2

Salad:
1 teaspoon extra-virgin olive oil (optional)
2 medium sweet potatoes, peeled and diced small
Pinch of salt (optional)
1 cup frozen corn
2 cups stemmed and chopped kale
1 cup shredded red cabbage

¼ cup pepitas
Dressing:
1 avocado, peeled and pitted
Juice of 1½ limes
Pinch of salt (optional)
Pinch red pepper flakes (optional)
3 tablespoons chopped fresh cilantro leaves
½ cup water

1. Make the Salad: Preheat the oven to 425ºF (220ºC). Grease a sheet pan with the olive oil. 2. Spread the sweet potato on the prepared sheet pan in one layer and sprinkle with salt (if using). Bake for 10 minutes. Using a spatula, turn the potatoes and continue to bake for another 5 minutes. Add the corn to the sheet pan and bake everything for 5 minutes more. 3. Make the Dressing: In a blender, combine the avocado, lime juice, salt, red pepper flakes (if using), cilantro, and water and blend until smooth. 4. Assemble the Salad: In a large bowl, combine the kale and cabbage, add half of the dressing, and toss gently. Add the sweet potatoes, corn, and the remaining dressing and toss until combined. The warm corn and sweet potatoes will help soften the kale slightly. Divide the salad between 2 bowls, top with the pepitas, and serve.

Per Serving:
calories: 488 | fat: 25g | protein: 13g | carbs: 64g | fiber: 16g

You Won't Believe It's Cashew Ranch Dressing

Prep time: 5 minutes | Cook time: 0 minutes | Serves 12

1¼ cups raw cashews
¾ cup water, plus more as needed
1 tablespoon plus 1½ teaspoons fresh lemon juice
1 tablespoon apple cider vinegar

1½ teaspoons onion powder
1 teaspoon dried dill
1 teaspoon salt (optional)
½ teaspoon dried basil
½ teaspoon garlic powder
¼ teaspoon black pepper

1. Blend all the ingredients in a high-speed blender until smooth. Taste and adjust the seasoning if necessary. If you prefer a thinner consistency, gradually add water, 1 tablespoon at a time, until desired thickness is reached. Transfer the dressing to an airtight container and refrigerate for up to 1 week. Note that the dressing may thicken in the refrigerator, so simply stir in water as needed to thin it out before serving.

Per Serving:
calories: 81 | fat: 6g | protein: 2g | carbs: 5g | fiber: 0g

Lemon Garlic Chickpeas Salad

Prep time: 10 minutes | Cook time: 0 minutes | Serves 2

1 cup cooked or canned chickpeas
½ cup fresh spinach
¼ cup lemon juice
¼ cup tahini

1 clove garlic minced
¼ cup water
Optional Toppings:
Fresh cilantro
Raisins

1. When using dry chickpeas, soak and cook ⅓ cup of dry chickpeas if necessary. 2. Meanwhile, add the tahini, minced garlic, lemon juice and water to a small airtight container or bowl. 3. Whisk the tahini, lemon juice, garlic and water in the bowl to form a thinner and smooth dressing, adding more water if necessary. Alternatively, shake the container with tahini, lemon juice, garlic and water until everything is thoroughly mixed, adding more water if you want a thinner and less creamy dressing. 4. Put the spinach in a strainer, rinse well to clean it thoroughly and then drain well. 5. Add the spinach and chickpeas to a large bowl and mix thoroughly. 6. Divide the salad between two bowls, garnish with the tangerines and the optional toppings, serve and enjoy! 7. Store the salad in an airtight container in the fridge, and consume within 2 days. Alternatively, store in the freezer for a maximum of 30 days and thaw at room temperature. The salad can be served cold.

Per Serving:
calories: 406 | fat: 22g | protein: 19g | carbs: 33g | fiber: 11g

Chickpea Apple Salad

Prep time: 15 minutes | Cook time: 15 minutes | Serves 2

1 cup cooked or canned chickpeas
½ cup dry quinoa
½ cup pomegranate seeds
¼ cup tahini

1 large apple, peeled and cored
Optional Toppings:
Fresh mint
Black pepper

1. When using dry chickpeas, soak and cook ⅓ cup of dry chickpeas if necessary. Cook the quinoa for about 15 minutes. 2. Meanwhile, cut the peeled and cored apple into small bits and set them aside for now. 3. Add the cooked chickpeas and quinoa to a large bowl and mix. 4. Add the pomegranate seeds and apple bits to the same bowl and mix thoroughly using a spatula. Optionally leave some pomegranate seeds and apple bits for garnishing later. 5. Stir the tahini into the chickpea and quinoa salad and make sure everything is mixed well. 6. Divide the salad between two bowls, optionally garnish with the leftover pomegranate seeds, apple bits and a swirl of tahini, any of the optional toppings and enjoy! 7. Store the salad in an airtight container in the fridge, and consume within 2 days. Alternatively, store in the freezer for a maximum of 30 days and thaw at room temperature. The salad can be served cold.

Per Serving:
calories: 234 | fat: 6g | protein: 11g | carbs: 32g | fiber: 6g

Bulgur Lettuce Cups

Prep time: 10 minutes | Cook time: 20 minutes | Serves 2 to 4

Sauce:
½ cup unsweetened natural peanut butter
¼ cup soy sauce
3 tablespoons seasoned rice vinegar
2 tablespoons lime juice
1 teaspoon liquid aminos
1 teaspoon sriracha
Cups:
1 cup bulgur

½ cup soy sauce
¼ cup seasoned rice vinegar
½ teaspoon garlic powder
½ teaspoon ground ginger
¼ teaspoon red pepper flakes
1 cup shredded carrots
1 cup shredded cabbage
½ cup sliced scallions, green and white parts
1 head red leaf lettuce or Bibb lettuce

Make the Sauce: 1. In a small bowl, whisk together the peanut butter, soy sauce, vinegar, lime juice, liquid aminos, and sriracha until well combined. Make the Cups: 2. In a medium saucepan, cook the bulgur for about 12 minutes. Remove from heat and drain any excess water. 3. In a small bowl, mix together the soy sauce, vinegar, garlic powder, ginger, and red pepper flakes. 4. Add the carrots, cabbage, scallions, and soy sauce mixture to the cooked bulgur. Mix thoroughly. 5. Serve the filling scooped into individual lettuce leaves and drizzle with the peanut sauce.

Per Serving:
calories: 532 | fat: 17g | protein: 25g | carbs: 79g | fiber: 18g

Warm Lentil Salad

Prep time: 10 minutes | Cook time: 15 minutes | Serves 2

2 teaspoons extra-virgin olive oil (optional)
2 garlic cloves, chopped
1 tablespoon Italian seasoning
½ head cauliflower, cut into florets (about 2 cups)
1 large carrot, peeled and diced small
2 medium tomatoes, diced small
10 Kalamata olives, pitted and

halved
1 teaspoon salt (optional)
½ teaspoon black pepper
2 tablespoons balsamic vinegar
1 (15-ounce / 425-g) can brown lentils
1 cup water
4 cups baby spinach
1 tablespoon sunflower seeds

1. Heat olive oil in a large saucepan over medium heat. Add garlic and Italian seasoning, cooking until fragrant for about 2 to 3 minutes. 2. Stir in cauliflower, carrot, tomatoes, olives, salt (if desired), and black pepper. Cook, stirring frequently, for another 2 to 3 minutes. Pour in balsamic vinegar and cook for an additional 2 to 3 minutes to caramelize the sugars in the vinegar. 3. Add lentils and water to the saucepan. Bring to a boil and cook for 2 to 3 minutes until heated throughout. Remove from heat. 4. In a large bowl, combine spinach and sunflower seeds. Add the lentil mixture and toss until the spinach wilts.

Per Serving:
calories: 363 | fat: 10g | protein: 21g | carbs: 53g | fiber: 19g

Thai-ish Cabbage Salad

Prep time: 20 minutes | Cook time: 0 minutes | Serves 6

Dressing:
3 tablespoons fresh lime juice
1 clove garlic, finely grated
1 (½-inch) piece of fresh ginger, peeled and finely grated
1 tablespoon pure maple syrup (optional)
Sriracha or other hot sauce, to taste
Salt and pepper, to taste (optional)
¼ cup plus 1 tablespoon coconut oil

Salad:
½ head of green or red cabbage, shredded
1 large carrot, peeled
1 red bell pepper
1 barely ripe mango, peeled
3 green onions, thinly sliced
¼ cup fresh mint leaves
¼ cup fresh cilantro leaves
¼ cup fresh basil leaves
Salt and pepper, to taste
½ cup roasted cashews or peanuts or both, chopped, for garnish

1. Make the Dressing: In a small jar with a tight-fitting lid, combine the lime juice, garlic, ginger, maple syrup, Sriracha, salt, pepper, and coconut oil, if using. Tightly secure the lid, and shake the jar vigorously until the dressing has a creamy and smooth consistency. Taste and adjust seasoning, if necessary. Set aside. 2. Make the Salad: Place the shredded cabbage in a large bowl. Using a vegetable peeler, make long strips from the carrot, and add these to the bowl with the cabbage. Remove the seeds and stem from the bell pepper, cut it into strips, and add these to the bowl. 3. Carefully cut around the large pit of the mango. After you have all of the usable mango you can get, cut the fruit into thin strips and add it to the bowl. 4. Add the sliced green onions. If you like, you can add the mint, cilantro and basil leaves whole to the salad, or you can simply give them a quick chop before adding them. Season the vegetables in the bowl with some salt and pepper, if using, and toss to mix. 5. Pour the dressing over the salad and toss to evenly coat. Garnish the salad with the chopped cashews or peanuts. Serve immediately.

Per Serving:
calories: 218 | fat: 15g | protein: 5g | carbs: 19g | fiber: 4g

Chickpea Salad with Vegetables

Prep time: 5 minutes | Cook time: 0 minutes | Serves 1

1 cup canned chickpeas
1 small avocado, peeled, pitted, and sliced
1 medium tomato, diced
1 Persian cucumber, diced
¼ cup thinly sliced red onion

1 tablespoon freshly squeezed lemon juice (optional)
1 tablespoon chopped cilantro
Pinch freshly ground black pepper
Pinch garlic powder

1. Drain the chickpeas. Place them in a medium mixing bowl. 2. Add the avocado, tomato, cucumber, and onion to the bowl. Drizzle with the lemon juice (if using). 3. Add the cilantro, pepper, and garlic powder. 4. Mix well and enjoy.

Per Serving:
calories: 636 | fat: 34g | protein: 20g | carbs: 72g | fiber: 28g

Perfect Potluck Pasta Salad

Prep time: 20 minutes | Cook time: 30 minutes | Serves 8

1 pound (454 g) bowtie pasta	marinated artichoke quarters
2 tablespoons olive oil	with their juices
(optional)	Juice of 1 lemon
¾ cup diced red, white, or	½ teaspoon minced lemon zest
yellow onion	¼ teaspoon salt (optional)
1 teaspoon minced garlic	Cherry tomatoes, halved
1 (6½ ounces / 184 g) jar	Freshly ground pepper, to taste

1. In a large pot over medium-high heat, boil water and cook the pasta according to the directions on the package. Remove from the heat and drain. 2. While the pasta cools, begin on the veggies. In a large pan over medium-high heat, heat the olive oil (if desired) and sauté the onion and garlic for 3 minutes or until the onion becomes tender and translucent. 3. Add the artichokes and their juices, lemon juice, lemon zest, and salt (if desired) and simmer over medium heat for 5 minutes. 4. Add the drained pasta and mix well. 5. Garnish with the cherry tomatoes and sprinkle with pepper. 6. Serve warm if you're rushed, or serve chilled if you have 30 minutes to spare.

Per Serving:

calories: 122 | fat: 4g | protein: 3g | carbs: 20g | fiber: 5g

Fiery Couscous Salad

Prep time: 5 minutes | Cook time: 5 minutes | Serves 3

1 cup cooked or canned	¼ cup tahini
chickpea	½ cup water
½ cup dry couscous	Optional Toppings:
3 tangerines	Cinnamon
1 (2-inch) piece ginger,	Fresh mint
minced	Raisins

1. When using dry chickpeas, soak and cook ⅓ cup of dry chickpeas if necessary. Cook the couscous for about 5 minutes. 2. Meanwhile, add the tahini, minced ginger and water to a small airtight container or bowl. Whisk the tahini and ginger in the bowl into a smooth dressing, adding more water if necessary. Alternatively, shake the container with tahini, ginger and water until everything is thoroughly mixed, adding more water if you want a thinner and less creamy dressing. 3. Add the couscous, dressing and chickpeas to a large bowl and mix thoroughly. 4. Peel and section the tangerines and set them aside to garnish the salad. 5. Divide the salad between two bowls, garnish with the tangerines and the optional toppings, serve and enjoy! 6. Store the salad in an airtight container in the fridge, and consume within 2 days. Alternatively, store in the freezer for a maximum of 30 days and thaw at room temperature. The salad can be served cold.

Per Serving:

calories: 349 | fat: 14g | protein: 14g | carbs: 41g | fiber: 8g

Tabbouleh Salad

Prep time: 15 minutes | Cook time: 10 minutes | Serves 4

1 cup whole wheat couscous	1 tomato, diced small
1 cup boiling water	1 cup fresh parsley, chopped
Zest and juice of 1 lemon	¼ cup fresh mint, finely
1 garlic clove, pressed	chopped
Pinch sea salt (optional)	2 scallions, finely chopped
1 tablespoon olive oil or	4 tablespoons sunflower seeds
flaxseed oil (optional)	(optional)
½ cucumber, diced small	

1. Place couscous in a medium bowl and pour enough boiling water over it to submerge all the grains. Cover the bowl with a plate or wrap and set aside. 2. In a large salad bowl, combine lemon zest, lemon juice, garlic, salt, and olive oil (if using). Add cucumber, tomato, parsley, mint, and scallions to the bowl and toss to coat the vegetables with the dressing. 3. Remove the plate from the couscous and fluff it with a fork. Add the cooked couscous to the vegetables and toss to combine. 4. Serve the salad topped with sunflower seeds (if desired).

Per Serving:

calories: 259 | fat: 8g | protein: 8g | carbs: 38g | fiber: 4g

Lentil, Lemon and Mushroom Salad

Prep time: 10 minutes | Cook time: 25 minutes | Serves 2

½ cup dry lentils of choice	3 garlic cloves, minced
2 cups vegetable broth	¼ teaspoon chili flakes
3 cups mushrooms, thickly	1 tablespoon lemon juice
sliced	2 tablespoons cilantro,
1 cup sweet or purple onion,	chopped
chopped	½ cup arugula
4 teaspoons extra virgin olive	Salt and pepper to taste
oil (optional)	(optional)
2 tablespoons garlic powder or	

1. Sprout the lentils for 2 to 3 days. 2. In a deep saucepan, bring vegetable stock to a boil. Add the lentils to the boiling broth, cover the pan, and cook over low heat for about 5 minutes until the lentils are slightly tender. Remove from heat and drain any excess water. 3. Heat 2 tablespoons of olive oil in a frying pan over high heat. Add onions, garlic, and chili flakes. Cook, stirring, until the onions are almost translucent, about 5 to 10 minutes. Add mushrooms to the pan and mix well. Continue cooking until the onions are completely translucent and the mushrooms have softened. Remove from heat. 4. In a large bowl, combine the lentils, onions, mushrooms, and garlic. Add lemon juice and the remaining olive oil. Toss or stir to thoroughly combine all the ingredients. 5. Serve the mushroom and onion mixture over a bed of arugula in a bowl. Season with salt and pepper to taste, if desired. Alternatively, store the dish for later enjoyment!

Per Serving:

calories: 262 | fat: 10g | protein: 16g | carbs: 28g | fiber: 15g

Winter Sunshine Salad

Prep time: 15 minutes | Cook time: 0 minutes | Serves 6

2 small fennel bulbs, cored and thinly sliced

2 ruby red grapefruits with juice reserved

2 cups shredded red cabbage

1 red or orange bell pepper, thinly sliced

1 tablespoon fresh lime juice

Salt and black pepper (optional)

½ cup chopped cilantro

1 avocado, diced or sliced

¼ cup walnut pieces

1. Combine the fennel, grapefruit segments and juice, cabbage, bell pepper, and lime juice in a large bowl. Season with salt (if desired) and pepper to taste, then toss to combine. 2. When ready to serve, add the cilantro and toss to combine. Divide into bowls, then divide avocado and walnuts evenly between salads.

Per Serving:

calories: 157 | fat: 8g | protein: 4g | carbs: 21g | fiber: 7g

Detox Salad

Prep time: 10 minutes | Cook time: 0 minutes | Serves 2

2 cups purple sauerkraut

1 bunch flat-leaf parsley, roughly chopped

¼ cup mixed seeds (pumpkin,

sunflower, sesame, hemp)

2 tablespoons raisins, rinsed

1 avocado, peeled, pitted and sliced

1. In a large bowl, combine the sauerkraut, parsley, seeds and raisins and toss until well combined. To serve, transfer to smaller bowls or plates and top each serving with half of the sliced avocado. 2. The salad will keep for up to 3 days in the fridge.

Per Serving:

calories: 321 | fat: 23g | protein: 9g | carbs: 25g | fiber: 12g

Classic French Vinaigrette

Prep time: 5 minutes | Cook time: 0 minutes | Serves 4

3 tablespoons apple cider vinegar

2 tablespoons minced shallot

1 tablespoon balsamic vinegar

1 teaspoon gluten-free Dijon mustard

½ teaspoon dried thyme

2 teaspoons olive oil (optional)

Salt and black pepper (optional)

1. In a medium jar with a tight-fitting lid, combine apple cider vinegar, shallot, and balsamic vinegar. Allow it to sit for 5 minutes. Stir in mustard and thyme. Gradually whisk in the oil in a slow and steady stream. Season with salt and pepper to taste, if desired. Refrigerate the dressing for up to 5 days.

Per Serving:

calories: 24 | fat: 2g | protein: 0g | carbs: 2g | fiber: 0g

Strawberry-Pistachio Salad

Prep time: 10 minutes | Cook time: 0 minutes | Serves 6

¼ cup orange juice

2 tablespoons fresh lime juice

¼ teaspoon salt, plus more to taste (optional)

⅛ teaspoon black pepper, plus more to taste

½ small red onion, chopped or sliced

2 cups cooked grains, cooled

2 cups strawberries, hulled and chopped

1½ cups cooked cannellini beans, drained and rinsed

1 (5 to 6 ounces / 142 to 170 g) container mixed baby greens

½ cup chopped cilantro

½ cup roasted, shelled pistachios, chopped

½ avocado, diced

High-quality balsamic vinegar

1. In a large bowl, combine orange juice, lime juice, ¼ teaspoon of salt (if desired), and ⅛ teaspoon of pepper. Toss the onions in the dressing, then add the grains, strawberries, and beans. Mix everything together until well combined. 2. Season with salt and pepper to taste. If desired, you can refrigerate the salad at this point for up to 1 day before serving. 3. Just before serving, add the greens and cilantro to the bowl and toss to combine. Sprinkle with pistachios, top with avocado slices, and drizzle with vinegar. Serve immediately.

Per Serving:

calories: 393 | fat: 10g | protein: 11g | carbs: 67g | fiber: 8g

Orange, Beet and Bean Salad

Prep time: 20 minutes | Cook time: 20 minutes | Serves 4

4 to 6 medium beets (about 1½ pounds / 680 g), washed and peeled

2 oranges, zested, peeled, and segmented

2 cups cooked navy beans, or 1 (15-ounce / 425-g) can, drained and rinsed

¼ cup brown rice vinegar

3 tablespoons minced dill

Salt, to taste (optional)

½ teaspoon freshly ground black pepper

4 cups mixed salad greens

4 tablespoons slivered almonds, toasted (optional)

1. Place the beets in a saucepan and cover with water. Bring to a boil, cover, reduce the heat, and simmer for 20 minutes, or until the beets are tender. Drain the beets and set aside to cool. 2. Once the beets have cooled, cut them into wedges and place them in a large bowl. Add the orange zest and segments, beans, brown rice vinegar, dill, and salt (if using) and pepper to the beets. Toss lightly to combine. 3. To serve, divide the mixed salad greens among 4 individual plates. Top with the beet salad and garnish with the toasted almonds (if using).

Per Serving:

calories: 241 | fat: 3g | protein: 12g | carbs: 45g | fiber: 17g

Chapter

8

Staples, Sauces, Dips, and Dressings

Mexican Salsa

Prep time: 5 minutes | Cook time: 0 minutes | Serves 5

3 large quartered tomatoes
¼ chopped red onion
¼ cup fresh cilantro

1 jalapeño
1 clove garlic, minced

1. Start by removing the stem, seeds, and placenta from the jalapeño pepper, then slice the flesh. 2. Place all the ingredients into a food processor or blender and blend until you achieve a smooth consistency. 3. Serve the salsa chilled, and it's ready to enhance your dishes as a delightful topping or side! 4. Store the salsa in the refrigerator, using an airtight container, and enjoy it within 3 days. If you prefer to keep it for a longer period, store it in the freezer for up to 60 days and thaw it at room temperature when needed.

Per Serving:
calories: 27 | fat: 0g | protein: 1g | carbs: 5g | fiber: 1g

Spicy Tomato and Pepper Sauce

Prep time: 10 minutes | Cook time: 10 minutes | Makes 1 cup

2 medium ripe tomatoes, halved and seeded
½ cup chopped red bell pepper
¼ cup chopped walnuts
4 medium garlic cloves

1 tablespoon ground coriander
1 teaspoon red pepper flakes
1 teaspoon ground fenugreek
½ teaspoon freshly ground black pepper

1. In a food processor, blend together the tomatoes, red bell peppers, walnuts, garlic, coriander, red pepper flakes, fenugreek, and black pepper until the mixture reaches a thick salsa-like consistency. 2. Transfer the blended mixture to a small saucepan, bring it to a boil, and then let it simmer for 3 minutes. 3. Allow the mixture to cool down, then store it in an airtight container in the refrigerator. This delicious salsa can be kept fresh for up to 5 days.

Per Serving:
calories: 35 | fat: 2g | protein: 1g | carbs: 2g | fiber: 1g

Mild Harissa Sauce

Prep time: 10 minutes | Cook time: 20 minutes | Makes 3 to 4 cups

1 large red bell pepper, seeded, cored, and cut into chunks
1 yellow onion, cut into thick rings
4 garlic cloves, peeled
1 cup no-sodium vegetable broth or water

2 tablespoons tomato paste
1 tablespoon low-sodium soy sauce or tamari
1 tablespoon Hungarian paprika
1 teaspoon ground cumin

1. Preheat your oven to 450ºF (235ºC) and line a baking sheet with parchment paper or aluminum foil. 2. Arrange the bell pepper on the prepared baking sheet, with the flesh-side facing up. Place the onion and garlic around the pepper, ensuring even spacing. 3. Roast the vegetables on the middle rack of the oven for 20 minutes. Once done, carefully transfer them to a blender. 4. To the blender, add the vegetable broth, tomato paste, soy sauce, paprika, and cumin. Blend everything until a smooth consistency is achieved. This flavorful sauce can be served either warm or cold. 5. Store any remaining sauce in an airtight container in the refrigerator, where it will stay fresh for up to 2 weeks. Alternatively, you can freeze it for up to 6 months.

Per Serving: (¼ cup)
calories: 15 | fat: 0g | protein: 1g | carbs: 3g | fiber: 1g

Pico de Gallo

Prep time: 15 minutes | Cook time: 0 minutes | Makes 2 cups

4 tomatoes, chopped small
1 medium yellow onion, minced
1 jalapeño pepper, seeded and minced
Juice of 1 lime, plus more if

needed
Pinch of salt, plus more if needed (optional)
3 tablespoons chopped fresh cilantro

1. Combine the tomatoes, onion, jalapeño, lime juice, and cilantro in a large bowl. If desired, add a pinch of salt to taste and adjust the seasoning according to your preference. 2. After preparing the salsa, transfer it to an airtight container and store it in the refrigerator. It will remain fresh and flavorful for up to 4 days. Enjoy this delicious salsa as a refreshing topping or side to your favorite dishes!

Per Serving:
calories: 19 | fat: 0g | protein: 1g | carbs: 4g | fiber: 1g

Lemon and Poppy Seed Dressing

Prep time: 5 minutes | Cook time: 10 minutes | Makes 1 cup

½ cup plant-based milk
2 tablespoons freshly squeezed lemon juice
1 tablespoon apple cider vinegar

1 tablespoon maple syrup (optional)
2 teaspoons dried poppy seeds
2 teaspoons cornstarch
½ teaspoon garlic powder

1. In a small saucepan, whisk together the milk, lemon juice, vinegar, maple syrup (if using), poppy seeds, cornstarch, and garlic powder until the cornstarch is fully dissolved. 2. Place the saucepan over medium heat and bring the dressing to a rolling boil, whisking continuously. Once it thickens, remove it from the heat. 3. Let the dressing cool before transferring it to a container suitable for refrigeration. Store in the refrigerator for up to 4 days.

Per Serving: (2 tablespoons)
calories: 18 | fat: 1g | protein: 0g | carbs: 3g | fiber: 0g

Tahini-Maple Granola

Prep time: 10 minutes | Cook time: 40 minutes | Makes 2½ cups

1 cup rolled oats
¼ cup unsweetened raisins
¼ cup pecan pieces
¼ cup walnut pieces
¼ cup sliced almonds

¼ cup vegan chocolate chips
3 tablespoons tahini
3 tablespoons pure maple syrup

1. To begin, preheat your oven to 350ºF (180ºC) and line a baking sheet with parchment paper for easy cleanup. 2. In a large bowl, combine the oats, raisins, pecans, walnuts, almonds, and chocolate chips to create a delightful mix of flavors and textures. 3. Add the tahini and maple syrup to the bowl, ensuring each ingredient is evenly coated. Mix thoroughly to ensure a delicious and cohesive blend. 4. Next, spread the granola mixture out on the prepared baking sheet, aiming for a thin layer. If you prefer a chunkier granola, leave some small clusters together. 5. Place the baking sheet in the oven and bake for 35 to 40 minutes. Remember to stir the granola halfway through the baking time to ensure even cooking. Once the granola turns crispy and golden brown, remove it from the oven. 6. After cooling, transfer the granola to an airtight container for storage. This delicious homemade granola will stay fresh for up to 1 week, ready to be enjoyed as a delightful and nutritious treat.

Per Serving:

calories: 145 | fat: 8g | protein: 4g | carbs: 3g | fiber: 2g

Creamy Nut Sauce

Prep time: 15 minutes | Cook time: 20 minutes | Makes 2 cups

1 tablespoon extra-virgin coconut oil (optional)
1 medium onion, diced
3 large garlic cloves, finely chopped
½ teaspoon fine sea salt, plus more to taste (optional)

1 tablespoon mirin
¼ cup filtered water
1 cup raw or toasted cashews, walnuts, or almonds
¾ cup boiling filtered water
1 teaspoon tamari

1. Heat the oil in a medium skillet over medium-high heat. Sauté the onion for 6 to 8 minutes until it turns golden. Stir in the garlic and add salt if using, cooking for an additional 3 to 4 minutes until the garlic becomes fragrant and golden. Pour in the mirin and ¼ cup of water, then increase the heat and bring it to a simmer, stirring to deglaze the pan for a couple of minutes. 2. Remove the skillet from the heat and transfer the mixture to an upright blender, scraping the skillet with a rubber spatula to get all the ingredients. Add the nuts, boiling water, and tamari to the blender and blend until the mixture becomes smooth, making sure to scrape the sides as needed. Adjust the seasoning with more salt if desired. You can serve the sauce immediately or allow it to cool before storing it in an airtight jar in the fridge for up to 4 days.

Per Serving: (½ cup)

calories: 188 | fat: 16g | protein: 4g | carbs: 9g | fiber: 2g

Dulse Rose Za'atar

Prep time: 5 minutes | Cook time: 0 minutes | Makes 6 tablespoons

¼ cup raw unhulled sesame seeds, toasted
2 tablespoons dried organic rose petals
1 tablespoon toasted dulse

flakes
1 teaspoon ground sumac
1 teaspoon dried thyme
½ teaspoon flaky sea salt (optional)

1. In a small jar or bowl, mix together the sesame seeds, rose petals, dulse, sumac, thyme, and salt (if desired) until well combined. Seal the jar tightly to store the seasoning, and it will stay fresh for up to 3 months.

Per Serving: (1 tablespoon)

calories: 44 | fat: 4g | protein: 1g | carbs: 2g | fiber: 1g

Spicy Tahini Dressing

Prep time: 10 minutes | Cook time: 0 minutes | Serves 8

½ cup tahini
2 tablespoons lemon juice
1 clove garlic, minced

1 tablespoon paprika powder
½ cup water

1. Combine all the ingredients in a small bowl or jar, then whisk or shake vigorously until the dressing is smooth and well-blended. 2. Serve the tahini dressing chilled, and use it as a delightful topping or a side to your dishes. 3. Keep the tahini dressing in the fridge, stored in an airtight container, and enjoy it within 4 days. Alternatively, you can freeze the dressing for up to 60 days and thaw it at room temperature when needed. Remember to shake well before using after thawing.

Per Serving:

calories: 102 | fat: 8g | protein: 4g | carbs: 2g | fiber: 1g

Pineapple Salsa

Prep time: 5 minutes | Cook time: 0 minutes | Serves 8

1 pound (454 g) fresh or thawed frozen pineapple, finely diced, and juices reserved
1 white or red onion, finely

diced
1 bunch cilantro or mint, leaves only, chopped
1 jalapeño, minced (optional)
Salt (optional)

1. In a medium bowl, mix together the pineapple along with its juice, onion, cilantro, and optional jalapeño for an added kick. Season the salsa with a pinch of salt according to your taste preferences. Serve and enjoy this delightful concoction as desired.

Per Serving:

calories: 40 | fat: 0g | protein: 0g | carbs: 10g | fiber: 1g

Zucchini Dressing

Prep time: 10 minutes | Cook time: 0 minutes | Makes 1 cup

1 medium zucchini, cut into 1-inch chunks
1 (3-inch) piece scallion, white and light green parts only, coarsely chopped
3 tablespoons freshly squeezed

lime juice
3 tablespoons extra-virgin olive oil (optional)
½ teaspoon fine sea salt, plus more to taste (optional)

1. In an upright blender, combine the zucchini, scallion, lime juice, oil, and optional salt, if desired. Start blending on a lower speed and gradually increase it as the dressing begins to come together. You can use a rubber spatula (with the blender off) to assist in moving the ingredients around or use the tamper stick if your blender has one. Taste and adjust the seasoning as needed, then scrape down the sides and blend again for a smooth consistency. 2. Enjoy the dressing immediately, or store it in a glass jar in the refrigerator for up to 3 days. Before using, give the jar a good shake as the dressing may thicken when chilled. If needed, you can thin it out with a little water to achieve the desired consistency.

Per Serving: (¼ cup)
calories: 98 | fat: 10g | protein: 0g | carbs: 2g | fiber: 0g

Coconut Butter

Prep time: 5 minutes | Cook time: 0 minutes | Makes 1 cup

4 cups unsweetened shredded dried coconut or 7 cups

unsweetened flaked dried coconut

1. Add the coconut to a food processor and process for 10 to 15 minutes, making sure to scrape down the sides every couple of minutes. Continue processing until the coconut turns into a smooth and liquid-like butter consistency. Store the coconut butter in a tightly sealed glass jar at room temperature for up to 1 month.

Per Serving: (½ cup)
calories: 280 | fat: 28g | protein: 3g | carbs: 10g | fiber: 7g

Dreamy Lemon Curd

Prep time: 10 minutes | Cook time: 5 minutes | Makes 1 cup

¼ cup maple syrup or raw agave nectar (optional)
½ cup full-fat coconut milk
⅓ cup fresh lemon juice
¼ cup room temperature coconut oil (optional)

⅛ teaspoon ground turmeric
⅛ teaspoon sea salt (optional)
2 teaspoons lemon zest
2 tablespoons arrowroot powder

1. In a medium saucepan over medium heat, combine the maple syrup, coconut milk, lemon juice, coconut oil, ground turmeric, and a pinch of sea salt if desired, along with the lemon zest. Bring the mixture to a gentle boil, whisking occasionally. 2. Once the mixture starts to bubble slightly, add the arrowroot powder to the saucepan and whisk continuously as it simmers. Continue whisking until the curd thickens to a spoon-coating consistency. Remove the saucepan from the heat. 3. Quickly transfer the lemon curd into a jar or bowl. Allow it to cool slightly at room temperature before covering the surface with a piece of plastic wrap. Store the lemon curd in the refrigerator for up to 1 week.

Per Serving: (¼ cup)
calories: 249 | fat: 20g | protein: 1g | carbs: 17g | fiber: 1g

Basil Pesto

Prep time: 10 minutes | Cook time: 0 minutes | Makes about 1½ cups

1 cup fresh basil, chopped
½ cup pine nuts, or walnuts, or sunflower seeds
1 to 2 garlic cloves, pressed
Zest and juice of 1 small
⅛ teaspoon sea salt (optional)

lemon
2 tablespoons nutritional yeast (optional)
¼ cup avocado, or 2 tablespoons tahini (optional)

1. For the sweetest flavor from fresh basil, immerse the leaves in a large bowl of ice water for approximately 5 minutes before chopping. 2. To enhance the flavor, consider lightly toasting the nuts. Place them in a small skillet over medium heat, stirring often, or bake them in the oven at 300°F (150°C) for 8 to 10 minutes. Keep a close eye on them, as small nuts and seeds can burn quickly. Alternatively, you can skip this step and proceed directly to step 3. 3. Blend all the ingredients in a food processor or blender until the mixture becomes smooth. Taste the sauce and adjust with additional salt (if using) or seasonings as needed.

Per Serving: (1 tablespoon)
calories: 89 | fat: 8g | protein: 1g | carbs: 2g | fiber: 0g

Smoky Mushrooms

Prep time: 10 minutes | Cook time: 10 minutes | Makes 2 cups

2 tablespoons soy sauce
2 tablespoons pure maple syrup
1 tablespoon liquid smoke
1 tablespoon liquid aminos

¼ teaspoon freshly ground black pepper
1 pound (454 g) cremini mushrooms, cut into ½-inch-thick slices

1. In a sauté pan or skillet, combine the soy sauce, maple syrup, liquid smoke, liquid aminos, and pepper, and whisk until well blended. 2. Add the mushrooms to the pan and cook over medium-high heat, stirring frequently, for approximately 10 minutes, or until the liquid evaporates, and the mushrooms become tender and glossy. Remove the pan from the heat. Transfer the cooked mushrooms to an airtight container and store in the refrigerator until you're ready to use them.

Per Serving:
calories: 45 | fat: 0g | protein: 3g | carbs: 8g | fiber: 1g

Balsamic Vinaigrette

Prep time: 2 minutes | Cook time: 0 minutes | Makes 1 cup

½ cup flax oil, hemp oil or extra-virgin olive oil (optional)

½ cup high-quality balsamic vinegar

2 tablespoons agave nectar (optional)

1½ teaspoons stone-ground mustard

Pinch of sea salt (optional)

1. Take a lidded glass jar and add all the ingredients in the order mentioned. Secure the lid tightly and shake the jar vigorously until everything is thoroughly mixed. 2. Use the dressing on your favorite salad right away, or if you prefer to save it for later, store it in the refrigerator. The dressing will stay fresh for about 2 weeks. If it separates over time, simply give it a good shake before using it again.

Per Serving:

calories: 270 | fat: 27g | protein: 0g | carbs: 6g | fiber: 0g

White Bean and Chickpea Hummus

Prep time: 5 minutes | Cook time: 0 minutes | Makes 3 cups

1 (15-ounce / 425-g) can chickpeas

1 (15-ounce / 425-g) can white beans

3 tablespoons freshly squeezed lemon juice

2 teaspoons garlic powder

1 teaspoon onion powder

1. After draining and rinsing the chickpeas and white beans, place them in a food processor or blender. 2. Add lemon juice, garlic powder, and onion powder to the chickpeas and beans, then process the mixture for 1 to 2 minutes until it becomes smooth and creamy. 3. Your delicious bean dip is now ready to serve! Enjoy it immediately or store it in a refrigerator-safe container for up to 5 days.

Per Serving: (¼ cup)

calories: 40 | fat: 1g | protein: 2g | carbs: 7g | fiber: 2g

Pomegranate Ginger Sauce

Prep time: 5 minutes | Cook time: 0 minutes | Serves 8

2 cups fresh or frozen pomegranate seeds

10 dried pitted plums

1 (2-inch) piece ginger

1 tablespoon black pepper

1. Place all the ingredients in a blender or food processor and blend until you achieve a smooth sauce consistency. 2. Keep the pomegranate sauce in the refrigerator, using an airtight container, and enjoy it within 3 days. Alternatively, you can store it in the freezer for up to 60 days, and when needed, thaw it at room temperature.

Per Serving:

calories: 65 | fat: 0g | protein: 1g | carbs: 15g | fiber: 3g

Nut Milk

Prep time: 5 minutes | Cook time: 0 minutes | Makes 5 cups

1 cup raw cashews or almonds, soaked overnight and drained

3 dates, pitted (optional)

1 teaspoon vanilla extract (optional)

4 cups water

1. Place the soaked nuts, and dates if using, along with vanilla if desired, and water into a blender. Blend on high for 3 to 4 minutes until the nuts are completely pulverized and the liquid becomes creamy. 2. Strain the blended mixture through a nut milk bag, cheesecloth, or a fine-mesh sieve into an airtight storage container. Refrigerate the nut milk and use it within 4 days.

Per Serving:

calories: 25 | fat: 2g | protein: 0g | carbs: 1g | fiber: 0g

Kalamata Olives and White Bean Dip

Prep time: 5 minutes | Cook time: 0 minutes | Makes 1 cup

5 jumbo Kalamata olives, pitted

1 cup cooked cannellini beans (no added salt)

1 tablespoon tahini (no added

sugar or salt)

1 garlic clove

1 tablespoon freshly squeezed lemon juice

1 tablespoon water

1. In a food processor, blend together the olives, beans, tahini, garlic, lemon juice, and water until you achieve the desired consistency.

Per Serving:

calories: 95 | fat: 3g | protein: 5g | carbs: 13g | fiber: 4g

Lemon-Tahini Sauce

Prep time: 5 minutes | Cook time: 0 minutes | Makes 1½ cups

1 cup raw tahini

½ cup purified water, plus more, if needed

Juice of 2 lemons

1 tablespoon cider vinegar

1 (1½-inch) piece fresh ginger, peeled

1 teaspoon ground coriander

1 teaspoon ground cumin

1 teaspoon fennel seeds

1 teaspoon salt (optional)

½ teaspoon freshly ground black pepper

1. In a blender or food processor, blend all the ingredients (beginning with only ½ cup of water) until smooth. Gradually add more water as needed, blending again until the dressing reaches your desired consistency. 2. Store the dressing in the refrigerator, where it will keep for 4 to 5 days.

Per Serving:

calories: 202 | fat: 15g | protein: 7g | carbs: 11g | fiber: 4g

Coconut Whipped Cream

Prep time: 5 minutes | Cook time: 0 minutes | Serves 5

1 cup coconut cream
1 teaspoon vanilla extract

2 tablespoons cocoa powder (optional)

1. In a large bowl, combine all the ingredients and mix for approximately 5 minutes using an electric mixer with beaters or a whisk. 2. Serve the whipped cream chilled and enjoy it as a topping or a side! 3. Store the whipped cream in an airtight container in the refrigerator and consume within 2 days. Alternatively, you can store the whipped cream in the freezer for a maximum of 60 days and thaw it at room temperature when needed.

Per Serving:

calories: 40 | fat: 1g | protein: 0g | carbs: 7g | fiber: 0g

Lemon Mint Tahini Cream

Prep time: 5 minutes | Cook time: 0minutes | Serves 6

½ cup tahini
3 pitted dates
½ cup water

¼ cup lemon juice
2 cloves garlic
6 leaves mint

1. Combine all the ingredients in a blender or food processor and blend until a thick and smooth sauce is formed. 2. Keep the tahini cream in the refrigerator, using an airtight container, and use within 3 days. Alternatively, you can store it in the freezer for up to 60 days, and when needed, thaw it at room temperature.

Per Serving:

calories: 141 | fat: 11g | protein: 5g | carbs: 5g | fiber: 1g

Roasted Garlic Dressing

Prep time: 5 minutes | Cook time: 30 minutes | Makes 1 cup

1 head garlic
½ cup water
1 tablespoon white balsamic vinegar

1 tablespoon freshly squeezed lemon juice
1 tablespoon maple syrup (optional)

1. Preheat the oven to 400ºF (205ºC). 2. Remove the outermost paper-like covering from the head of garlic while still leaving the bulbs intact to the base. Slice the top of the head of garlic so that the flesh inside the bulbs is just showing. 3. Double-wrap the head of garlic in parchment paper and place it on a baking sheet. Bake for 30 minutes. 4. Remove the garlic from the oven, and unwrap the parchment paper. Squeeze the head of garlic from the base to remove the caramelized cloves. They should slide out easily. 5. In a blender, combine the caramelized garlic cloves, water, vinegar, lemon juice, and maple syrup (if desired). Blend on high for 1 minute, or until the dressing has a creamy

consistency. 6. Use right away, or store in a refrigerator-safe container for up to 5 days.

Per Serving: (2 tablespoons)

calories: 13 | fat: 0g | protein: 3g | carbs: 0g | fiber: 0g

Spicy Italian Vinaigrette

Prep time: 5 minutes | Cook time: 0 minutes | Makes 1 cup

1 cup apple cider vinegar
½ cup extra-virgin olive oil (optional)
2 teaspoons maple syrup (optional)

2 teaspoons Italian seasoning
¼ teaspoon salt (optional)
¼ teaspoon black pepper
½ teaspoon garlic powder
Pinch red pepper flakes

1. In a jar, combine the apple cider vinegar, olive oil, maple syrup, Italian seasoning, salt (if using), black pepper, garlic powder, and red pepper flakes. Cover the jar and shake until all the ingredients are well blended. The dressing can be stored in the refrigerator for up to 2 weeks.

Per Serving:

calories: 131 | fat: 14g | protein: 0g | carbs: 2g | fiber: 0g

Chipotle Relish

Prep time: 15 minutes | Cook time: 0 minutes | Makes 1½ cups

½ cup diced Persian cucumber
½ cup diced red bell pepper
1 small seedless orange, peeled and diced
½ tablespoon freshly squeezed

lime juice
¼ teaspoon chipotle chili powder
¼ cup diced jicama (optional)

1. Mix the cucumber, bell pepper, orange, lime juice, chili powder, and jicama (if using) in a medium bowl. 2. Enjoy immediately with chips or refrigerate, covered, until ready to serve.

Per Serving:

calories: 17 | fat: 0g | protein: 0g | carbs: 4g | fiber: 1g

Cashew Cream

Prep time: 10 minutes | Cook time: 0 minutes | Serves 6

1 cup raw cashews, soaked in hot water for 1 hour, and drained

1 teaspoon fresh lemon juice
½ teaspoon salt (optional)
½ to 1 cup water

1. In a high-speed blender, blend the cashews, lemon juice, and salt (if desired), using a tamper to help with the blending. Gradually add water, 2 tablespoons at a time, until the desired creamy consistency is achieved. Process until the mixture becomes thick and creamy.

Per Serving:

calories: 111 | fat: 9g | protein: 4g | carbs: 6g | fiber: 1g

Savory Chia Crackers

Prep time: 20 minutes | Cook time: 20 minutes | Makes 36 crackers

½ cup oat flour
½ cup brown rice flour
¼ cup water
2 teaspoons nutritional yeast

1 teaspoon chia seeds
¼ teaspoon freshly ground black pepper
¼ teaspoon onion powder

1. Preheat your oven to 350ºF (180ºC). Cut two sheets of parchment paper to fit your baking sheet and place them on a flat surface. 2. In a food processor, combine oat flour, brown rice flour, water, nutritional yeast, chia seeds, pepper, and onion powder. Process for 1 to 2 minutes until a dough forms. The dough should be easy to pinch between your fingers without sticking. 3. Transfer the dough onto one of the parchment paper sheets. Use your clean hands to shape it into a mound, then press and flatten it into a thick square. Place the other parchment paper sheet on top and use a rolling pin to roll the dough evenly to about ⅛ inch thickness. If it's too thick, the crackers won't be crispy. Keep the second parchment sheet for later use. 4. With a knife or pizza cutter, cut the dough into 36 rectangles measuring approximately 1 by 2 inches. Lightly prick holes in the center of each cracker using a fork. Carefully transfer the parchment paper with the cut dough onto a baking sheet. 5. Bake the crackers for 10 minutes, then flip them over and bake for an additional 10 minutes until the edges turn golden brown. Once done, transfer the crackers to a wire rack to cool; they will become crisp as they cool down. 6. Store the crackers in an airtight container at room temperature for up to 1 week, or freeze them for up to 1 month.

Per Serving: (4 crackers)
calories: 61 | fat: 1g | protein: 2g | carbs: 12g | fiber: 1g

Quick Mole Sauce

Prep time: 40 minutes | Cook time: 25 minutes | Makes 4 cups

4 dried pasilla chiles
2 dried ancho chiles
Boiling water, for soaking the peppers
1 yellow onion, cut into slices
6 garlic cloves, coarsely chopped
1 tablespoon water, plus more as needed
2 tablespoons tomato paste
1 jalapeño pepper, seeded and chopped

2 ounces (57 g) vegan dark chocolate
2 tablespoons whole wheat flour
2 tablespoons cocoa powder
2 tablespoons almond butter
2 teaspoons smoked paprika
1 teaspoon ground cumin
1 teaspoon ground cinnamon
½ teaspoon dried oregano
2½ cups no-sodium vegetable broth

1. Remove the stems and seeds from the pasilla and ancho chiles. Cut them in half and place them in a medium bowl. Pour boiling water over the chiles, soak for 20 minutes, and then drain. 2. In a large nonstick sauté pan or skillet over medium-high heat, cook the onion and garlic for 5 to 7 minutes. Add water, 1 tablespoon at a time, as needed to prevent burning. The onions should be dark brown but not burnt. Stir in the tomato paste and caramelize for 2 minutes. Transfer this mixture to a high-speed blender. 3. Add the soaked chiles, jalapeño pepper, chocolate, flour, cocoa powder, almond butter, paprika, cumin, cinnamon, oregano, and vegetable broth to the blender. Purée for about 3 minutes until smooth. 4. Return the sauté pan or skillet to medium-high heat. Pour in the sauce and cover the pan. Cook until the sauce starts to bubble. Reduce the heat to low and simmer uncovered for 5 minutes, stirring occasionally. 5. Serve immediately, or store in an airtight container in the refrigerator for up to 1 week, or freeze for up to 6 months.

Per Serving: (½ cup)
calories: 114 | fat: 7g | protein: 4g | carbs: 13g | fiber: 4g

Chili Spice Blend

Prep time: 5 minutes | Cook time: 0 minutes | Makes 7½ tablespoons

¼ cup chili powder
4 teaspoons onion powder
4 teaspoons ground cumin

1 teaspoon ground coriander
1 teaspoon garlic powder
½ teaspoon cayenne

1. Mix chili powder, onion powder, cumin, coriander, garlic powder, and cayenne in an airtight container with a lid (or use a repurposed spice jar). Shake or stir well to combine.

Per Serving:
calories: 24 | fat: 1g | protein: 1g | carbs: 4g | fiber: 2g

Quick Spelt Bread

Prep time: 5 minutes | Cook time: 45 minutes | Makes 1 loaf

420 grams whole-grain spelt flour (about 3¾ cups)
1 teaspoon baking soda
1 teaspoon baking powder
1½ cups unsweetened soy

milk
2 tablespoons pure maple syrup
1 tablespoon lemon juice

1. Preheat the oven to 350ºF (180ºC). 2. Cut parchment paper to evenly line a 9-by-5-inch loaf pan by cutting inward to make the corners fit snugly. Allow the parchment paper to pass the top of the loaf pan (you will use these to remove the loaf from the pan in step 7). 3. In a large bowl, mix together the flour, baking soda, and baking powder. 4. In a medium bowl, mix together the soy milk, maple syrup, and lemon juice. 5. Add the soy milk mixture to the flour mixture, and mix well until combined, all the flour has hydrated, gluten has started to form, and the dough gets a little harder to mix. Transfer to the prepared loaf pan. 6. Bake for 45 minutes, or until the loaf is golden brown and a wooden skewer inserted into the center comes out clean. Remove from the oven. 7. Using the parchment paper as a sling, remove the bread from the loaf pan, and let cool completely before cutting.

Per Serving:
calories: 204 | fat: 2g | protein: 8g | carbs: 42g | fiber: 6g

Roasted Bell Pepper Wedges

Prep time: 5 minutes | Cook time: 25 minutes | Makes 1½ cups

2 large red bell peppers, seeded and cut into wedges	pepper
1 tablespoon freshly squeezed lemon juice	½ teaspoon garlic powder (optional)
Pinch freshly ground black	½ teaspoon cumin seeds (optional)

1. Preheat the oven to 425ºF (220ºC). 2. Place the bell pepper wedges in a large mixing bowl; then add the lemon juice, black pepper, garlic powder (if using), and cumin seeds (if using). Toss to combine. 3. Place the bell pepper wedges cut-side down on a baking sheet lined with nonstick foil or parchment paper. 4. Bake for 20 to 25 minutes until soft and lightly charred. Remove from the oven and cool for up to 20 minutes. Store in the refrigerator in an airtight container for up to 5 days.

Per Serving:

calories: 53 | fat: 1g | protein: 2g | carbs: 10g | fiber: 4g

Creamy Chimichurri Sauce

Prep time: 15 minutes | Cook time: 0 minutes | Makes 1 cup

½ cup water	2 tablespoons chopped scallions
¼ cup freshly squeezed lemon juice	2 small garlic cloves, minced
1 cup fresh cilantro	¼ teaspoon red pepper flakes
1 cup flat-leaf parsley	Pinch freshly ground black pepper
1 large ripe avocado, peeled and pitted	

1. Place the water, lemon juice, cilantro, parsley, avocado, scallions, garlic, red pepper flakes, and black pepper in a food processor. Combine until smooth. 2. Store in a Mason jar in the refrigerator for up to 3 days. Shake well before using.

Per Serving:

calories: 47 | fat: 4g | protein: 1g | carbs: 4g | fiber: 2g

Cheesy Vegetable Sauce

Prep time: 10 minutes | Cook time: 25 minutes | Makes 4 cups

1 cup raw cashews	(or almond or cashew if gluten-free)
1 russet potato, peeled and cubed	1 tablespoon arrowroot powder, cornstarch, or tapioca starch
2 carrots, cubed	
½ cup nutritional yeast	1 onion, chopped
2 tablespoons yellow (mellow) miso paste	3 garlic cloves, minced
1 teaspoon ground mustard	1 tablespoon water, plus more as needed
2 cups unsweetened oat milk	

1. In an 8-quart pot, combine the cashews, potato, and carrots.

Add enough water to cover by 2 inches. Bring to a boil over high heat, then reduce the heat to simmer. Cook for 15 minutes. 2. In a blender, combine the nutritional yeast, miso paste, ground mustard, milk, and arrowroot powder. 3. Drain the cashews, potato, and carrot. Add to the blender but don't blend yet. 4. Rinse the pot, place it over high heat, and add the onion and garlic. Cook for 3 to 4 minutes, adding water 1 tablespoon at a time to prevent burning. Transfer to the blender. Purée everything until smooth. Scrape the sides and continue blending as needed. Pour the cheese sauce into the pot and place it over medium heat. Cook, stirring, until the sauce comes to a simmer. 5. Use immediately, or refrigerate in a sealable container for up to 1 week.

Per Serving: (½ cup)

calories: 191 | fat: 10g | protein: 9g | carbs: 20g | fiber: 4g

Plant-Powered "Sour Cream"

Prep time: 5 minutes | Cook time: 0 minutes | Makes 1 cup

8 ounces (227 g) silken tofu	1 teaspoon apple cider vinegar
2 tablespoons freshly squeezed lemon juice	1 teaspoon onion powder

1. In a blender, combine the tofu, lemon juice, vinegar, and onion powder. Blend for 1 minute, or until the mixture reaches a creamy consistency. 2. Store in a refrigerator-safe container for up to 5 days.

Per Serving: (1 tablespoon)

calories: 10 | fat: 0g | protein: 1g | carbs: 0g | fiber: 0g

Veggie Tofu Pasta

Prep time: 15 minutes | Cook time: 15 minutes | Serves 8

1 pound (454 g) of your favorite pasta	spinach
3 tablespoons water	1 (14-ounce / 397-g) block extra-firm tofu, pressed
½ cup diced red, white, or yellow onion	2 teaspoons dried oregano
1½ teaspoons minced garlic	1 (25-ounce / 709-g) jar marinara sauce
3½ cups packed chopped	

1. In a medium pot over medium-high heat, cook the pasta according to the directions on the package. 2. While the pasta cooks, begin the veggie sauce. In a large pot over medium-high heat, heat the water. Add the onion and garlic and sauté for 2 to 3 minutes or until the onion is tender and translucent. Add the spinach and let it wilt. 3. Using your fingers, crumble the tofu into the pot and cook for another 5 minutes. 4. Stir in the oregano. Add the marinara sauce and cook for 5 minutes. 5. While the sauce cools, check on the pasta. When it's cooked, remove from the heat and drain. 6. Divide the pasta into bowls and top with the sauce.

Per Serving:

calories: 174 | fat: 5g | protein: 9g | carbs: 25g | fiber: 5g

Toasted Sesame Miso Dressing

Prep time: 5 minutes | Cook time: 0 minutes | Makes ⅓ cup

2 tablespoons miso
2 tablespoons apple cider vinegar or rice vinegar
1 tablespoon tamari or soy sauce
1 tablespoon water
½ teaspoon toasted sesame oil

(optional)
½-inch piece ginger, grated
½ teaspoon maple syrup
(optional)
1 tablespoon sesame seeds
(optional)

1. Put all the ingredients together in a bowl and stir together until smooth and creamy.

Per Serving:

calories: 79 | fat: 4g | protein: 3g | carbs: 6g | fiber: 1g

Strawberry Chia Jam

Prep time: 2 minutes | Cook time: 10 minutes | Makes 1½ cups

3 cups frozen strawberries
4 dates, pitted and chopped small

¼ cup water
3 tablespoons chia seeds

1. In a medium saucepan over medium-high heat, combine the strawberries, dates, and water and bring to a boil. Lower the heat to medium-low and simmer, stirring occasionally, for 10 minutes. Remove from the heat. 2. Using a potato masher, mash the mixture until the jam is smooth but with some chunks remaining. Add the chia seeds and stir well. Transfer the mixture to a small jar, cover, and let cool. The jam will thicken as it cools. The jam can be stored in the refrigerator for up to 5 days.

Per Serving:

calories: 43 | fat: 1g | protein: 1g | carbs: 8g | fiber: 3g

Easy Guacamole

Prep time: 15 minutes | Cook time: 0 minutes | Serves 4

2 large Hass avocados, peeled, stoned and halved
¼ cup lemon juice
1 red onion, minced
1 clove garlic, minced

½ cup chopped fresh cilantro
Optional Toppings:
Jalapeño slices
Sweet corn

1. Put all ingredients in a food processor and blend until smooth. Alternatively, for a chunky guacamole, mash the ingredients in a medium-sized bowl with a fork. 2. Serve right away with the optional toppings and enjoy! 3. Store the guacamole in an airtight container in the fridge and consume within 2 days. Alternatively, store in the freezer for a maximum of 90 days, and thaw at room temperature before serving.

Per Serving:

calories: 181 | fat: 14g | protein: 2g | carbs: 11g | fiber: 6g

Super-Simple Guacamole

Prep time: 10 minutes | Cook time: 0 minutes | Makes 1½ cups

2 avocados, peeled and pitted
Juice of ½ lime
Pinch of salt (optional)
2 tablespoons chopped fresh

cilantro
1 tomato, chopped
1 scallion, white and green parts, chopped

1. In a medium bowl, combine the avocados, lime juice, and salt (if using) and mash together until it reaches your desired consistency. Add the cilantro, tomato, and scallion and mix well. Serve immediately.

Per Serving:

calories: 113 | fat: 10g | protein: 2g | carbs: 7g | fiber: 5g

Hemp Heart "Parmesan"

Prep time: 5 minutes | Cook time: 0 minutes | Makes 1 cup

½ cup plus 2 tablespoons hemp hearts

½ cup nutritional yeast
¼ teaspoon garlic powder

1. In a small container with a lid, combine the hemp hearts, nutritional yeast, and garlic powder. Shake or stir. Store in the refrigerator for up to 1 month.

Per Serving:

calories: 54 | fat: 3g | protein: 4g | carbs: 2g | fiber: 2g

Raw Date Paste

Prep time: 10 minutes | Cook time: 0 minutes | Makes 2½ cups

1 cup Medjool dates, pitted and chopped

1½ cups water

1. In a blender, combine the dates and water and blend until smooth. Store in an airtight container in the refrigerator for up to 7 days.

Per Serving:

calories: 21 | fat: 0g | protein: 0g | carbs: 5g | fiber: 1g

Creamy Balsamic Dressing

Prep time: 10 minutes | Cook time: 0 minutes | Makes ¾ cup

¼ cup tahini
¼ cup balsamic vinegar
¼ cup fresh basil, minced
⅛ cup water
1 tablespoon maple syrup

(optional)
1 garlic clove, pressed
Pinch sea salt (optional)
Pinch freshly ground black pepper (optional)

1. Put all the ingredients in a blender or food processor and blend until smooth. You could whisk this together without a blender, if you mince the basil very fine.

Per Serving: (1 tablespoon)

calories: 157 | fat: 10g | protein: 3g | carbs: 12g | fiber: 2g

BBQ Sauce

Prep time: 5 minutes | Cook time: 0 minutes | Serves 16

2 cups canned or fresh tomato cubes

5 pitted dates

3 tablespoons smoked paprika

2 tablespoons garlic powder

2 tablespoons onion powder

1. Add all the ingredients to a blender or food processor and blend to form a smooth sauce. 2. Store the BBQ sauce in the fridge, using an airtight container, and consume within 3 days. Alternatively, store it in the freezer for a maximum of 60 days and thaw at room temperature.

Per Serving:

calories: 11 | fat: 0g | protein: 0g | carbs: 2g | fiber: 0g

Sugar-Free Ketchup

Prep time: 5 minutes | Cook time: 20 minutes | Makes 2 cups

1 (15-ounce / 425-g) can tomato sauce

3 tablespoons apple cider vinegar

3 tablespoons maple syrup (optional)

½ teaspoon salt (optional)

1 teaspoon onion powder

1 teaspoon garlic powder

2 tablespoons tomato paste

1. In a medium saucepan, combine the tomato sauce, vinegar, maple syrup, salt (if using), onion powder, garlic powder, and tomato paste and bring to a boil over medium-high heat. 2. Lower the heat to medium-low and simmer, stirring often, for 20 minutes. Let cool and store in an airtight container in the refrigerator for up to 10 days.

Per Serving:

calories: 20 | fat: 0g | protein: 0g | carbs: 5g | fiber: 1g

Chapter 9

Desserts

Stone Fruit Chia Pudding

Prep time: 10 minutes | Cook time: 10 minutes | Makes 3 cups

1¼ pounds (567 g) stone fruit, halved, pitted, and cut into 1-inch dice
¾ cup freshly squeezed orange juice or ½ cup filtered water
Pinch of fine sea salt
(optional)
½ cup raw cashews or macadamia nuts
2 tablespoons coconut butter
1 teaspoon vanilla extract
¼ cup chia seeds

1. In a medium pot, combine the fruit, orange juice, and salt (if using). Bring the mixture to a boil over high heat. Cover the pot, reduce the heat to low, and let it simmer for 8 to 10 minutes until the fruit is fully cooked. Remove from the heat and allow it to cool slightly. 2. Transfer the cooked fruit mixture to an upright blender. Add the cashews, coconut butter, and vanilla, then blend until it becomes smooth and creamy. Pour the mixture into a wide-mouthed quart jar or a medium bowl. Add the chia seeds and whisk thoroughly, ensuring there are no clumps of seeds. Let it sit for a few minutes, then whisk again. Keep the whisk in place and refrigerate the pudding for at least 1 hour, or until it is fully chilled, whisking occasionally to evenly distribute the chia seeds and speed up the cooling process. The pudding will thicken further overnight; if it becomes too thick, stir in a splash of water or nut milk. Store the pudding in an airtight glass jar or container in the fridge for up to 5 days.

Per Serving: (½ cup)

calories: 199 | fat: 15g | protein: 3g | carbs: 17g | fiber: 5g

Nutty Raspberry Thumbprint Cookies

Prep time: 5 minutes | Cook time: 12 minutes | Makes 18 cookies

⅓ cup unsweetened applesauce
¼ cup almond butter
½ cup date sugar (optional)
1 tablespoon ground flaxseeds
2 teaspoons pure vanilla extract
1¾ cups oat flour
½ teaspoon baking soda
½ teaspoon salt (optional)
½ cup rolled oats
½ cup finely chopped walnuts
⅓ cup raspberry jam, or to taste

1. Preheat your oven to 350ºF (180ºC) and line a large baking sheet with parchment paper or a Silpat baking mat. 2. In a large mixing bowl, use a sturdy fork to beat together the applesauce, almond butter, date sugar (if using), and flaxseeds until relatively smooth. Add the vanilla and mix well. 3. Add the oat flour, baking soda, and salt (if using), and thoroughly combine the ingredients. Fold in the oats and walnuts. 4. Take about 2 tablespoons of the batter and roll it into a ball, placing it on the prepared baking sheet. Continue with the remaining batter, making 18 balls in total. Since they don't spread much during baking, they can all fit on one sheet. Moisten your thumb or index finger and create a deep indent in the center of each cookie. Fill each indentation with about ½ teaspoon of jam. 5. Bake the cookies for 10 to 12 minutes, or until the bottoms are golden brown. 6. Once out of the oven, let the cookies cool on the sheets for 5 minutes, then transfer them to a cooling rack to cool completely.

Per Serving:

calories: 114 | fat: 5g | protein: 3g | carbs: 14g | fiber: 2g

Superfood Caramels

Prep time: 10 minutes | Cook time: 10 minutes | Makes 12 pieces

12 to 14 Medjool dates, pitted
½ cup raw tahini
1 tablespoon lucuma powder
1 teaspoon Himalayan pink
salt, plus more for sprinkling (optional)
1 (80-g) bar dark organic chocolate

1. In a food processor, blend dates, tahini, lucuma, and salt (if using) until well mixed, forming a cohesive ball in the processor. 2. Transfer the "caramel" mixture onto a piece of parchment paper and cover with another piece. Use a rolling pin to flatten it into a square or rectangular shape about ½ inch thick. Freeze for at least 20 minutes until firm enough to cut. 3. While the caramel is chilling in the freezer, prepare a large plate lined with parchment paper near your stovetop. 4. In a double boiler or a heat-safe medium bowl over a saucepan of boiling water, gently melt the chocolate over low heat. Stir occasionally to avoid overcooking the chocolate. Once fully melted, lower the heat or turn it off. 5. Retrieve the chilled caramels from the freezer and place them on a cutting board. Cut them into square or rectangular pieces of average caramel size. 6. Using a spoon, carefully dip each caramel piece into the melted chocolate, ensuring it is fully covered. Place the coated caramels on the parchment-lined plate. 7. Optionally, sprinkle Himalayan pink salt over the coated caramels before the chocolate hardens. Proceed with the remaining pieces and then place the plate in the freezer. 8. Allow the chocolate to harden for at least 30 minutes. Enjoy some of the chocolate-covered caramels, and store the rest in an airtight container in the freezer.

Per Serving:

calories: 163 | fat: 7g | protein: 3g | carbs: 23g | fiber: 3g

Blueberry-Lime Sorbet

Prep time: 5 minutes | Cook time: 0 minutes | Serves 6

1 cup frozen blueberries
1 cup fresh blueberries
3 to 6 ice cubes
¼ cup unsweetened raisins
2 tablespoons lime juice

1. Using a high-efficiency blender, blend together the frozen blueberries, fresh blueberries, ice, raisins, and lime juice for about 30 seconds until you achieve a smooth consistency. You might need to use the tamping tool to push the frozen ingredients toward the blades. Serve the delicious blueberry concoction immediately.

Per Serving:

calories: 116 | fat: 1g | protein: 2g | carbs: 30g | fiber: 4g

Zesty Orange-Cranberry Energy Bites

Prep time: 10 minutes | Cook time: 0 minutes | Makes 12 bites

2 tablespoons almond butter, or cashew or sunflower seed butter

2 tablespoons maple syrup or brown rice syrup (optional)

¾ cup cooked quinoa

¼ cup sesame seeds, toasted

1 tablespoon chia seeds

½ teaspoon almond extract or vanilla extract

Zest of 1 orange

1 tablespoon dried cranberries

¼ cup ground almonds

1. Combine the nut or seed butter with syrup (if using) in a medium bowl, mixing until smooth and creamy. 2. Add the remaining ingredients and stir until the mixture forms a cohesive ball. 3. Shape the mixture into 12 balls and place them on a baking sheet lined with parchment or waxed paper. Refrigerate for about 15 minutes to set.

Per Serving: (1 bite)

calories: 71 | fat: 4g | protein: 2g | carbs: 6g | fiber: 1g

Caramel-Coconut Frosted Brownies

Prep time: 10 minutes | Cook time: 25 minutes | Makes 12 brownies

Brownies:

1 (15-ounce / 425-g) can black beans, drained and rinsed

½ cup rolled oats

6 tablespoons pure maple syrup

⅓ cup cocoa powder

⅓ cup unsweetened applesauce

2 tablespoons unsalted, unsweetened almond butter

1 teaspoon vanilla extract

Pinch ground cinnamon

Frosting:

1 cup pitted dates

6 tablespoons unsweetened plant-based milk

2 tablespoons nutritional yeast

¼ teaspoon vanilla extract

⅛ teaspoon red miso paste

¼ cup chopped pecans

3 tablespoons unsweetened coconut flakes

To Make the Brownies: 1. Preheat your oven to 350ºF (180ºC) and line a 12-cup cupcake tin with liners. 2. In a food processor, blend the beans, oats, maple syrup, cocoa powder, applesauce, almond butter, vanilla, and cinnamon until smooth. 3. Spoon about 2 tablespoons of the mixture into each cupcake liner, and then evenly divide the remaining mixture among the cups. 4. Bake for 20 to 22 minutes or until the tops are crispy and a toothpick inserted into the center of a cupcake comes out mostly clean. Remove from the oven, take the brownies out of the tin, and place them on a wire rack to cool for about 5 minutes. To Make the Frosting: 5. While the brownies are cooling, combine the dates, milk, nutritional yeast, vanilla, and miso in a food processor. Process until the mixture is mostly smooth. 6. Pulse in the pecans and coconut until well mixed, leaving some texture. 7. Spread about 1 heaping tablespoon of the frosting onto each brownie and serve.

Per Serving:

calories: 235 | fat: 11g | protein: 10g | carbs: 30g | fiber: 12g

Nice Cream

Prep time: 10 minutes | Cook time: 0 minutes | Serves 2

2 cups frozen banana chunks

1 tablespoon soy milk

½ teaspoon vanilla extract

1. Place the bananas in a food processor and process them until they become crumbly. 2. Add the soy milk and vanilla to the processor, and continue processing until the mixture starts to come together, resembling soft-serve ice cream. Serve right away.

Per Serving:

calories: 112 | fat: 1g | protein: 2g | carbs: 28g | fiber: 3g

Creamy Dreamy Brown Rice Pudding

Prep time: 5 minutes | Cook time: 2 to 3 hours | Serves 6 to 8

Nonstick cooking spray (optional)

1 cup brown rice

4 cups unsweetened vanilla plant-based milk

¼ cup maple syrup or date

syrup (optional)

2 teaspoons ground cinnamon

2 teaspoons vanilla extract

½ cup raisins, for topping (optional)

1. Prepare the slow cooker by either coating the inside with cooking spray or lining it with a slow cooker liner. 2. Add the rice, milk, and optionally the syrup, cinnamon, and vanilla to the slow cooker, and mix everything together. 3. Cover the slow cooker and cook the mixture on High for 2 to 3 hours or on Low for 3 to 4 hours. Stir the pudding when there's about an hour left to check for desired doneness and texture. For a creamier pudding, cook it longer; for a firmer texture, cook it shorter. Just before serving, add the raisins if desired for added sweetness and texture. Enjoy!

Per Serving:

calories: 157 | fat: 3g | protein: 3g | carbs: 34g | fiber: 3g

Baked Apples

Prep time: 5 minutes | Cook time: 20 minutes | Serves 4

3 green apples, cored and evenly sliced

¼ cup apple juice

1½ teaspoons cinnamon

Optional Toppings:

1 tablespoon chopped pecans

1. Begin by preheating your oven to 365ºF (185ºC). 2. Take a 9 × 9-inch baking pan and spread the apple slices in a single layer across the bottom. 3. Drizzle the apple juice over the apples and sprinkle the cinnamon on top, ensuring a delightful flavor throughout. 4. Cover the baking pan with aluminum foil to lock in moisture, and bake for 15 to 18 minutes until the apples become a lighter color and achieve a soft, tender texture.

Per Serving:

calories: 81 | fat: 0g | protein: 1g | carbs: 21g | fiber: 4g

Chocolate Lava Mug Cake

Prep time: 10 minutes | Cook time: 5 minutes | Makes 1 cake

¼ cup almond milk
1 tablespoon cooked, unsweetened adzuki or black beans, mashed well
1 tablespoon sugar (optional)
½ teaspoon vanilla extract
2 tablespoons unsweetened

cocoa powder
¼ cup whole wheat pastry flour
⅛ teaspoon salt (optional)
¼ teaspoon baking powder
2 tablespoons mini chocolate chips (optional)

1. In a mug, mix together the almond milk, beans, sugar, and vanilla. Stir in the cocoa, flour, and optionally the salt and baking powder, until the mixture is just combined. Drop the chocolate chips into the center of the batter. 2. Microwave the mug cake for about 90 seconds, until the edges are set but the center remains soft. Allow it to sit for 5 minutes, then enjoy your delicious treat!

Per Serving:

calories: 209 | fat: 3g | protein: 7g | carbs: 45g | fiber: 8g

Vanilla Corn Cake with Roasted Strawberries

Prep time: 20 minutes | Cook time: 50 minutes | Makes 1 cake

¾ cup full-fat coconut milk
1 teaspoon fresh lemon juice
1 cup cornmeal
1 cup whole spelt flour
1 teaspoon lemon zest
1 tablespoon aluminum-free baking powder
¼ teaspoon baking soda
1 teaspoon fine sea salt (optional)

½ teaspoon ground turmeric (optional)
½ cup plus 2 tablespoons pure maple syrup (optional)
½ cup coconut oil, plus extra to grease pan
1 teaspoon vanilla bean paste or pure vanilla extract
4 cups whole strawberries

1. Preheat your oven to 350ºF (180ºC) and lightly grease a 9-inch round cake pan with coconut oil. Cut a circle of parchment paper to fit the bottom of the pan and place it inside. Lightly grease the parchment, and set it aside. 2. In a medium bowl, whisk together the coconut milk and lemon juice. Let the mixture sit for 5 minutes to allow the milk to slightly curdle. 3. In a large bowl, whisk together the cornmeal, spelt flour, lemon zest, baking powder, baking soda, sea salt, and turmeric (if using). 4. Create a well in the center of the cornmeal mixture and add the maple syrup, oil (if using), vanilla, and the coconut milk mixture. Gently mix with a spatula until the batter becomes smooth and well combined, being careful not to overmix. 5. Scrape the batter into the prepared cake pan and place it in the oven. Bake the cake for 25 to 28 minutes or until the top turns golden and a toothpick inserted into the center comes out clean. Allow the cake to cool completely. Preheat your oven to 400ºF (205ºC). 6. Cut the strawberries into halves or quarters (depending on their size) and arrange them on a baking sheet lined with parchment paper.

Roast the strawberries in the oven until they become juicy and jammy, which should take about 20 minutes. 7. To serve, slice the corn cake and top each piece with a few roasted strawberries. Enjoy this delightful treat!

Per Serving: (⅛ cake)

calories: 394 | fat: 20g | protein: 6g | carbs: 52g | fiber: 5g

Molasses-Ginger Oat Cookie Balls

Prep time: 10 minutes | Cook time: 15 minutes | Makes 1 dozen cookies

1 cup pitted dates
3 tablespoons unsalted, unsweetened almond butter
2 tablespoons blackstrap molasses
1 teaspoon vanilla extract
1 cup oat flour

¼ cup rolled oats
½ teaspoon baking powder
1 teaspoon ground ginger
½ teaspoon ground cinnamon
⅛ teaspoon ground nutmeg
⅛ teaspoon ground cardamom

1. Preheat your oven to 350ºF (180ºC) and line a baking sheet with parchment paper.
2. Using a food processor, blend the dates and almond butter until they form a smooth, creamy paste. Transfer this mixture to a large bowl. 3. Stir in the molasses and vanilla into the bowl with the date and almond butter mixture. 4. In a separate medium bowl, thoroughly combine the flour, oats, baking powder, ginger, cinnamon, nutmeg, and cardamom. 5. Gently fold the flour mixture into the molasses mixture until well combined. 6. Using about 1 tablespoon of dough per cookie, drop 12 dough balls onto the prepared baking sheet, spacing them about 1 inch apart. 7. Bake for 12 to 15 minutes, until the edges turn golden brown, and the cookies feel slightly firm to the touch. Remove the cookies from the oven. Enjoy your delightful treats!

Per Serving:

calories: 275 | fat: 10g | protein: 6g | carbs: 44g | fiber: 6g

Sweet Red Beans

Prep time: 10 minutes | Cook time: 30 minutes | Serves 6

1 cup adzuki beans, soaked overnight, drained and rinsed
¼ teaspoon vanilla bean powder or ½ teaspoon vanilla extract

2 cup water
3 tablespoons maple syrup (optional)
⅛ teaspoon salt (optional)

1. Place the beans and vanilla in a medium saucepan. Add the water and bring to a boil. Cover and continue to boil until tender, about 30 minutes. (If your beans are still tough and need more water to cook, add it sparingly; you don't want soupy beans.) 2. Remove from the heat and stir in the sugar and salt, if desired. Let cool before serving.

Per Serving:

calories: 76 | fat: 0g | protein: 3g | carbs: 16g | fiber: 3g

Triple Chocolate Icebox Cake

Prep time: 10 minutes | Cook time: 0 minutes | Makes 1 cake

1 (13½-ounce / 383-g) can light or full-fat coconut milk
¼ cup unsweetened cocoa powder
2 tablespoons maple syrup (optional)

1 (13-ounce / 369-g) package double chocolate sandwich cookies
2 tablespoons mini chocolate chips (optional)

1. In a blender, blend together the coconut milk, cocoa powder, and maple syrup (if using) until the mixture is smooth and creamy. 2. Take a 9 × 5-inch loaf pan (preferably glass) and create a single layer of cookies at the bottom. Spread approximately a quarter of the filling on top. Repeat this process with the remaining cookies and filling to create layers. Cover the pan and refrigerate for at least 1 hour or overnight to set. 3. When ready to serve, use a butter knife to gently loosen the edges and carefully invert the dessert onto a plate. For an extra touch, sprinkle mini chocolate chips on top before serving, if desired.

Per Serving: (¼ cake)
calories: 272 | fat: 4g | protein: 24g | carbs: 17g | fiber: 4g

Golden Banana Bread

Prep time: 5 minutes | Cook time: 50 minutes | Serves 10

Coconut oil, for pan (optional)
Dry Ingredients:
2 cups almond meal (ground almonds)
1 cup certified gluten-free rolled oats
¼ cup ground flaxseeds
2 tablespoons whole psyllium husk
2 teaspoons ground cinnamon
½ teaspoon ground turmeric
½ teaspoon Himalayan pink salt (optional)
Wet Ingredients:

4 very ripe bananas
¼ cup date syrup (optional)
3 tablespoons raw agave nectar (optional)
1 teaspoon vanilla bean powder
Suggested Add-Ins (optional):
½ cup raisins
½ cup chopped walnuts
1 cup diced banana
Garnish (optional):
1 very ripe banana, sliced
¼ cup chopped dark vegan chocolate

1. Preheat your oven to 375ºF (190ºC) and grease the bottom and sides of an 8½ × 4½-inch loaf pan with coconut oil (if desired). 2. Prepare the dry ingredients: In a high-speed blender or food processor, combine all the dry ingredients and pulse until well mixed, leaving some oats whole. Set this mixture aside. 3. Prepare the wet ingredients: Take four ripe bananas and mash them until smooth in a large bowl using a fork. Add date syrup, agave (if using), and vanilla bean powder, and mix everything thoroughly. Now, add the dry mixture to the wet ingredients and blend until well combined. The mixture should take on a dough-like texture due to the ground flaxseeds and psyllium husk. 4. Personalize your loaf by adding your choice of mix-ins to the dough. 5. Scoop the dough mixture into the prepared pan and press it firmly to remove any air pockets. If desired, you can slice a ripe banana into four pieces lengthwise and place them side by side on top of the loaf. 6. Bake the loaf for about 50 minutes. To ensure it's thoroughly baked, insert a toothpick into the center – it should come out clean. 7. Once baked, remove the loaf from the oven and let it cool in the pan. For a delightful finishing touch, garnish with banana slices or chocolate (if desired). Enjoy your scrumptious creation!

Per Serving:
calories: 284 | fat: 15g | protein: 8g | carbs: 39g | fiber: 7g

Almond Truffles with Toasted Coconut

Prep time: 10 minutes | Cook time: 0 minutes | Makes 8

¼ cup almond meal
¼ cup toasted shredded coconut

2 tablespoons cacao powder
2 tablespoons maple syrup (optional)

1. In a medium bowl, mix together the almond meal, coconut, cacao, and maple syrup (if desired) until you achieve a smooth consistency. You can use a fork or mix it by hand. 2. Take about 1 tablespoon of the dough and roll it into a small ball. Continue this process with the remaining dough until you have 8 truffles. 3. You can enjoy the truffles right away, or for a slightly firmer texture, refrigerate them for 10 to 20 minutes before serving. Savor these delightful treats!

Per Serving:
calories: 42 | fat: 3g | protein: 1g | carbs: 5g | fiber: 1g

Chocolate Chip Oat Cookies

Prep time: 10 minutes | Cook time: 15 minutes | Makes 20 cookies

¾ cup oat flour
¾ cup rolled oats
2 tablespoons hemp hearts or chia seeds
¼ cup pure maple syrup
3 tablespoons unsalted, unsweetened almond butter or

other nut butter
2 tablespoons tahini
1 tablespoon unsweetened soy milk
1 teaspoon vanilla extract
¼ cup vegan mini chocolate chips

1. Preheat the oven to 350ºF (180ºC). Line a baking sheet with parchment paper. 2. In a large bowl, mix together the flour, oats, and hemp hearts. 3. Add the maple syrup, almond butter, tahini, soy milk, and vanilla. Mix thoroughly. 4. Stir in the chocolate chips. 5. Drop 20 (1-tablespoon) dough balls, evenly spaced, onto the prepared baking sheet, and gently press down to create flat cookies. 6. Transfer the baking sheet to the oven, and bake for 12 minutes, or until the edges are golden brown. Remove from the oven. Let the cookies cool on the baking sheet for 10 minutes, then move to a wire rack to cool completely. Store in an airtight container.

Per Serving:
calories: 151 | fat: 8g | protein: 5g | carbs: 16g | fiber: 3g

Chocolate-Covered Strawberries

Prep time: 10 minutes | Cook time: 1 minute | Serves 20 strawberries

1 (12-ounce / 340-g) bag vegan semisweet chocolate chips

1 (1-pound / 454-g) carton strawberries, washed and dried

1. Prepare a baking sheet by lining it with parchment paper. 2. Take a medium-sized microwave-safe bowl and heat the chocolate chips in 30-second intervals, stirring after each session, until the chocolate turns smooth and creamy. 3. Hold each strawberry by its stem and dip it into the melted chocolate, ensuring a delectable coating. Place the chocolate-dipped strawberries onto the parchment-lined baking sheet. Continue this process until all the strawberries are coated. 4. Transfer the baking sheet to the refrigerator and let it chill for approximately 20 to 25 minutes, allowing the chocolate to firm up. For optimal taste and texture, store these delightful treats in the fridge until it's time to serve.

Per Serving: (5 strawberries)

calories: 439 | fat: 25g | protein: 4g | carbs: 62g | fiber: 7g

Poached Pears

Prep time: 10 minutes | Cook time: 20 minutes | Serves 2 to 4

2 cups apple juice
¼ cup unsweetened raisins
½ teaspoon ground cinnamon

½ teaspoon vanilla extract
4 to 6 slightly ripe Bosc pears, peeled

1. In a large flat-bottomed pan, combine the apple juice, raisins, cinnamon, and vanilla. Place the pan over high heat. 2. Quarter the pears and use a melon baller or paring knife to remove the seeds. 3. Add the pears to the liquid and bring it to a boil. Reduce the heat to medium, partially cover the pan, and simmer for about 20 minutes until the pears become tender (you can easily slide a paring knife into them). Once done, remove from the heat. 4. Serve the beautifully poached pears with a delightful drizzle of the cooking liquid.

Per Serving:

calories: 343 | fat: 2g | protein: 0g | carbs: 89g | fiber: 4g

Salted Caramel Bites

Prep time: 5 minutes | Cook time: 0 minutes | Makes 18 bites

1 cup raw cashews
1 cup soft and sticky Medjool dates, pitted

½ cup tahini
1 teaspoon pure vanilla extract
¼ teaspoon sea salt (optional)

1. In a food processor with the chopping blade, pulse the cashews until they are finely chopped. Add the dates and process until a thick, sticky paste forms. Make sure to scrape down the sides of the bowl as needed. 2. Add the tahini, vanilla, and salt (if using) to the mixture and process until it forms a dough. If the mixture is not holding together well, you can add a tiny bit of water and process again. 3. Take a heaping teaspoon of the dough and roll it into a ball about 1½ inches in diameter. Continue this process to form approximately 18 balls. Freeze them on a baking sheet until firm, then transfer to an airtight container and store at room temperature for up to 5 days.

Per Serving:

calories: 112 | fat: 6g | protein: 2g | carbs: 11g | fiber: 1g

Chocolate Dirt Yogurt Cup

Prep time: 15 minutes | Cook time: 0 minutes | Serves 2

¼ cup vegan chocolate chips
3 tablespoons sliced almonds
3 teaspoons cocoa powder, divided
2 teaspoons plus 2 tablespoons

pure maple syrup, divided
1 cup nondairy vegan yogurt
2 tablespoons tahini
½ teaspoon vanilla extract
½ cup blueberries

1. In a food processor, combine the chocolate chips, almonds, 2 teaspoons of cocoa powder, and 2 teaspoons of maple syrup. Process until crumbly, like dirt. 2. In a medium bowl, mix together the yogurt, remaining 2 tablespoons of maple syrup, the tahini, vanilla, and remaining 1 teaspoon of cocoa powder. 3. In a small serving dish, layer 1 tablespoon of the chocolate "dirt" mixture, ¼ cup of blueberries, and a layer of chocolate yogurt. Repeat with a second layer, and top with the remaining "dirt mixture." Refrigerate until ready to serve.

Per Serving:

calories: 299 | fat: 17g | protein: 15g | carbs: 50g | fiber: 6g

Sweet Potato Spice Cake

Prep time: 5 minutes | Cook time: 45 minutes | Serves 6

1 sweet potato, cooked and peeled
½ cup unsweetened applesauce
½ cup plant-based milk
¼ cup maple syrup (optional)

1 teaspoon vanilla extract
2 cups whole-wheat flour
½ teaspoon baking soda
½ teaspoon ground cinnamon
¼ teaspoon ground ginger

1. Preheat the oven to 350°F (180°C). 2. In a large mixing bowl, use a fork or potato masher to mash the sweet potato. 3. Mix in the applesauce, milk, maple syrup (if desired), and vanilla. 4. Stir in the flour, baking soda, cinnamon, and ginger until the dry ingredients have been thoroughly combined with the wet ingredients. 5. Pour the batter into a nonstick baking dish or one lined with parchment paper. Bake for 45 minutes, or until you can stick a knife into the middle of the cake and it comes out clean. 6. Cool, slice, and serve.

Per Serving:

calories: 238 | fat: 1g | protein:5 g | carbs: 52g | fiber: 2g

Pumpkin Pie Oatmeal Parfaits

Prep time: 20 minutes | Cook time: 7 hours | Makes 6 parfaits

Nonstick cooking spray (optional)
1 (15-ounce / 425-g) can coconut cream
2 cups steel-cut oats
4 cups water
1 (15-ounce / 425-g) can pumpkin purée
2 teaspoons ground cinnamon, divided

1 teaspoon ground nutmeg, divided
½ teaspoon ground cloves
½ teaspoon ground ginger
½ cup maple syrup, plus 3 to 4 tablespoons more for serving (optional)
1½ cups rolled oats
¾ cup chopped pecans (optional)

1. Prepare the slow cooker by either coating the inside with cooking spray or using a slow cooker liner. Place the unopened can of coconut cream in the refrigerator to chill. 2. In the slow cooker, combine the steel-cut oats, water, pumpkin purée, 1 teaspoon of cinnamon, ½ teaspoon of nutmeg, cloves, ginger, and maple syrup (if using). Stir everything together until well combined. Cover the slow cooker and cook on Low for 7 hours. Once cooked, give it a good stir. 3. While the steel-cut oats cook, preheat your oven to 350ºF (180ºC). On a baking sheet lined with parchment paper, spread out the rolled oats and pecans (if using) in a single layer. Sprinkle them with the remaining 1 teaspoon of cinnamon and ½ teaspoon of nutmeg. Bake for 10 minutes. Set the crumble aside to cool and store it loosely covered at room temperature until the steel-cut oats are done cooking. 4. Just before serving, take the chilled coconut cream and pour it into a medium bowl. Using an electric beater, whip the cream for about 1 minute until it thickens. 5. For each parfait, layer 3 tablespoons of the crumble, about ½ teaspoon of maple syrup (if using), 2 to 3 tablespoons of the warm pumpkin oatmeal, and approximately 2 tablespoons of the whipped cream. Continue layering in this order until your glass is full, finishing with the whipped cream on top, a sprinkle of the crumble, and a tiny drizzle of maple syrup.

Per Serving:
calories: 497 | fat: 18g | protein: 11g | carbs: 76g | fiber: 10g

Berry Chia Pudding

Prep time: 5 minutes | Cook time: 5 minutes | Makes 3 cups

4 cups fresh or frozen berries
1½ cups freshly squeezed orange juice
Pinch of fine sea salt (optional)

½ cup raw cashews or macadamia nuts
2 tablespoons coconut butter
2 teaspoons vanilla extract
6 tablespoons chia seeds

1. Combine the berries, orange juice, and salt, if using, in a medium pot and bring to a boil over high heat. Cover, reduce the heat to low, and simmer for 5 minutes, or until the berries have softened and released their juices. Remove from the heat and allow to cool slightly. 2. Transfer the mixture to an upright blender, add the cashews, coconut butter, and vanilla, and blend until completely smooth. Pour into a widemouthed quart jar or a medium bowl, add the chia seeds, and whisk thoroughly, making sure there are no clumps of seeds hiding anywhere. Allow to sit for a few minutes and then whisk again. Leave the whisk in place and refrigerate for at least 1 hour, or until completely chilled, whisking every now and then to distribute the chia seeds evenly and to help cool the pudding quickly. The pudding will thicken further overnight; if it gets too thick, stir in a splash of water or nut milk. Store the pudding in an airtight glass jar or other container in the fridge for up to 5 days.

Per Serving: (½ cup)
calories: 211 | fat: 14g | protein: 2g | carbs: 21g | fiber: 5g

Cherry Chocolate Bark

Prep time: 5 minutes | Cook time: 0 minutes | Serves 8

1 cup vegan semisweet chocolate chips
1 cup sliced almonds
1 cup dried tart cherries,

chopped
½ teaspoon flaky sea salt, for sprinkling (optional)

1. Line a rimmed baking sheet with parchment paper and place in the fridge or freezer to get very cold. 2. In a heatproof glass bowl set over a pan of simmering water, melt the chocolate, stirring occasionally. Be careful not to let water droplets get into the bowl or the chocolate will seize. 3. Remove the bowl from the heat (or the microwave) when some pieces of unmelted chocolate still remain. Stir well until the remaining chocolate melts, but do not stir too vigorously or air bubbles will form. 4. Pour the melted chocolate onto the chilled prepared pan and use a thin spatula to spread it evenly almost to the edges of the pan. Immediately sprinkle the almonds and cherries evenly over the chocolate, followed by a sprinkling of salt (if using). Refrigerate until firm. 5. Break the bark into pieces and store in an airtight container in the refrigerator for up to 1 week.

Per Serving:
calories: 189 | fat: 12g | protein: 3g | carbs: 17g | fiber: 3g

Homemade Caramel with Dates and Peanut Butter

Prep time: 20 minutes | Cook time: 0 minutes | Serves 8

5 Medjool dates, pitted
1 tablespoon peanut butter (no sugar or salt added)

2 teaspoons molasses
8 small apples, cored and sliced into 8 wedges

1. Soak the dates in hot water for 10 minutes. 2. Drain the dates and place them in a food processor. Add the peanut butter and molasses and blend to a smooth consistency. 3. Refrigerate the caramel mixture for 20 to 30 minutes. 4. Serve 1 tablespoon of the caramel mixture with each sliced apple. Refrigerate the remaining caramel mixture for up to 5 days.

Per Serving:
calories: 145 | fat: 1g | protein: 1g | carbs: 36g | fiber: 6g

Peanut Butter Cookies

Prep time: 10 minutes | Cook time: 15 minutes | Makes 10 cookies

2 tablespoons ground flaxseeds

6 tablespoons cold water

¼ cup maple syrup (optional)

1 tablespoon baking powder

1 cup natural peanut butter

½ cup whole-wheat flour

1. Preheat the oven to 350ºF (180ºC). Line a sheet pan with parchment paper. 2. In a large bowl, mix together the ground flaxseeds and water to make "flax eggs" and let sit until it gels, about 10 minutes. 3. Add the maple syrup (if using), baking powder, peanut butter, and flour to the bowl and mix well with a fork. 4. Put rounded tablespoons of the batter onto the prepared sheet pan. Flatten each cookie and, using the back of a fork, press a crisscross pattern into each one. Bake for 13 to 15 minutes, or until they are firm and slightly golden.

Per Serving:

calories: 409 | fat: 28g | protein: 14g | carbs: 33g | fiber: 5g

Poppy's Carrot Cake

Prep time: 20 minutes | Cook time: 3 hours | Serves 6 to 8

Carrot Cake:

Nonstick cooking spray (optional)

1 tablespoon ground flaxseed

2½ tablespoons water

2¼ cups rolled oats, divided

1¾ teaspoons ground cinnamon

¾ teaspoon ground nutmeg

¾ teaspoon ground ginger

2 teaspoons baking powder

1 teaspoon baking soda

1 cup unsweetened plant-based milk

¾ cup raisins, divided

¼ cup unsweetened

applesauce

⅓ cup date syrup or maple syrup (optional)

1 medium banana, peeled and broken into pieces

1 teaspoon vanilla extract

2 cups grated carrots

½ cup walnut pieces (optional)

Frosting:

¾ cup raw cashews

6 pitted Medjool dates, chopped

½ teaspoon ground ginger

⅓ to ½ cup water

2 tablespoons coconut cream

1. Prepare the slow cooker by folding two long sheets of aluminum foil and placing them perpendicular to each other (crisscross) in the bottom of the slow cooker to create "handles" that will come out over the top of the slow cooker. Coat the inside of the slow cooker and foil with cooking spray (if using) or line it with a slow cooker liner. 2. Make the carrot cake: Make a flax egg in a small bowl by mixing together the flaxseed and the water. Set aside. 3. In a blender or food processor, combine 1¾ cups of oats, the cinnamon, nutmeg, ginger, baking powder, and baking soda. Blend until the oats are turned into a flour. Pour into a large bowl and set aside. Add the remaining ½ cup of whole oats to the dry

ingredients. 4. Without rinsing the blender or food processor, add the milk, ¼ cup of raisins, applesauce, syrup (if using), banana, vanilla, and the flax egg. Process until smooth and the raisins are broken down. Pour over the dry ingredients. Add the carrots, the remaining ½ cup of raisins, and the walnuts (if using), and stir well to combine. 5. Pour the mixture into the prepared slow cooker. Stretch a clean dish towel or a few layers of paper towels over the top of the slow cooker and cover. Cook on Low for 3 hours. The carrot cake is ready when a toothpick inserted in the center comes out clean. Remove the insert from the slow cooker and cool on a wire rack for at least 30 minutes before removing the cake from the insert. Allow to cool completely before frosting. 6. Make the frosting: Put the cashews, dates, and ginger in a blender or food processor. Cover with just enough water to submerge the cashews and dates. Let the mixture soak for up to 1 hour to soften. Add the coconut cream and blend well until creamy. The frosting will thicken slightly as it sits.

Per Serving:

calories: 436 | fat: 11g | protein: 9g | carbs: 81g | fiber: 9g

No-Bake Mocha Cheesecake

Prep time: 15 minutes | Cook time: 10 minutes | Makes 1 cake

Crust:

12 chocolate sandwich cookies

Filling:

1 (13½-ounce / 383-g) can full-fat coconut milk

1 tablespoon agar flakes

1 tablespoon plus 1 teaspoon instant coffee

¼ cup maple syrup (optional)

¼ cup water

½ teaspoon vanilla extract

1 cup raw cashews, soaked in hot water for at least 10 minutes, and drained

2 tablespoons unsweetened cocoa powder

1. To make the crust, place the cookies in the bowl of a food processor. Pulse until roughly chopped, then process until they resemble crumbs. Pour into a 9-inch pie plate and press the crumbs to form a crust. Freeze it while you make the filling. 2. To make the filling, transfer the solids from the coconut milk to a high-speed blender. Pour the liquid into a small saucepan. (Don't worry if some of the solids get in there. They'll melt.) 3. Add the agar, coffee, maple syrup (if desired), water, and vanilla to the saucepan with the liquids and whisk to combine. Place over medium heat and allow the mixture to come to a simmer, with tiny bubbles breaking the surface. Let cook for 3 minutes, whisking often, until the agar is completely dissolved. 4. Add the cashews and cocoa to the blender with the coconut milk solids. Process, pausing as needed to scrape down the sides, until smooth. 5. With the blender running on low, pour in the contents of the saucepan and process until the filling is smooth and thoroughly combined. Pour the filling into the prepared crust and refrigerate until set, at least 30 minutes. Serve chilled.

Per Serving: (⅛ cake)

calories: 325 | fat: 23g | protein: 5g | carbs: 29g | fiber: 3g

Prep time: 15 minutes | Cook time: 20 minutes | Makes 10 scones

2 cups whole spelt flour

1 tablespoon aluminum-free baking powder

1 teaspoon ground cinnamon

½ teaspoon fine sea salt (optional)

⅓ cup pure maple syrup (optional)

⅓ cup liquid refined coconut oil, plus extra for greasing the measuring cup (optional)

2 teaspoons pure vanilla extract

½ cup mashed ripe banana

2 tablespoons hot water

⅓ cup chopped walnuts

⅓ cup Medjool dates, pitted and chopped

Serve:

Coconut butter

Jam

1. Preheat the oven to 350ºF (180ºC). Line a baking sheet with parchment paper, and set aside. 2. In a large bowl, whisk together the spelt flour, baking powder, cinnamon, and sea salt, if using. Make a small well in the center of the flour mixture and add the maple syrup, coconut oil, if using, vanilla, and mashed banana to the bowl. Gently stir the mixture with a spatula until the ingredients are slightly combined but there are still jags of flour throughout. 3. Add the hot water, chopped walnuts, and dates to the bowl and stir until everything is evenly combined. Avoid overmixing. 4. Lightly grease a ⅓ cup measuring cup with coconut oil. Scoop the scone batter up with the measuring cup and drop onto the prepared baking sheet with a little force. The portion of scone dough should come out in a nice puck shape. Repeat with remaining dough, spacing each scone 2 inches apart, and re-greasing the measuring cup if necessary. 5. Bake the scones for 20 minutes. Allow them to cool slightly on a wire rack before enjoying with coconut butter and jam.

Per Serving: (2 scones)

calories: 492 | fat: 21g | protein: 11g | carbs: 72g | fiber: 9g

Chapter
10

Basics

Coriander Chutney

Prep time: 15 minutes | Cook time: 0 minutes | Makes about 1 cup

½ teaspoon cumin seeds, toasted and ground
½ teaspoon yellow mustard seeds, toasted and ground
1 large bunch cilantro
1 small yellow onion, peeled and chopped (about ½ cup)

¼ cup unsweetened coconut
3 tablespoons grated ginger
2 serrano chiles, stemmed (for less heat, remove the seeds)
Zest and juice of 2 lemons
Salt, to taste (optional)

1. Put all the ingredients in a blender and blend on high speed until you get a smooth mixture. Add water as necessary to reach a thick paste consistency.

Per Serving: (¼ cup)
calories: 38 | fat: 1g | protein: 0g | carbs: 5g | fiber: 1g

5-Minute Tofu Cheese Sauce

Prep time: 5 minutes | Cook time: 0 minutes | Makes about 2 cups

1 (12-ounce / 340-g) package silken tofu
½ cup nutritional yeast
1½ teaspoons onion powder
½ teaspoon garlic powder
¼ teaspoon paprika

2 teaspoons Dijon mustard
1 tablespoon white wine vinegar
1 teaspoon salt (optional)
½ cup unsweetened plant-based milk

1. In a blender or food processor, combine the tofu, nutritional yeast, onion powder, garlic powder, paprika, mustard, vinegar, and add salt if desired. Blend the mixture for 30 to 60 seconds until thoroughly combined. If the mixture is too thick, you can add some milk to achieve the desired consistency. 2. Heat the sauce on the stove or in the microwave before serving. You can store the sauce in the refrigerator for up to 4 days.

Per Serving:
calories: 54 | fat: 2g | protein: 7g | carbs: 4g | fiber: 2g

Pineapple Chutney

Prep time: 25 minutes | Cook time: 15 minutes | Makes 1½ cups

½ medium yellow onion, peeled and diced small
1 tablespoon grated ginger
2 jalapeño peppers, seeded and minced
½ tablespoon cumin seeds,

toasted and ground
½ fresh pineapple, peeled, cored, and diced
½ cup finely chopped cilantro
Salt, to taste (optional)

1. In a large skillet or saucepan, sauté the onion over medium heat for 7 to 8 minutes. To prevent sticking, add 1 to 2 tablespoons of water as needed while cooking. 2. Afterward, add the ginger, jalapeño peppers, and cumin seeds, and cook for an additional 4 minutes. Introduce the pineapple and remove the pan from the heat. Stir in the cilantro and optionally add salt to taste.

Per Serving: (½ cup)
calories: 98 | fat: 0g | protein: 2g | carbs: 24g | fiber: 3g

Fava Bean Spread

Prep time: 15 minutes | Cook time: 0 minutes | Makes about 3½ cups

4 cups cooked fava beans, or 2 (15-ounce / 425-g) cans, drained and rinsed
8 cloves garlic, peeled and chopped

Zest of 1 lemon and juice of 2 lemons
1 teaspoon cumin seeds, toasted and ground
Salt, to taste (optional)

1. In the food processor, blend together the fava beans, garlic, lemon zest, lemon juice, cumin, and optional salt with 1 cup of water until the mixture becomes smooth and creamy. Add more water as necessary to achieve the desired consistency.

Per Serving: (½ cup)
calories: 103 | fat: 1g | protein: 5g | carbs: 17g | fiber: 5g

Croutons

Prep time: 5 minutes | Cook time: 15 minutes | Serves 4

½ day-old baguette, sliced
2 tablespoons olive oil (optional)

½ tablespoon garlic salt (optional)

1. Preheat your oven to 350ºF (180ºC). 2. Brush olive oil onto the baguette slices and optionally sprinkle with garlic salt. 3. Cut the bread into cubes, spread them on a baking sheet, and bake for 10 to 15 minutes until they turn golden brown. 4. Let the croutons cool before serving. 5. For the best taste and texture, enjoy the croutons immediately after baking.

Per Serving:
calories: 94 | fat: 7g | protein: 1g | carbs: 7g | fiber: 0g

Apple Cider Vinaigrette

Prep time: 5 minutes | Cook time: 0 minutes | Makes ½ cup

2 tablespoons apple cider vinegar
¼ cup olive oil (optional)
½ tablespoon Dijon mustard
1 tablespoon maple syrup

(optional)
1 teaspoon minced garlic
Pinch of salt (optional)
Freshly ground pepper, to taste

1. Combine all the ingredients in a small bowl and whisk until thoroughly mixed. 2. Transfer the mixture into an airtight container and store it in the refrigerator for up to 7 days.

Per Serving: (½ cup)
calories: 272 | fat: 27g | protein: 0g | carbs: 8g | fiber: 0g

Spicy Cilantro Pesto

Prep time: 10 minutes | Cook time: 0 minutes | Makes about 1 cup

2 cups packed cilantro
¼ cup hulled sunflower seeds, toasted (optional)
1 jalapeño pepper, coarsely chopped (for less heat, remove the seeds)
4 cloves garlic, peeled and chopped

Zest and juice of 1 lime
Salt, to taste (optional)
½ package extra-firm silken tofu (about 6 ounces / 170 g), drained
¼ cup nutritional yeast (optional)

1. In a food processor, blend together cilantro, sunflower seeds (optional), jalapeño pepper, garlic, lime zest and juice, salt (optional), tofu, and nutritional yeast (optional) until a smooth and creamy mixture is achieved.

Per Serving: (¼ cup)

calories: 143 | fat: 8g | protein: 11g | carbs: 10g | fiber: 5g

Mayonnaise

Prep time: 5 minutes | Cook time: 0 minutes | Makes 1½ cups

1 (12-ounce / 340-g) package extra-firm silken tofu, drained
1 teaspoon dry mustard
½ teaspoon onion powder
½ teaspoon garlic powder

½ teaspoon salt, or to taste (optional)
3 tablespoons red wine vinegar

1. In the food processor, blend all the ingredients until the mixture becomes smooth and creamy.

Per Serving: (½ cup)

calories: 110 | fat: 6g | protein: 11g | carbs: 3g | fiber: 0g

Plant-Based Fish Sauce

Prep time: 10 minutes | Cook time: 20 minutes | Makes 3 to 4 cups

4 cups water
1 (4-by-8-inch) sheet of kombu
½ cup dried shiitake mushrooms

¼ cup low-sodium soy sauce, tamari, or coconut aminos
3 garlic cloves, crushed
2 teaspoons rice vinegar

1. In a medium saucepan, bring water, kombu, mushrooms, soy sauce, garlic, and vinegar to a boil. Reduce heat to low, cover, and simmer for 15 to 20 minutes. 2. Remove from heat and let it steep overnight or at least 8 hours, keeping it covered. 3. Strain the mixture to remove any solids. Store the plant-based fish sauce in a glass bottle in the refrigerator for up to 3 weeks, shaking well before each use.

Per Serving:

calories: 4 | fat: 0g | protein: 0g | carbs: 1g | fiber: 0g

Herbed Millet Pizza Crust

Prep time: 5 minutes | Cook time: 40 minutes | Makes 1 large thin-crust pizza crust

½ cup coarsely ground millet
1½ cups water
1 tablespoon mixed dried Italian herbs

¼ teaspoon sea salt (optional)
1 to 2 tablespoons nutritional yeast

1. Preheat the oven to 350ºF (180ºC). Line an 8-inch-round pie dish or springform pan with parchment paper to easily lift the crust after cooking. A nonstick pan is recommended as the crust can be fragile until it cools and may stick. 2. In a small pot, combine millet, water, and a pinch of salt. Bring it to a boil, then cover and simmer for 15 to 20 minutes, stirring occasionally to prevent sticking. For a more intense flavor, add dried herbs while cooking, or stir them in after the millet is cooked. 3. Once the millet is cooked, add salt (if using) and nutritional yeast. Spread the seasoned millet evenly in the pan, reaching the edges. 4. Bake the crust in the oven for 20 minutes or until lightly browned around the edges.

Per Serving: (1 crust)

calories: 378 | fat: 4g | protein: 11g | carbs: 72g | fiber: 8g

Tahini Dressing

Prep time: 5 minutes | Cook time: 0 minutes | Makes ½ cup

¼ cup tahini
1 teaspoon minced garlic
3 tablespoons lemon juice
1 tablespoon maple syrup (optional)
1 teaspoon soy sauce

1 teaspoon ground cumin
1 tablespoon olive oil (optional)
1 tablespoon hot water
Pinch of salt and pepper (optional)

1. Combine all the ingredients in a small bowl and whisk until thoroughly combined. 2. Transfer the mixture to an airtight container and store it in the refrigerator for up to 7 days.

Per Serving: (½ cup)

calories: 283 | fat: 24g | protein: 6g | carbs: 16g | fiber: 3g

Tofu Sour Cream

Prep time: 5 minutes | Cook time: 0 minutes | Makes 1½ cups

1 (12-ounce / 340-g) package extra-firm silken tofu, drained
1 tablespoon fresh lemon juice
1 tablespoon red wine vinegar
Salt, to taste (optional)

Mix all the ingredients in a blender and blend until the texture is smooth and creamy. Refrigerate until it's time to serve.

Per Serving: (½ cup)

calories: 105 | fat: 6g | protein: 11g | carbs: 2g | fiber: 0g

Pure Nut Mylk

Prep time: 2 minutes | Cook time: 0 minutes | Makes 3 cups

1 cup raw, unsalted nuts (almonds, hazelnuts, Brazil nuts, pecans, macadamias, walnuts)

3 cups purified water for blending, plus more if desired

1. In a bowl, soak the nuts in 2 to 3 cups of water overnight. 2. After soaking, drain and rinse the nuts thoroughly. Transfer them to a blender along with 3 cups of purified water. Blend on high speed for 2 to 3 minutes until you get a smooth consistency. 3. Strain the blended nut mixture using a cheesecloth or nut milk bag, ensuring you squeeze out all the liquid. 4. For a thinner nut mylk, add more purified water to your preference. 5. Store the nut mylk in a glass jar in the refrigerator. It will remain fresh for 3 to 4 days.

Per Serving:

calories: 276 | fat: 23g | protein: 10g | carbs: 10g | fiber: 6g

Chipotle Peppers in Adobo Sauce

Prep time: 30 minutes | Cook time: 20 minutes | Makes 20 to 25 peppers

1 (2 ounces / 57 g) package morita chiles (about 17 to 20)

1 (2 ounces / 57 g) package chipotle chiles (about 10 to 12)

1 to 2 cups boiling water

½ onion, chopped

1 garlic clove, crushed

½ teaspoon ground cumin

½ teaspoon dried oregano

½ teaspoon dried marjoram

¼ cup apple cider vinegar

¼ cup rice vinegar

2 tablespoons date syrup (optional)

2 tablespoons tomato paste

1. Preheat your oven to 350ºF (180ºC) and line a baking sheet with aluminum foil. Place the morita and chipotle chiles on the prepared baking sheet and roast for 5 minutes. Then transfer them to a medium glass bowl and cover them with boiling water. Submerge the chiles using a small plate or bowl and let them soak for 30 minutes to rehydrate. 2. While the chiles are soaking, use a nonstick skillet over medium-high heat to dry sauté the onion for about 5 minutes. Add 1 teaspoon of water as needed to prevent sticking, and cook until the onion becomes translucent. Add the garlic, cumin, oregano, and marjoram, and sauté for an additional minute until fragrant. Remove from heat. 3. Transfer the sautéed onion mixture to a blender. Add the apple cider vinegar, rice vinegar, date syrup (if using), and tomato paste. After the chiles have rehydrated, remove the stems from 6 to 7 of the morita chiles and slice them open to remove the seeds. Add the deseeded chiles to the blender along with ¾ cup of their soaking liquid. Blend until smooth, discarding any leftover liquid. 4. Pour the sauce back into the skillet and add the remaining chiles. Cook over medium heat, stirring occasionally, for 15 minutes or until the sauce is reduced by half.

Per Serving:

calories: 30 | fat: 0g | protein: 1g | carbs: 6g | fiber: 2g

Strawberry Dressing

Prep time: 5 minutes | Cook time: 0 minutes | Makes 1½ cups

1½ cups chopped fresh strawberries

1 to 2 tablespoons agave, or

maple syrup (optional)

½ tablespoon lemon juice

1. Combine all the ingredients in a food processor or blender and blend until you achieve a smooth consistency. 2. Transfer the mixture to an airtight container and store it in the refrigerator for up to 7 days.

Per Serving: (1 cup)

calories: 51 | fat: 0g | protein: 1g | carbs: 13g | fiber: 2g

Quinoa Mylk

Prep time: 5 minutes | Cook time: 20 minutes | Makes 4 cups

½ cup uncooked quinoa

4 cups purified water, for

blending

4 dates

1. Begin by soaking the quinoa overnight in 1 cup of water. Before cooking, make sure to drain and rinse the quinoa thoroughly until the water runs clear. 2. To cook the quinoa, bring 2 more cups of water to a boil in a medium saucepan. Add the quinoa, bring to a second boil, then cover and simmer on low heat for 15 minutes. Once cooked, allow the quinoa to cool down. Next, place the cooled quinoa in a blender with 4 cups of purified water. Blend on high speed for 1 to 3 minutes until you achieve a smooth consistency. 3. Strain the blended quinoa mixture using a cheesecloth or a nut milk bag. The straining process may be slow, but you can gently squeeze and massage the bottom of the cloth to speed it up. 4. Pour the quinoa mylk back into the blender, add the dates, and blend until smooth. 5. Transfer the quinoa mylk to a glass jar with a tight lid and store it in the refrigerator for 3 to 4 days.

Per Serving:

calories: 98 | fat: 1g | protein: 3g | carbs: 19g | fiber: 2g

Maple-Dijon Dressing

Prep time: 5 minutes | Cook time: 0 minutes | Serves 4

¼ cup apple cider vinegar

2 tablespoons maple syrup

2 teaspoons gluten-free Dijon mustard

¼ teaspoon black pepper

2 tablespoons water

Salt (optional)

1. Combine the vinegar, maple syrup (if desired), mustard, pepper and water in a small jar with a tight-fitting lid. Season with salt to taste, if desired. Refrigerate for up to 5 days.

Per Serving:

calories: 31 | fat: 0g | protein: 0g | carbs: 7g | fiber: 0g

Tempeh Bacon

Prep time: 5 minutes | Cook time: 10 minutes | Serves 4

2 tablespoons soy sauce
1 tablespoon water
1 tablespoon maple syrup (optional)
½ tablespoon liquid smoke

1 (8-ounce / 227-g) package tempeh
1 tablespoon canola oil (optional)

1. In a medium bowl, whisk together the soy sauce, water, maple syrup (if using), and liquid smoke. Set the mixture aside. 2. Take the tempeh block and cut it in half lengthwise. Then, slice it as thinly as possible. 3. Heat the oil, if using, in a large pan over high heat. Add the sliced tempeh in a single layer and cook for 2 minutes. Flip the slices and cook for an additional 2 minutes. 4. While the tempeh is still in the pan, pour in the liquid mixture. Sauté the tempeh for 3 minutes, then flip the slices and cook for another 3 minutes or until the liquid is fully absorbed. 5. The Tempeh Bacon is at its best when served immediately. Enjoy!

Per Serving:

calories: 17 | fat: 11g | protein: 11g | carbs: 11g | fiber: 0g

Tomato Sauce

Prep time: 10 minutes | Cook time: 40 minutes | Makes 4 cups

1 medium yellow onion, peeled and diced small
6 cloves garlic, peeled and minced
6 tablespoons minced basil

2 tablespoons minced oregano
1 (28-ounce / 794-g) can diced tomatoes, puréed
Salt, to taste (optional)

1. Place the onion in a large saucepan and sauté over medium heat for 10 minutes. Add water 1 to 2 tablespoons at a time to keep the onion from sticking to the pan. 2. Add the garlic, basil, and oregano and cook for another 3 minutes. Add the puréed tomatoes and salt (if using) and cook, covered, over medium-low heat for 25 minutes.

Per Serving: (1 cup)

calories: 48 | fat: 0g | protein: 2g | carbs: 10g | fiber: 4g

Quinoa

Prep time: 5 minutes | Cook time: 5 minutes | Makes 3 cups

1 cup quinoa

1½ cups vegetable broth

1. Rinse the quinoa in cold water using a fine-mesh strainer. 2. Put the quinoa and broth into the pressure cooker and cook on high pressure for 5 minutes. 3. Let the pressure out, remove the lid, and fluff the quinoa with a fork. 4. Store in an airtight container in the fridge for up to 5 days.

Per Serving: (1 cup)

calories: 214 | fat: 3g | protein: 8g | carbs: 38g | fiber: 4g

Hemp Mylk

Prep time: 5 minutes | Cook time: 0 minutes | Makes 3 cups

½ cup hemp hearts
3 cups purified water, for blending

½ teaspoon ground cinnamon
2 dates, pitted

1. In a blender, combine all the ingredients and blend until smooth and creamy. 2. Pour into a glass jar with a tight lid and refrigerate. Your hemp mylk will last for up to 5 days in the fridge.

Per Serving:

calories: 47 | fat: 0g | protein: 1g | carbs: 11g | fiber: 1g

Piecrust

Prep time: 10 minutes | Cook time: 0 minutes | Serves 4

1 cup all-purpose flour, plus more for rolling
½ teaspoon baking powder
¼ teaspoon salt (optional)
2 tablespoons canola oil, plus more if storing dough for later

(optional)
½ teaspoon lemon juice
3½ tablespoons plant-based milk
4 tablespoons water

1. In a medium bowl, use a wooden spoon to thoroughly combine all the ingredients until they form a cohesive ball of dough. 2. Wrap the dough in plastic wrap and refrigerate it for 1 hour. 3. If you plan to use the dough immediately, sprinkle a work surface with flour, place the chilled dough on it, and roll it out with a lightly floured rolling pin into a thin, 11-inch circle. Transfer the rolled-out dough to a 9-inch pie dish. Fill it with your desired fillings and bake following the recipe's instructions. 4. If you don't intend to use the dough right away, prevent it from drying out by lightly coating the exterior with 1 teaspoon of oil (or less, if preferred). Place the lightly oiled dough in a medium bowl, cover it tightly with plastic wrap, or use an airtight container, and refrigerate for up to 7 days.

Per Serving:

calories: 183 | fat: 8g | protein: 4g | carbs: 25g | fiber: 1g

Green Split Peas

Prep time: 5 minutes | Cook time: 45 minutes | Makes 2 cups

1 cup split peas, rinsed

1½ cups water

1. Put the split peas and water into a large pot with a lid. 2. Over high heat, bring to a boil. 3. Cover the pot with the lid and reduce the heat to low. 4. Simmer for 45 minutes. 5. Store in an airtight container in the fridge for up to 5 days.

Per Serving: (1 cup)

calories: 347 | fat: 1g | protein: 24g | carbs: 63g | fiber: 25g

Nitter Kibbeh

Prep time: 20 minutes | Cook time: 25 minutes | Makes 1½ cups

2 pounds (907 g) yellow onions, peeled and diced small

9 cloves garlic, peeled and minced

1 tablespoon grated ginger

½ tablespoon turmeric

¼ teaspoon ground cardamom

½ teaspoon ground cinnamon

⅛ teaspoon ground cloves

⅛ teaspoon ground nutmeg

1. Place the onions in a large skillet over medium heat. Stir frequently, adding water only as needed to keep the onions from sticking to the pan, and cook for about 20 minutes, or until the onions are browned. Add the garlic, ginger, turmeric, cardamom, cinnamon, cloves, and nutmeg and cook for 5 minutes. Add ¼ cup of water and scrape the bottom of the pan with a spatula to pick up and incorporate the bits on the bottom of the pan.
2. Transfer the mixture to a blender and purée, adding water as needed to make a smooth and creamy consistency. This will keep, refrigerated, for up to 7 days.

Per Serving: (½ cup)

calories: 119 | fat: 0g | protein: 3g | carbs: 27g | fiber: 3g

Easy-Peasy Almond Milk

Prep time: 5 minutes | Cook time: 0 minutes | Makes 2 cups

2 to 3 tablespoons raw almond butter

2 cups water

Pinch sea salt (optional)

1 to 2 dates, or 10 drops pure

stevia (or vanilla stevia), or 1 to 2 tablespoons unrefined sugar (optional)

¼ teaspoon pure vanilla extract (optional)

1. Put everything in a blender and purée until smooth. 2. Strain the fiber from the almonds through a piece of cheesecloth or a fine-mesh sieve. 3. Keep in an airtight container in the fridge for up to 5 days.

Per Serving: (1 cup)

calories: 110 | fat: 8g | protein: 3g | carbs: 5g | fiber: 2g

Roasted Red Pepper Sauce

Prep time: 10 minutes | Cook time: 0 minutes | Makes 2 cups

1 (12 ounces / 340 g) package extra-firm silken tofu, drained

2 large red bell peppers, roasted and seeded

3 cloves garlic, peeled and chopped

2 tablespoons chopped dill

1 teaspoon salt (optional)

½ teaspoon freshly ground black pepper

zest of 1 lemon

1. Combine all ingredients in the bowl of a food processor and purée until smooth and creamy. Refrigerate in an airtight container until ready to use.

Per Serving: (1 cup)

calories: 205 | fat: 11g | protein: 19g | carbs: 14g | fiber: 3g

Creamy Herbed Hemp Dressing

Prep time: 10 minutes | Cook time: 0 minutes | Serves 6

½ cup hemp seeds

¼ cup chopped flat-leaf parsley

2 tablespoons raw cashews

1 scallion, sliced

1 tablespoon apple cider vinegar

1 tablespoon fresh lemon juice

2 teaspoons capers, drained

1 teaspoon nutritional yeast

½ teaspoon garlic powder

½ teaspoon coconut sugar (optional)

¼ teaspoon dried dill

Salt and black pepper (optional)

1 or 2 tablespoons water (optional)

1. Process the hemp seeds, parsley, cashews, scallion, vinegar, lemon juice, capers, nutritional yeast, garlic powder, sugar, and dill in a high-speed blender until smooth. Season with salt (if desired) and pepper and add water, 1 tablespoon at a time, as needed to achieve desired consistency. Refrigerate in an airtight container for up to 5 days.

Per Serving:

calories: 106 | fat: 9g | protein: 4g | carbs: 5g | fiber: 2g

Fresh Tomato Salsa

Prep time: 15 minutes | Cook time: 0 minutes | Makes about 4 cups

3 large ripe tomatoes, diced small

1 small red onion, peeled and diced small

½ cup chopped cilantro

1 to 2 jalapeño peppers,

minced (for less heat, remove the seeds)

2 cloves garlic, peeled and minced

3 tablespoons fresh lime juice

Salt, to taste (optional)

1. Combine all ingredients in a large bowl and mix well. Store refrigerated until ready to serve.

Per Serving: (1 cup)

calories: 38 | fat: 0g | protein: 1g | carbs: 8g | fiber: 2g

Mango-Orange Dressing

Prep time: 5 minutes | Cook time: 0 minutes | Serves 8

1 cup diced mango

½ cup orange juice

2 tablespoons fresh lime juice

2 tablespoons gluten-free rice vinegar

1 teaspoon coconut sugar (optional)

¼ teaspoon salt (optional)

2 tablespoons chopped cilantro

1. Process the mango, orange juice, lime juice, rice vinegar, sugar, and salt (if desired) in a blender until smooth. Stir in the cilantro. Refrigerate in an airtight container for up to 2 days.

Per Serving:

calories: 23 | fat: 0g | protein: 0g | carbs: 6g | fiber: 0g

10-Minute White Bean Cheese Sauce

Prep time: 10 minutes | Cook time: 0 minutes | Makes about 3 cups

1 cup canned white beans, drained and rinsed

½ cup unsweetened plant-based milk

5 tablespoons nutritional yeast

¼ teaspoon garlic powder

½ teaspoon apple cider vinegar

1 teaspoon Dijon mustard

¼ teaspoon paprika

¼ teaspoon ground turmeric

Salt (optional)

1. Place the beans, milk, nutritional yeast, garlic powder, vinegar, mustard, paprika, and turmeric in a blender or food processor. Season with salt (if using). Blend for 30 to 60 seconds, until creamy. 2. Heat the sauce on the stove or in the microwave. This will keep for up to 4 days in the refrigerator.

Per Serving:

calories: 32 | fat: 0g | protein: 3g | carbs: 4g | fiber: 2g

Measurement Conversion Chart

VOLUME EQUIVALENTS(DRY)

US STANDARD	METRIC (APPROXIMATE)
1/8 teaspoon	0.5 mL
1/4 teaspoon	1 mL
1/2 teaspoon	2 mL
3/4 teaspoon	4 mL
1 teaspoon	5 mL
1 tablespoon	15 mL
1/4 cup	59 mL
1/2 cup	118 mL
3/4 cup	177 mL
1 cup	235 mL
2 cups	475 mL
3 cups	700 mL
4 cups	1 L

VOLUME EQUIVALENTS(LIQUID)

US STANDARD	US STANDARD (OUNCES)	METRIC (APPROXIMATE)
2 tablespoons	1 fl.oz.	30 mL
1/4 cup	2 fl.oz.	60 mL
1/2 cup	4 fl.oz.	120 mL
1 cup	8 fl.oz.	240 mL
1 1/2 cup	12 fl.oz.	355 mL
2 cups or 1 pint	16 fl.oz.	475 mL
4 cups or 1 quart	32 fl.oz.	1 L
1 gallon	128 fl.oz.	4 L

TEMPERATURES EQUIVALENTS

FAHRENHEIT(F)	CELSIUS(C) (APPROXIMATE)
225 °F	107 °C
250 °F	120 °C
275 °F	135 °C
300 °F	150 °C
325 °F	160 °C
350 °F	180 °C
375 °F	190 °C
400 °F	205 °C
425 °F	220 °C
450 °F	235 °C
475 °F	245 °C
500 °F	260 °C

WEIGHT EQUIVALENTS

US STANDARD	METRIC (APPROXIMATE)
1 ounce	28 g
2 ounces	57 g
5 ounces	142 g
10 ounces	284 g
15 ounces	425 g
16 ounces (1 pound)	455 g
1.5 pounds	680 g
2 pounds	907 g

Appendix 2

The Dirty Dozen and Clean Fifteen

The Environmental Working Group (EWG) is a nonprofit, nonpartisan organization dedicated to protecting human health and the environment Its mission is to empower people to live healthier lives in a healthier environment. This organization publishes an annual list of the twelve kinds of produce, in sequence, that have the highest amount of pesticide residue-the Dirty Dozen-as well as a list of the fifteen kinds ofproduce that have the least amount of pesticide residue-the Clean Fifteen.

THE DIRTY DOZEN

- The 2016 Dirty Dozen includes the following produce. These are considered among the year's most important produce to buy organic:

Strawberries	Spinach
Apples	Tomatoes
Nectarines	Bell peppers
Peaches	Cherry tomatoes
Celery	Cucumbers
Grapes	Kale/collard greens
Cherries	Hot peppers

- *The Dirty Dozen list contains two additional itemskale/collard greens and hot peppers-because they tend to contain trace levels of highly hazardous pesticides.*

THE CLEAN FIFTEEN

- The least critical to buy organically are the Clean Fifteen list. The following are on the 2016 list:

Avocados	Papayas
Corn	Kiw
Pineapples	Eggplant
Cabbage	Honeydew
Sweet peas	Grapefruit
Onions	Cantaloupe
Asparagus	Cauliflower
Mangos	

- *Some of the sweet corn sold in the United States are made from genetically engineered (GE) seedstock. Buy organic varieties of these crops to avoid GE produce.*

Appendix

3

Recipe Index

T

V

W

Y

Z

Made in the USA
Las Vegas, NV
16 January 2024

84436996R00059